THE ILLUSTRATED BOOK
OF GARDEN FLOWERS

ACKNOWLEDGEMENTS

This title first appeared as **The Oxford Book of Garden Flowers** and Peerage Books gratefully acknowledge the co-operation of the Oxford University Press who gave permission for this edition to be published.

The flowers illustrated in this book have been drawn from live specimens, a very large number of which have come from John Scott & Co., Royal Nurseries, Merriott, Somerset. The annual plants, selected by A. P. Balfour, came from Sutton's Gardens at Reading. Other specimens have come from the various authors' gardens, especially from Waterperry School of Horticulture rock gardens.

We wish to thank the Director, Rosewarne Experimental Station and also Mr. J. B. Hindley for help in providing specimens.

All the text was checked and proof-read by E. B. Anderson, whose painstaking care, especially in checking the spelling of the scientific names, has been an important contribution to the book. He is also mainly responsible for the entries at the end of the book.

We also wish to acknowledge with appreciation the patient and skilled work of the plate-makers on the 96 colour plates in this book. Without this, so faithful a reproduction of the artist's drawings in an inexpensive book would have been impossible.

In general, in naming the plants in this book we have followed the R.H.S. Dictionary (Oxford 1956). The common or country name, where there is one, is given in brackets after the scientific name.

THE ILLUSTRATED BOOK
OF GARDEN FLOWERS

Illustrations by
B.E. NICHOLSON
from specimens mainly selected by
MICHAEL WALLIS
Royal Nurseries, Merriott, Somerset

Text by

E.B. ANDERSON

(SHRUBS AND BULBS)

MARGERY FISH

(HERBACEOUS PLANTS)

A.P. BALFOUR

(ANNUALS)

MICHAEL WALLIS

(ROSES)

VALERIE FINNIS

(ROCK PLANTS)

PEERAGE
BOOKS

First published in Great Britain by Oxford University Press as
The Oxford Book of Garden Flowers

This edition published by Peerage Books
59 Grosvenor Street
London W1

© 1963 Oxford University Press
1979 Revised
Reprinted 1984

ISBN 0 907408 59 1

Printed in Czechoslovakia
50532

Contents

BARBARA NICHOLSON
AN APPRECIATION

Barbara Nicholson began her artistic career as a medical illustrator; then, in 1960, she prepared the illustrations for *The Oxford Book of Wild Flowers*, which was followed by *The Oxford Book of Garden Flowers* and *The Oxford Book of Flowerless Plants* (now reprinted as *The Illustrated Books of Wild Flowers, Garden Flowers* and *Flowerless Plants*), also illustrated by her. In 1972 she began a series of paintings for the British Museum (Natural History) illustrating the plants that are typical of fifteen important habitats of the British Isles. Each painting has its own particular charm and combines the highest artistic merit with accurate portrayal of the habitat and the plants within it. She also illustrated *The Oxford Book of Food Plants* as well as *The Oxford Book of Trees* (the latest edition of which is entitled *The Illustrated Book of Trees)* and by 1977 the series was completed. She died in 1978.

Barbara Nicholson's work was always preceded by field studies and, as far as possible, she painted from fresh material so that she had the rare quality of producing illustrations that were botanically precise and very beautiful.

INTRODUCTION

The main purpose of this book is to show interested but amateur gardeners, whether children or adults, what possibilities there are in planting up their gardens. This is a companion book to *The Illustrated Book of Wild Flowers* (originally published as *The Oxford Book of Wild Flowers*), but its purpose is rather different. Here, we are concerned not so much with identification and classification as with suggestions for suitable plants which the ordinary gardener can grow with success, subject to his soil and climate. We are also concerned with particular needs and interests, such as for annuals to fill gaps in the herbaceous border; half-hardy annuals for bedding out; plants which will flourish in shady damp situations, or in dry soils; carpeting and trailing plants; plants for woodland and wild gardens; flowers which can be dried for winter decoration; daisies from America; or bulbs from Africa. The general pattern of the book is seasonal, beginning in January with the winter-flowering shrubs and herbaceous flowers and ending in the late autumn with the shrubs grown for their autumn foliage and fruit. For example, *Crocus chrysanthus* appears on p. 11 with other early spring bulbs and *Crocus nudiflorus* comes on p. 183 with the autumn bulbs. Within this seasonal pattern every page has its own particular story to tell and its own unity, for the plants grouped together on a page belong to each other in some sense – in family, in place of origin, in type of growth, or in choice of situation.

It is not the purpose of this book to serve instead of a dictionary of gardening or a horticulturist's catalogue, but rather to show the amateur gardener what to look for in the catalogues for his particular purpose. We have chosen for the illustrations recommended named varieties, and further varieties are mentioned in the text; but the selection is of necessity arbitrary and is intended to show the range of types available. With plants such as roses, dahlias, chrysanthemums, and sweet peas, the specialist catalogues will give all the varieties available, including the newest ones. We give comparatively little space to these well-known groups, and comparatively more space to species less well-known and equally satisfactory and easy to grow.

This book is concerned mainly with those flowers which can be grown in ordinary garden conditions. Where a plant is tender or needs particular conditions, this is stressed in the text. Hothouse plants are not included at all, though there is one page of greenhouse plants used for bedding out and two or three pages of half-hardy annuals which can be sown under glass and then planted out. Also a few half-hardy plants such as dahlias and gladioli, which must be lifted for the winter, do appear. It is obviously impossible in a book of this size to include even every plant which is easy to grow, and any selection is bound to be a personal one. Plants which are very expensive or difficult to obtain have for the most part been excluded, and only a few flowering trees are included, mostly in the sections on plants grown for their autumn berries and foliage.

This book is not a manual of gardening, and there are no articles on making a rock garden, preparing seed beds, etc. But a good deal of advice is given incidentally all the way through on the culture of the different plants described. It is hoped that the lists at the end of the book may also prove to be of practical use in making successful selections. Every attempt is made to ensure that the ambitious gardener experimenting with plants new to him shall meet with success, not failure.

WINTER-FLOWERING SHRUBS. 1

British winters are so capricious compared with Continental ones that it is never possible to be sure what weather any winter month will produce. There may be days or even weeks in December to February when the weather is almost spring-like, and when a number of plants, particularly shrubs, will flower. The shrubs shown here and on page 3 are all hardy, and though their flowers may be spoilt by severe frost and snow, they will do well in the milder periods. Obviously they should, as far as is possible, be given positions in the garden where they are sheltered from cold winds. That is why walls are often recommended for many of them. Any cutting back and thinning should be done immediately after the flowers fade before the new growth has started.

1 MAHONIA japonica. Mahonia used to be classed as a Berberis, to which it is closely related. It is an evergreen shrub which was introduced to Britain from Japanese gardens; hence its name, though its home is China. *M. japonica* is sometimes confused with *M. bealei*, but can be easily distinguished because its flowers are pendulous, whereas those of *M. bealei* are erect. *M. japonica* is far the better plant, with handsome leaves and sprays of delicate-looking flowers which have a scent like lily-of-the-valley. It forms a rounded bush and will grow 10 ft. tall, but it can be cut back with impunity. It will grow under small deciduous trees, which provide a little shelter.

2 CHIMONANTHUS praecox (Winter Sweet). This deciduous shrub, a native of China, produces wax-like, pale-greenish-yellow flowers with dull purple centres from November to March. It is named from Greek words *cheimon* = winter, and *anthos* = flower. *C. praecox*, which has a very strong sweet scent and grows well against a south or west wall, is easy to obtain, but is not so showy as *C. p. luteus*, the one illustrated, which is difficult to obtain, or *C. p. grandiflorus* which has large flowers yellower than *C. praecox* but not so fragrant. Chimonanthus will grow up to 8 ft. as a bush or higher on a wall.

3 GARRYA elliptica. A hardy, evergreen shrub from California and Oregon named after Nicholas Garry of the Hudson's Bay Company, who helped in plant-collecting expeditions in the early 19th century. The flowers are borne on catkins, male plants producing striking long catkins sometimes a foot long, whereas the female catkins are only half to a third as long. Garrya does best if grown on a wall or sunny bank, and in some areas will grow and flower freely on a north wall. It grows quickly, reaching 6–12 ft. in height.

CORNUS mas (Cornelian Cherry). This European shrub or small tree, long known in Britain, differs from other cornels, including the native Dogwood, in flowering early — February and March — on leafless stems. The fluffy yellow flowers are in little bunches ¾ in. across. It does not fruit readily in Britain, but the 'cherries' when they do form are bright red and edible.

Some species of cornus, such as *C. alba siberica*, flowering from May to August, are often grown more for their decorative stems and fruit (*see* p. 189) than their flowers.

LONICERA x purpusii (Winter-flowering Honeysuckle). This hybrid between *L. standishii* and *L. fragrantissima* is superior to the former and more free-flowering than the latter. The small creamy-white flowers do not make much show but have an attractive lemony scent which makes them valuable for cutting. These semi-evergreen shrubs grow up to 6 ft. tall and flower from December to March.

PRUNUS subhirtella autumnalis. Most of the plums and cherries are spring-flowering (*see* pp. 25, 60), but this variety of *P. subhirtella* from Japan makes a small twiggy tree which flowers from late autumn through the winter. It is one of the best winter-flowering plants, the leafless branches being covered with small pompon-like flowers, usually white but pink in the variety *rosea*. If cut when in bud, they will develop perfectly in the house and so not be spoilt by bad weather.

1 MAHONIA JAPONICA   2 CHIMONANTHUS PRAECOX LUTEUS
3 GARRYA ELLIPTICA

1

WINTER-FLOWERING SHRUBS. 2

1 JASMINUM **nudiflorum**. The most common and valuable of winter flowers, which was introduced from China in 1844 by Robert Fortune, a wonderful plant collector. It will grow in almost any position, even on a shady north wall, and flowers freely. Though frosts destroy open blossoms, more come as soon as the weather is milder. It is really a rambling shrub and may be grown as a bush in the open; but it is usually seen as a climber. If cut back to the base each year after flowering, it will make long annual shoots. Treated this way it grows attractively on the top of a dry bank or wall. For the summer-flowering jasmine *see* p. 165.

2 VIBURNUM **fragrans candidum**. This is the white variety of the most popular winter-flowering hardy species of a large genus. It flowers better in a poor soil, and even then it tends to sucker and grow into a thicket unless rigorously thinned. Also, though it needs sun, it is better in not too warm a place, for in such it tends to flower on and off through the winter instead of making a good display in February. It is very sweet-scented, and some forms of the original species are more pink than others.

V. grandiflorum has larger flowers of apple-blossom pink and is just as sweet-scented; but it is slow in starting to flower. The hybrid *V. x. bodnantense*, a cross between *V. fragrans* and *V. grandiflorum*, including the forms 'Dawn' and 'Deben', is half way in all characters.

3 HAMAMELIS **mollis (Witch-hazel)**. A very hardy winter-flowering shrub which will withstand even severe frosts. It looks well planted against a background of evergreens, which show up the leafless branches covered with delicately scented, golden-yellow, strap-petalled flowers. *H. mollis brevipetala*, the variety illustrated, has rather shorter petals of a deeper yellow. *H. mollis pallida* has sulphur-yellow flowers. Hamamelis prefers a rich, light, but not too dry soil, with peat and leaf-mould; it does not do well on chalky soils. The foliage turns a lovely yellow in the autumn.

4 HAMAMELIS **'Ruby Glow'**. Several new varieties and hybrids with reddish flowers have appeared recently, possibly derived from *H. japonica*. H. 'Jelena' is another of these, with attractive red and yellow flowers.

5 ERICA x **darleyensis (Winter-flowering Heath)**. This is a hybrid between the dwarf, bushy, winter-flowering *E. carnea* and the larger, more upright; early-spring-flowering *E. mediterranea*. It is a vigorous, quick-growing, spreading shrub about 2 ft. tall, which flowers very freely from November to May. If it grows too big it can be clipped back after flowering. It prefers a soil with peat or leaf-mould but, like all the varieties of *E. carnea*, will tolerate some lime.

Other good varieties or hybrids include: white, 'Snow Queen', 'Springwood White'; pink, 'Alan Coates', 'Springwood Pink'; carmine, 'Eileen Porter'; dark red, 'rubra'. The hybrids E. x 'Arthur Johnson' (deep pink) and 'Silberschmelze' (white) with attractive grey foliage. For other ericaceous plants *see* p. 57.

RHODODENDRON x **praecox**. This hybrid between *R. ciliatum* and *R. dauricum*, made in 1885 at Ormskirk, Lancs., is a semi-evergreen shrub producing clusters of rosy-purple flowers in the milder periods of February and March, or even earlier. *R. mucronulatum* is a rather larger deciduous rhododendron which in mild winters will be in bloom by Christmas. Both these should be planted in a sheltered position so that frost does not damage the flowers. Rhododendrons will not grow on limy soil. For spring and later-flowering species *see* pp. 26 and 57.

6 DAPHNE **mezereum**. A very popular early-flowering daphne to be seen in many cottage gardens. The ordinary form is less attractive in colour than some of the pink, crimson, and white varieties. Birds eat the scarlet or pale yellow berries and thereby distribute the seeds, which produce self-sown seedlings. These can be moved when about 4 ins. tall and planted where they are wanted. Daphnes have a way of dying suddenly from no apparent cause, but seem to do this less in a limy soil. For *D. odora*, also an early-flowering species, *see* p. 27, and for later-flowering species *see* p. 59.

1 Jasminum nudiflorum   2 Viburnum fragrans candidum   3 Hamamelis mollis brevipetala
4 Hamamelis 'Ruby Glow'   5 Erica x darleyensis   6 Daphne mezereum

WINTER HERBACEOUS FLOWERS

There are not many herbaceous plants that flower in the winter months, and most of these, though they will grow quite happily anywhere, need particular conditions if they are to flower satisfactorily. In general, these conditions are not difficult to provide. All the plants illustrated here, except the iris, belong to the Buttercup family.

1 **IRIS unguicularis (stylosa).** This Algerian and eastern mediterranean iris needs to be planted in very poor limy soil in a position where it will be sun-parched in summer, such as the base of a south wall, with stones among the rhizomes to help retain the heat of summer. It usually flowers best after a hot dry summer, and will produce often a great many flowers which may appear any time from September till April, and are sweetly scented. Slugs are prone to eat through the stems, so it is a good idea to pick the buds as soon as they are big enough and bring them indoors to open. Iris *unguicularis* dislikes being disturbed.

There are various colour forms — *alba* (white); *speciosa* (deep lavender-blue with bright yellow keel); *grandiflora* (deep purple); and *lilacina* (pale lilac).

2 **HELLEBORUS atrorubens.** One of the earliest of the Lent roses to flower, its plum-purple flowers may start opening as early as December. They begin to open near the ground, and as the stalk grows, more buds open until there are several flowers on foot-high stems. The leaves are large and divided into leaflets. Like all hellebores it needs a shady site, with rich moist soil, and should not be disturbed.

The species *H. abchasicus* from the Caucasus is a maroon-crimson, usually speckled with a deeper colour and with some green. There are also green-flowered hellebores (*see* p. 13).

3 **HELLEBORUS niger.** The Christmas rose is not always easy to make flower, though it sometimes does extremely well in quite unexpected places, and will flower from December to March. It needs rich, moist soil and a shady position, and is improved by a dressing of well-rotted manure in spring. The plant is perfectly hardy but, to produce long-stemmed flowers and to keep their petals undamaged, the plants are often boxed and covered with glass when the buds are forming. The leaves are very dark and leathery, and the white flowers are sometimes flushed with pink.

The variety *altifolius* (high leaves) has flowers usually tinged rose and hidden among the leaves. 'Potter's Wheel' has large white flowers on stalks about 1 ft. tall.

4 **ANEMONE hepatica** (now classified in a separate genus, Hepatica). These little plants, flowering from February to April, do best in a firm, retentive, limy soil, with a cool root-run. The bottom of a north wall is a good place for them, with pieces of stone on the surface of the bed. As with most winter-flowering plants, they hate disturbance. The common *H. triloba* has been grown in Britain for a long time, and there are several varieties — *alba* (white); *rubra* (reddish-pink); *caerulea* (deep blue); and double forms of the pink and the blue, *H. transsilvatica*, the species illustrated, is larger in all parts and a stronger grower.

5 **RANUNCULUS ficaria major (Giant Celandine)** is a large form of the common celandine, but not to be confused with the greater celandine, which belongs to the poppy family. Like the wild flower, it is one of the earliest herbaceous flowers to appear, and also needs a cool moist position. The name 'ranunculus' comes from the Latin *rana* = a frog, because many of the genus like marshy places where frogs abound.

R. ficaria major is about four times the size of the common celandine, making an imposing plant about a foot high. There is a white variety of *R. ficaria* (*alba*) and also a copper-orange (*cupreus*), and *R. ficaria flore-pleno* is a double form. All these are only 3–4 ins. tall.

VIOLA odorata (Sweet Violet). There are many garden forms of this common native plant, with bigger flowers, some double, and in various shades of violet, blue, rose, and white. Many of these are useful for growing in a cold frame for early blossom. They do best in a moderately heavy, rich soil. For other violas *see* p. 55.

1 IRIS UNGUICULARIS   2 HELLEBORUS ATRORUBENS   3 HELLEBORUS NIGER
4 ANEMONE HEPATICA   5 RANUNCULUS FICARIA MAJOR

EARLY SHADE-TOLERANT BULBS

All the winter and early-spring flowering bulbs illustrated here, excepting the leucojum, prefer a shady or half shady situation. Leucojum requires sun or half shade. All also prefer a well-drained, moist, leaf-mouldy soil, though some are more tolerant than others.

1 **ERYTHRONIUM**, from *erythros* = red, the colour of the flowers in the European species *E. dens-canis*, 'Dog's Tooth Violet'. Erythroniums are native to Europe, Asia, Japan, and America, the greatest number and the most beautiful coming from the western states of the U.S.A. *E. tuolumnense* comes from Tuolumne County in California, and grows up to a foot tall, with several flowers on a stem. Some other American species, such as *E. oregonum* (white) and *E. revolutum* (deep pink), have leaves beautifully marked in brown, which has led to the local names of 'Trout' or 'Faun' lilies. The natural hybrids 'White Beauty' and 'Pink Beauty' are good garden plants also. The European *E. dens-canis* also has leaves marbled with brown and varies in colour from white, through pink, to deep violet. All erythroniums like plenty of humus and moisture while in growth.

2 **ANEMONE ranunculoides** (from *anemos* = wind, the Wind Flower). This native of Europe is closely related to the wood anemone, *A. nemorosa*, a common British wild plant with garden forms in white, pink, or blue and also double white. The best variety of *A. ranunculoides* is that illustrated, which is also known as *superba*. The young foliage is bronzy in tint. There is also a double form *A. ranunculoides plena*.

3-4 **GALANTHUS** (**Snowdrop**), *gala* = milk, *anthos* = flower. In most gardens snowdrops are the first plants to flower in the year. *G. nivalis*, the common snowdrop, is a native of Britain, but for the garden there are improved forms of *G. nivalis* and other species from Greece, South Russia, and Turkey, which are more worth growing. They appear to cross fertilize readily, producing many varieties which differ in height, size of flower, markings, and time of flowering. The two illustrated, *G. nivalis* 'S. Arnott' (probably an Italian form) and *G. nivalis atkinsii*, are very good choices for the ordinary garden and increase freely. *G. elwesii* is a very variable species which prefers sun and has handsome wide leaves and green markings not only at the top of the inner segments but also at their base. There are autumn-flowering forms of *G. nivalis* — *reginae-olgae* and *corcyrensis* — and several double forms which in fact are less graceful than the singles. There are two rare varieties in which the markings are yellow, but these are not generally available.

5 **LEUCOJUM** (**Snowflake**). In contrast to snowdrops, snowflakes have all the petals the same size, giving a bell-shaped flower. Like snowdrops, they naturalize readily. *L. vernum*, the spring snowflake, comes from Central Europe, and has a strong-growing variety with two flowers on a stem, *L. vernum vagneri*, as well as one in which the spots are yellow. *L. aestivum*, Summer Snowflake, found wild on river banks in Britain, is taller and does not usually flower until April or later. It has up to five rather smaller flowers on a stem, and will grow in a wet soil.

6 **CYCLAMEN**. Hardy cyclamen are also called Sow-Bread from the delight with which pigs will root them up in the wild. There are spring and autumn flowering cyclamen (*see* p. 177), natives of Central and Southern Europe, Turkey, and Northern Persia. A collection of the species available will give bloom from August to April, except in freezing weather, starting with the sweet-scented carmine *C. europaeum* in August and ending with the bright crimson *C. repandum* in April-May. The parent of the greenhouse plants is the wild *C. persicum* from the Eastern Mediterranean.

The naming of these plants is very confusing. The plant illustrated has been called *C. ibericum, atkinsii,* or *vernum*, and an exactly similar plant but plain green leaves is known as *C. coum* or *C. orbiculatum coum*. Whatever the name, all these hardy species require a well-drained, stony, leafy soil, and do well under deciduous trees and even high-branched pines.

7 **ERANTHIS** (**Winter Aconite**). Together with the snowdrops, these are among the first flowers of the garden year, appearing in late January or early February and dying away before the leaves appear on the trees. The best for the garden is the sterile hybrid *E. x tubergeniana*, a cross between *E. cilicica* from Greece and Turkey and the early-flowering *E. hyemalis*. This latter is suitable for the wild part of the garden where it will seed itself and spread, but may be a nuisance elsewhere. E. 'Guinea Gold' is another excellent hybrid, producing large, golden-yellow blooms about March.

1 Erythronium tuolumnense 2 Anemone ranunculoides major 3 Galanthus nivalis 'S. Arnott'
4 Galanthus nivalis atkinsii 5 Leucojum vernum 6 Cyclamen vernum
7 Eranthis x tubergeniana

SUN-LOVING SPRING BULBS

These are all plants which prefer full sun though, except for Anemone *blanda*, they will tolerate some shade, but not for more than half a day. They all look much more effective if concentrated in a limited area rather than dotted about the garden. They are very easy to grow in any ordinary soil, and will seed themselves freely if undisturbed.

1 PUSCHKINIA **scilloides (Striped Squill).** The name is in honour of Count Mussin-Pushkin, a Russian who collected plants in the Lebanon, Turkey, and the Caucasus, the home of puschkinia. Neither this nor the very lovely white variety is as much grown as it should be, for they offer no difficulty.

2 ANEMONE **blanda.** This is one of a group of anemones which have tuberous roots and come from places with hot summers, such as Greece and the Near East. *A. blanda*, a native of Greece, needs full sun to open its large flowers — up to 2 ins. across. 'Blue Star', 'Charmer' (pink), and 'White Splendour' are good varieties, and *A. blanda scythinica* is a very attractive white variety with a blue reverse to the petals.

A. apennina is very similar, but has rather smaller flowers on 6-in. stems. It does very well in shade and will colonize beneath and around shrubs and trees.

3 CHIONODOXA, from *chion* = snow, *doxa* = glory, for they flower as the snow melts on the Turkish mountains. The best garden species come from Turkey, though they are also found in Crete and Cyprus. The commonest is *C. luciliae*, a soft blue with a white eye, and there are also white and pink varieties. *C. gigantea rosea* is larger, and there is also an excellent white form. *C. sardensis* is almost a gentian blue with no white eye; and *C. tmoli* is a small bright blue later-flowering species.

4-5 MUSCARI **(Grape Hyacinth).** These bulbs from Mediterranean countries grow so easily and increase so freely that they can become a nuisance; therefore, except for rare species, it is better to cut off the seed heads before the seeds ripen. *M. tubergeniana* (4), however, is a choicer species which does not increase too fast. M. 'Old Blue' (5) and also the paler blue 'Cantab' are probably seedlings from the large-flowered *M. armeniacum*. There are two lovely white varieties, *M. botryoides album* and the later-flowering *M. argeae album*. Some, particularly *M. moschatum* (Musk Hyacinth), have a sweet musk scent and prefer to grow in a hot place. *M. macrocarpum* has bright yellow flowers and is highly scented.

An unusual variety is *M. comosum monstrosum*, the Feather or Plume Hyacinth. It produces a profusion of bluish-violet flowers in dense, loose plumes in May. The flowers last a long time but set no seed.

6 HYACINTHUS **azureus (Muscari azureum).** This is a true hyacinth, about 3–6 ins. high, which looks charming in March if a number are planted together. There is also a white form and a larger, later-flowering one, *H. azureus amphibolis*, which has many more flowers to a spike.

The Pyrenean *H. amethystinus*, which is like a miniature bluebell, about 8 ins. tall, flowers in May and has a white form also.

7 SCILLA **(Squill** or **Wild Hyacinth).** The most common species to be found in gardens is the bright blue *S. siberica*, the best variety of which is 'Spring Beauty'. The Spanish form of the bluebell, *S. hispanica* (now usually classed as *Endymion hispanicus*) is also common but later flowering, and has blue, purple, pink, and white forms. The species illustrated, *S. bifolia*, from Southern Europe and Turkey is a rarer plant and the best forms are not yet easy to obtain.

There are several good May and June flowering scillas, in particular *S. pratensis* and its variety *amethystina*, which grow 6–12 ins. tall and have crowded spikes of violet, starlike flowers.

1 PUSCHKINIA SCILLOIDES   2 ANEMONE BLANDA   3 CHIONODOXA GIGANTEA ROSEA
4 MUSCARI TUBERGENIANA   5 MUSCARI 'OLD BLUE'   6 HYACINTHUS AZUREUS
7 SCILLA BIFOLIA

EARLY SUN-LOVING BULBS. 2

The plants on this page are all fairly easy to grow. They need a well-drained, preferably limy soil and a position in full sun with some shelter from north and east winds, as, for example, in open spaces between deciduous shrubs. In such conditions they will flower in February and March, even after severe winters when the flowers of shrubs have been browned off by frost. Heavy soils must be lightened with gravel, humus, and such materials, and these bulbs benefit always from a generous feed of bone meal, applied during the winter.

1 IRIS **danfordiae**. This very early-flowering, short-stemmed iris is named after a Mrs. Danford and comes from the Taurus Mts. of southern Turkey. The leaves are short at flowering time but grow longer later and must not be cut back. The bulbs, after flowering, tend to split into many bulblets which take several years to reach flowering size again. A light dusting of dried-blood fertilizer helps them to mature more quickly, but as the bulbs are cheap, it is best to renew them annually.

2 IRIS **histrioides major**. The word *histrio* means 'actor', and this species and *I. histrio* are so named because their brilliant colouring is like an actor painted for the show. This iris flowers at the same time as *I. danfordiae* and looks well planted with it. The form *I. h. major* has flowers up to 4 ins. across on short stems. The bulbs should be lifted every 2–3 years after the foliage has died down, dried in an airy place, and replanted in the autumn.

3 IRIS **reticulata**. An iris from the Caucasus which flowers rather later than Nos. 1 and 2 and has a delicate scent of violets. It grows about 6 ins. tall, and the flowers appear with the leaves. There are several varieties and hybrids. The variety 'Cantab' is pale blue; 'J. S. Dijt', red-purple; 'Royal Blue', dark blue; and 'Wentworth', purple-blue. The hybrid 'Harmony' is sky-blue; 'Clarette', pale and deep blue; and 'Spring Time', blue and violet flaked white.

4 NARCISSUS **cyclamineus**. This Portuguese plant, which grows about 6 ins. tall, differs from the other bulbs on this page in preferring a damp, though not boggy, situation. When it has a situation it likes it will sow itself freely.

Many of the hybrids, including the one illustrated, 'February Gold', grow rather taller — up to 12 ins. —

except for 'Snipe', a cream and yellow hybrid. The hybrid 'Beryl' is primrose-yellow with a small orange cup; 'Charity May' is a soft clear yellow; 'Dove Wings' has a creamy-white perianth and canary-yellow cup.

5 NARCISSUS **asturiensis**. A native of Spain and Portugal which used to be called *N. minimus* because it is the smallest of the trumpet daffodils. It varies both in height and shape of trumpet, but is usually about 4 ins. tall. In its native surroundings, it flowers just below the melting snow, but is dry later.

Other dwarf trumpet daffodils are a little taller, about 6–8 ins., and are slightly scented. *N. minor* is deep yellow; *N. pumilus*, bright yellow; and *N. nanus*, pale yellow and sulphur.

6 CROCUS **sieberi atticus**. A good and easily grown crocus from the mountains of Greece, with several varieties such as 'Violet Queen' and 'Hubert Edelsten', which has the outer petals marked with crimson and purple.

7-8 CROCUS **chrysanthus**. 'Warley White' and 'Zwanenberg Bronze' are two of many varieties of the wild *C. chrysanthus* which comes from Turkey and Greece. Some of the best blue crocuses belong to this species.

There are a great many species of spring-flowering crocuses, and some, such as *C. biflorus*, have several colour forms. *C. susianus* (Cloth of Gold Crocus) is a golden yellow with bronze exterior. *C. tomasinianus* from Dalmatia has pale lavender flowers with a white throat and spreads so fast it may become a weed; but the variety 'Whitewell Purple', a lovely reddish-purple, does not have this disadvantage.

Mice have a tendency to dig down to and eat the corms of all crocuses. For autumn-flowering crocuses *see* p. 183.

1 IRIS DANFORDIAE   2 IRIS HISTRIOIDES MAJOR   3 IRIS RETICULATA
4 NARCISSUS CYCLAMINEUS   5 NARCISSUS ASTURIENSIS   6 CROCUS SIEBERI ATTICUS
7 CROCUS CHRYSANTHUS 'WARLEY WHITE'   8 CROCUS CHRYSANTHUS 'ZWANENBERG BRONZE'

WOODLAND PLANTS WITH GREENISH FLOWERS

Many of the flowers that bloom very early in the year, especially those which grow in the shade, are green or greenish white or yellow. If they flowered later, when other plants had grown up round them, they would hardly be noticed; but early in the year they show up well. They prefer a cool soil with plenty of humus and moisture during the growing period.

1 EPIMEDIUM **pinnatum** (*epi* = upon, *media* = land of the Medes). These plants, sometimes called Barren-wort or Bishop's Hat, will grow anywhere, though they prefer semi-shade and cool soil. The more common varieties make good ground cover as weeds cannot penetrate their tough congested roots. The foliage is delicately shaped and the young leaves a lovely pinkish colour. The old leaves get coarse and tattered, but they protect the fragile flowers from late May frosts, and so should not be cut off in places where frosts are likely, such as low-lying gardens.

Most epimediums flower later than the other plants on this page — in May. *See* also p. 49.

2 HELLEBORUS **corsicus.** The hellebores, members of the buttercup family, are some of the best very early-flowering plants (*see* p. 5). This species comes from Corsica, where it grows in stony soil on banks, and the trusses of flowers, when heavy with seed, rest on the bank. In English gardens it will grow under trees, but the plants may need staking if they grow tall. The evergreen leaves are decorative all through the year, and the flowers persist from January till June. The plant grows from 1–1½ ft. tall.

3 ARUM **italicum marmoratum.** The leaves of this arum are more interesting than the flower, which is much like the native *A. maculatum* (Lords and Ladies). The flower, however, produces a sturdy spike about a foot high of orange-scarlet fruit in the summer. The leaves appear in the late autumn or very early spring. The plants naturalize easily in woodland.

4 HACQUETIA **epipactis,** named after a German botanist, B. Hacquet. Very early in the year the green-gold flowers open at ground level, and as the flower stalks grow, the bracts of the flower become greener until, by May, when they are about 6 ins. tall, they are the same colour as the leaves. The pincushion of seed vessels remains slightly gold. Hacquetia prefers a heavy loam soil, and very much dislikes being disturbed. This plant is now often called *Dondia epipactis.*

5 EUPHORBIA **(Spurge),** named after Euphorbus, physician to an ancient king of Mauritania. This is a very large family of annual and perennial herbs, shrubs, and trees. Some, such as the poinsettias (*E. pulcherrima*), are greenhouse plants. Many are succulent plants, mostly from South Africa, and these are not hardy. Several of the hardy herbaceous euphorbias are wild plants in Britain.

The evergreen euphorbias are useful in the garden as they will grow in any position in any soil, and their handsome blue-green leaves last throughout the year. The showy part of the flowers is not the flower itself but the yellow-green or burnt-orange bracts round the flower. Some species start flowering very early in the year, even in the winter, and the flower-heads survive for many weeks.

E. wulfeni, the species illustrated, forms a clump up to 4 ft. tall and flowers from March to July. *E. epithymoides* is a more slender plant, about 1 ft. tall. *E. myrsinites* has a prostrate growth, yellow flowers, and light glaucous-green fleshy leaves. Other species flower later in the year. *E. lathyrus* (Caper Spurge) flowers in May and has large green bracts; and *E. marginata* is an annual which flowers in September and has large white bracts and white margined leaves.

DAPHNE **laureola (Spurge Laurel).** This early-flowering evergreen daphne, a native of Britain, grows from 2–4 ft. tall and is more useful for its foliage than its flowers. The flowers are greenish-yellow and fragrant and appear from February. For other daphnes *see* pp. 3, 27 and 59.

SARCOCOCCA (*sarkos* = fleshy, *kokkas* = berry). *S. confusa,* an evergreen shrub up to 6 ft. tall, and *S. humilis,* only 1–1½ ft. tall, are hardy plants which will grow in any well-drained, reasonably rich soil and prefer a shady position. The white flowers appear as early as January in small clusters and are very fragrant. They produce round shining black fruits, and sometimes there are flowers and fruit at the same time.

1 Epimedium pinnatum   2 Helleborus corsicus   3 Arum italicum (leaf)
4 Hacquetia epipactis   5 Euphorbia wulfeni

PRIMROSES AND POLYANTHUS

Primroses and polyanthus (primulas) are among the easiest plants to grow if certain basic principles are remembered. Their chief requirements are semi-shade, humus, regular division, and moisture. The dappled shade of apple trees, which allows a certain amount of sunshine to filter through, or that from tall perennials, gives all the shade needed. Humus can be in the form of leaf-mould, old rotted manure, peat, spent hops, or even wool shoddy. Primroses do not like waterlogged soil and will not do well in heavy clay unless a certain amount of sand or grit is added, as well as plenty of humus. Watering is important in dry weather, and where watering is difficult a mulch of peat, straw, or very old manure helps to keep the plants from drying out.

There is a vast number of species and varieties of garden primulas growing from 2–3 ins. to 3–4 ft. tall and flowering from February or March to June or July. Here are given a few early flowering kinds, mostly belonging to the two groups, Vernales and Auricula. *See also* pp. 21, 44 and 75.

1-2 PRIMULA vulgaris x veris (Polyanthus). A hybrid of the common primrose and the oxlip which has been grown since 1564. Coloured forms as distinct from yellow ones began to appear in the mid-17th century, and today good strains, such as the Blackmore and Langdon's or the Toogoods Excelsior strains, produce large heads of a wide variety of brilliant colours, growing 8–12 ins. tall and flowering from April to June. Seeds can be sown in June in a prepared seed-bed in the open or in boxes, and the seedlings planted into their permanent positions in the autumn. The seed sometimes takes a long time to germinate, especially if the soil is dry.

Hose-in-Hose, sometimes called the Duplex Primrose, has one flower inside another, and there are hose-in-hose forms of primrose, polyanthus, or cowslip. Special varieties of hose-in-hose primulas can be obtained, such as 'Dark Beauty', deep crimson; 'Irish Molly', lavender; 'Lady Lettice', pale yellow flushed apricot; 'Sparkler', vivid scarlet.

3 PRIMULA denticulata, so called because its leaves become toothed as they get older and longer. These 'drumstick' primulas do best in moist loam, with some shade, and are suitable for the wild garden as well as the border or rock garden. They may often be in flower in March. There is a white variety (*alba*), and also pink (*rosea*), and red (*rubra*).

4 PRIMULA auricula (ear-shaped). The old name was Bear's Ears, and the garden varieties were popular flowers among miners and weavers in earlier days. Unlike other primulas they do best in well-drained rocky crevices in full sun. There are two main groups: the show auriculas which have powdered flowers and stems and need the protection of a cold house, and the alpine auriculas which are hardy garden plants, but some need protection from bad weather. There are a great number of named varieties, attractive ones being *auricula alpina*, golden yellow; 'Blairside Yellow'; 'Blue Velvet'; and 'Old Red Dusty Miller', brick red. Auriculas produce particularly beautiful crimson-maroon, purple, and lilac varieties. It is important to protect the plants from slugs.

5 PRIMULA vulgaris. Jack-in-the-Green, or 'Jack-in-the-Pulpit', has an enlarged leaf-like calyx, resembling an Elizabethan ruff. Some are in the form of primroses, others of polyanthus, and they can be in various colours. Attractive varieties are 'Tipperary Purple', pinkish-purple; 'Eldorado', gold; 'Orlando', primrose; and 'Salamander', crimson with golden centre.

6 PRIMULA vulgaris flore plena. The double primroses are among the most difficult plants to grow, succeeding in some places and refusing to grow in others, for no apparent reason. They need constant division and feeding with decayed manure or bone meal. Many of the old varieties no longer exist, and others are extremely scarce. There are many varieties, of which these are some: *lilacina plena* (lavender), *alba plena* (white), 'Bon Accord', forms in cerise, bright rose, magenta, and lavender; 'Chevithorne Purple'; 'Cloth of Gold' (sulphur); 'Crimson King'; 'Mme. de Pompadour' (dark crimson); 'Our Pat' (violet); 'Prince Silverwings' (lilac-crimson silver edged, splashed orange). All are 6 ins. tall and flower in April and May.

7 PRIMULA vulgaris heterochroma (Blue Primrose). Many strains of primroses in various shades of blue are in cultivation, some of polyanthus habit. Two good ones are 'Blue Horizon' and 'Blue Ribbon'. There are also white, purple, and yellow forms. *P. vulgaris sibthorpii* is an early-flowering variety with red or pink flowers.

8 PRIMULA x pruhoniciana 'Garryarde Guinivere'. A hybrid of *P. juliae*, which is itself an early-flowering dwarf, compact species with green leaves. This strain has wrinkled red-bronze leaves and flowers, often frilled. Other varieties are 'Enid' (rose-pink with orange eye); 'Galahad' (frilled white); 'Grail' (deep purple-red); 'Victory' (crimson-purple). These are all about 3–4 ins. tall and are suitable for growing in moist places such as the margin of a pool.

9 PRIMULA x pruhoniciana (juliana) 'Lady Greer'. These miniature polyanthus are early and free-flowering and like moist, fairly shady places. The well-known 'Wanda' primroses belong to this group, and there are other varieties in crimson, purple, pink, and lilac.

1 Primula 'Polyanthus' 2 Primula 'Hose-in-Hose' 3 Primula denticulata
4 Primula auricula alpina 5 Primula v. 'Jack-in-the-Green' 6 Primula v. lilacina plena
7 Primula v. heterochroma 8 Primula 'Garryarde Guinivere' 9 Primula x pruhoniciana 'Lady Greer' 15

SPRING WOODLAND HERBS

Evergreen plants that flower early in the year are valuable for two reasons. Their flowers are welcome when colour is scarce, and afterwards their foliage makes good ground cover. The large shining leaves of bergenia, for example, cover much space and are always attractive, and the long spotted leaves of the pulmonarias become more conspicuous after flowering is over, when they brighten up dark corners and add interest under trees.

1-2 PULMONARIA (Lungwort), from *pulmo* = a lung; the spotted leaves of *P. officinalis* were supposed to resemble diseased lungs, and the plant was used at one time to treat lung diseases. *P. longifolia* (Narrow-leaved Lungwort), and *P. officinalis* (Jerusalem Cowslip) are natives of Europe and the former a wild plant of Southern England. Pulmonarias are easily grown, even in poor soil, and are useful for rough parts of the garden, growing about 1-1½ ft. tall. *P. angustifolia azurea*, the blue Cowslip (1), has pink buds which turn blue as they open. Mawson's variety is an improved form. *P. saccharata* has even more rose-pink buds and is a rather smaller plant. The bright brick-red flowers of *P. rubra* (2) appear so early in the spring that the plant has been called the Christmas Cowslip.

3 SYMPHYTUM (Comfrey), from *sympho* = to heal. Another member of the Forget-me-not family which was used in old days for medicinal purposes. Symphytum is a native of Europe and Western Asia, and the white or purplish *S. officinale* and the yellowish *S. tuberosum* are British wild flowers. A blue-flowered Comfrey, probably *S. peregrinum*, has also established itself in woods and by roadsides. In gardens the pink and blue *S. peregrinum*, growing up to 4 ft. tall, the smaller gentian-blue *S. caucasicum*, and the early-flowering dwarf *S. grandiflorum* with pale yellow flowers and red-tipped buds are all easy to grow in almost any soil or situation. Their showy flowers and coarse hairy leaves make them useful for the wild garden or for growing in clumps under trees.

4 VINCA (Periwinkle). The hardy species are shrubby, trailing natives of Europe, *V. minor* and *V. major* being British wild flowers. The large-leaved forms are excellent for covering large areas or for thickening the lower part of a hedge, but if introduced to places where choice plants are grown, they may well swamp them. The small-leaved forms do not have this disadvantage and make excellent and neat ground cover.

The pale blue *V. acutiflora* from South Europe and the deeper blue variety *dubia* start flowering in the late autumn and continue through the winter and spring. Other species, such as *V. major* and *V. minor* and varieties of these, start flowering in April and continue

through the summer. Both these last two species have white, blue, lavender, and red-purple, as well as double and semi-double, forms. *V. minor variegata* has silver and green leaves.

5 BRUNNERA macrophylla. This used to be called *Anchusa myosotidiflora*, because of its forget-me-not-like flowers in loose sprays. It is now named after a Swiss botanist, Samuel Brunner. It starts flowering in late April or May and continues intermittently throughout the summer. After flowering, the leaves get bigger and coarser, making an excellent ground cover under trees or shrubs. It does best in fairly moist soil in shade, such as a shady border or woodland, and grows about 18 ins. tall.

OMPHALODES verna (Blue-eyed Mary). Most of these forget-me-not-like perennials flower later in the summer, but *O. verna* is spring-flowering. It has large blue flowers with white throats on graceful racemes growing up to 8 ins. tall. It spreads rapidly by runners and is suitable for naturalizing in light woodlands. The June-August-flowering *O. cappadocica* is a rather tufted plant up to 6 ins. tall, with lovely clear blue flowers, which is easy to grow in full or partial shade in leafy soil.

6 BERGENIA (Elephant-leaved Saxifrage). Its large leathery leaves, beautiful at all times, often turn to vivid shades of mahogany and scarlet in winter. Its flowers are carried on stout stems 9 ins. to a foot high and appear early in the year. It is an excellent ground-cover plant, looking particularly attractive growing against paving, and it will flourish in sun or shade.

Two very good species, *B. ligulata* (white or pale pink) and the rather smaller *B. ciliata* (pink), may suffer in a hard winter, but most are very hardy. *B. cordifolia alba* is white and *B. c. purpurea* is purplish-pink. *B. crassifolia* has large red flowers, and *B. delavayi* large crimson-purple flowers and crimson leaves in winter. The hybrid 'Ballawley', a cross between *B. delavayi* and *B. beesii*, has very striking large crimson flowers.

1 PULMONARIA ANGUSTIFOLIA   2 PULMONARIA RUBRA   3 SYMPHYTUM PEREGRINUM
4 VINCA DUBIA   5 BRUNNERA MACROPHYLLA   6 BERGENIA CORDIFOLIA 'CROESUS'

DAFFODILS AND NARCISSI

All daffodils are botanically narcissi, a word derived from *narkau*=to grow stiff, and relating to their narcotic properties. Daffodil, applied originally to the wild Lent Lily, *N. pseudo-narcissus*, comes from an early English word *affodille*. We now use the name daffodil for narcissi with long trumpets. The hundreds of named varieties have been derived from a limited number of wild species from France, Spain, Portugal, and Northern Italy. In Britain, as well as the widespread *N. pseudo-narcissus*, there is the Tenby Daffodil *N. obvallaris*, which is a deep golden-yellow with a shorter, broader tube. The bunch-flowered narcissi have been derived from *N. tazetta* which ranges from Spain eastwards to Japan and is also found in North Africa and the Canaries.

In order to bring some order into the vast number of varieties of narcissi, the Royal Horticultural Society has grouped them into eleven divisions. Three are based on the size of the trumpet or cup in relation to the outer petals or perianth; one includes all double garden forms; and five include those in which the characteristics of other wild species are clearly evident in the hybrid. The two remaining divisions are for wild species and wild hybrids. The division is put in brackets for each group described.

All garden narcissi like a good loam in sun or half shade and to be divided when they become too crowded. They should not be lifted until the foliage has become yellow; then they can be dried in a cool shady place, and replanted in the autumn. If lifted or not, foliage should not be removed until it has died down. *Narcissi* for show need a special technique.

1 TRUMPET NARCISSI (**Daffodils**) (I), are those with the trumpet as long as or longer than the perianth. 'Mount Hood' together with 'Beersheba' remain the best of the reasonably priced pure white daffodils. Of pure yellows 'Golden Harvest' and 'King Alfred' are as good as any. 'Foresight' has an ivory perianth and a primrose trumpet.

2 JONQUILLA HYBRIDS (VII). These usually retain the perfume of the single sweet jonquil *N. jonquilla*, and are all some shade of yellow or orange. 'Lanarth' (golden yellow) and 'Trevithian' (pale lemon) are well tried varieties, as also is the dainty, butter-yellow, late-flowering 'Baby Moon'. The variety painted, 'Polnesk', is a good garden variety which stands up well to rough weather, but is still not easily obtained and more expensive.

3 LARGE-CUPPED NARCISSI (II) have several colour combinations. 'Carbineer' is a characteristic variety of those with yellow perianth and coloured cup; 'Carlton' is all soft yellow; 'Fortune' has a coppery-red cup. Some large-cupped narcissi have a white or whitish perianth and a coloured cup. 'Coverack Perfection' is cream with a reddish edge to the cup; 'Kilworth' has an orange-red cup; 'Papillon Blanche' has a white and yellow fluted crown. A few large-cupped narcissi have white perianths and cups; the only two reasonably priced ones at present are 'Castella' and 'White Nile'.

4 POETICUS NARCISSI (IX). The best known is the sweet-scented late-flowering 'Old Pheasant's Eye' Narcissus, *N. recurvus*, which grows in millions in the alpine meadows, and also varieties of *N. poeticus* also called 'Pheasant's Eye'. *N. recurvus* is a plant for naturalizing; for the garden N. 'Actaea' or, perhaps, 'Queen of Narcissi' are the best choices.

5 TAZETTA VARIETIES (VIII). The original poetaz varieties were derived from crossing varieties of the bunch-flowered narcissi *N. tazetta* and *N. poeticus*. The result produced fewer but larger flowers on the stem than on *N. tazetta*. Of the varieties available, 'Geranium' is a very good one; 'Scarlet Gem' has a yellow perianth and orange-scarlet cup; and 'St. Agnes' has a pure white perianth and shallow red cup.

6 SMALL-CUPPED NARCISSI (III). There are still only a few varieties, some of which are expensive. These narcissi are very suitable for a small garden, and the following are reasonable in price: 'La Riante' (illustrated); 'Firetail', cream perianth and scarlet cup; 'Polar Ice', white perianth and white flat cup, green in the centre; 'Verger' white with orange cup.

DOUBLE NARCISSI (IV). Doubles belong to various groups. There are the old ones, still in cultivation, such as *N. poeticus plenus*, the double white poeticus; the double sweet jonquil, *N. jonquilla plena*: the double campanelle jonquil, *N. odorus rugulosus plenus*: and the older still, *N. telamonius plenus*, the Van Sion daffodil. Of newer doubles the most popular are 'Mary Copeland', creamy-white with lemon and orange-red segments; 'Mrs. William Copeland', white with creamy-yellow segments; and a little more expensive, the exquisite primrose-yellow self 'Camellia'.

CYCLAMINEUS NARCISSUS (VI) *see* p. 11.

1 TRUMPET NARCISSUS 'MOUNT HOOD'
3 LARGE-CUPPED NARCISSUS 'CARBINEER'
5 TAZETTA VARIETY 'GERANIUM'

2 JONQUILLA HYBRID 'POLNESK
4 POETICUS NARCISSUS 'ACTAEA'
6 SMALL-CUPPED NARCISSUS 'LA RIANTE'

CUSHION PLANTS FOR ROCK GARDENS

The plants on this page are natives of alpine or sub-alpine regions, either in Europe or other parts of the world, or garden hybrids. In their native environment they have to survive through the winter·in frozen soil with little moisture, and in the dark under a deep covering of snow; and in summer are subjected to intense light, strong drying winds, and night frosts. Consequently, to withstand these conditions they tend to form compact cushions with long roots. When the snows melt in the spring, the plants burst into bloom suddenly, earlier in lower places and later higher up. In England in a cold spring some of them may not flower until towards the end of April and into May.

1 MORISIA **monantha.** A densely tufted plant from near the sea in Sardinia and Corsica, and it grows well in sandy soil but tends to damp off in rich soil. Its stemless flowers appear very early in the spring.

2 SOLDANELLA **villosa.** The name comes from the Italian *soldo* = a coin, because of the shape of the leaves. Soldanella are not difficult to grow in the rock garden but they do often fail to flower, for the buds, which form in the autumn and lie dormant through the winter, may have been eaten by slugs. They grow best in half shade in a soil rich in humus. *S. alpina* is a wild flower of the Alps and Pyrenees. *S. villosa* and *S. montana* have rather larger flowers, and the former is the most free-flowering; *S. minima* has small white and pink bells.

3 PRIMULA **marginata.** This miniature primula from the Maritime Alps has thick, notched, leathery leaves, and flowers very early. 'Linda Pope' is a hybrid of *P. marginata*. These particular alpine primulas prefer a well-drained loam, rich in leaf-mould, but grow and flower freely under most conditions. *See also p. 15.*

DOUGLASIA **vitaliana.** Douglasia is another of the Primrose family, five species of which come from North America and are pink, while *D. vitaliana* is bright yellow and is abundant in the European alps, especially on acid soils, but will grow in lime. Although this plant is easy to cultivate in a sunny well-drained situation, it is often reluctant to flower, especially if it has been disturbed. The grey-leaved variety *D. v. praetutiana* flowers freely.

ANDROSACE. Another of the Primrose family, closely related to douglasia and primula. There are many species, mostly dwarf, tufted, alpine plants with rose, pink, or white flowers. Most of them flower rather later than the plants on this page, but some, such as *A. villosa arachnoidea*, begin flowering in April. *A. villosa superba* has large heads of snow-white flowers; *A. jaquemontii*, a new introduction, has deep pink flowers; *A. sarmentosa* 'Brilliant' blossoms rather later and has silver rosettes of foliage, and rich pink flowers with crimson eyes. *A. lanuginosa* is a rather larger plant with silvery, trailing foliage and lilac-pink flowers which appear in the summer.

4 DRABA **(Whitlow Grass).** These bright green or grey-green cushions send up slender stems carrying bright yellow, white, or violet flowers in April. They grow best in a sharp scree in full sun. There are a great many species, most of which are perennial. The one illustrated, *D. aizoides*, is very easy to grow. *D. dedeana* from the Pyrenees has dainty white flowers. *D. bryoides imbricata* is a tiny variety with bright yellow flowers ideal for a miniature or sink garden (*see* p. 94).

5-7 SAXIFRAGA. The name comes from *saxum* = rock, and *frango* = break, and many species of this very large genus look best in a crevice in a wall or rock. They also do well in a sunny scree, or bed of rubble, which gives the essential good drainage. The Kabschia group are the best of the early-flowering cushion saxifrages. They form dense tufts with flowers on stems about 2 ins. or less long. They like open, but partly shaded positions and, except for the amethyst-coloured *S. lilacina*, they prefer a limy soil. The flowers are sometimes spoilt by heavy spring rains unless the plants are protected by glass when the buds are opening. *S. x. jenkinsae* (5) is a hybrid, probably bred from the white *S. burseriana* and *S. lilacina*. Other good Kabschia hybrid saxifrages are *S. haagii*, bright yellow; *S. irvingii*, lilac pink; and S. 'Cranbourne', deep pink.

Another group allied to Kabschia is Engleria, of which *S. grisebachii* (7) is typical. It is a native of the mountains of Greece and Albania, and the Wisley variety has also been found wild in Albania. The purple *S. porophylla*, the yellow *S. stuartii*, and some of the hybrids between species of Kabschia and Engleria are excellent.

S. oppositifolia (6) belongs to the Porphyrion group, which have large rose-purple flowers and are mat-forming plants.

For later-flowering Saxifrages, *see* pp. 43 and 49.

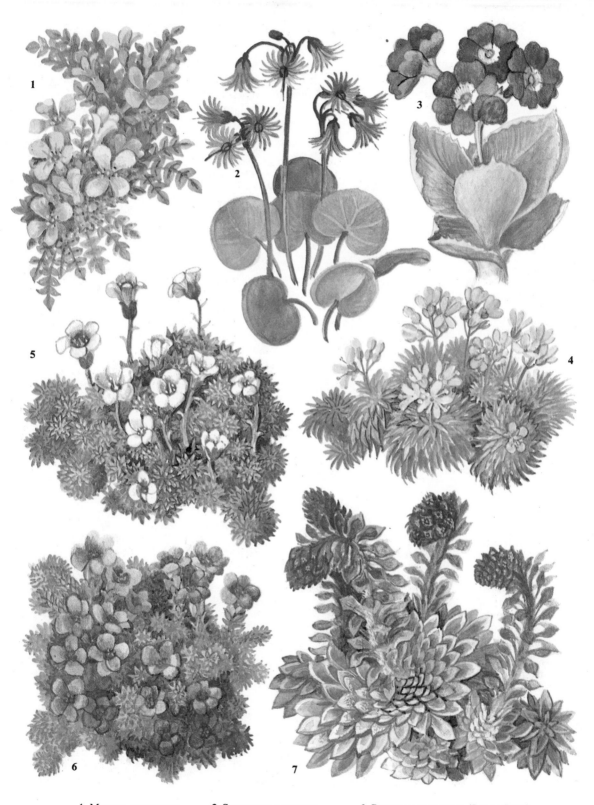

1 Morisia monantha   2 Soldanella villosa   3 Primula marginata 'Linda Pope'
4 Draba aizoides   5 Saxifraga x jenkinsae   6 Saxifraga oppositifolia
7 Saxifraga grisebachii 'Wisley' Variety

MARCH SHRUBS. 1

With March the shrub season may truly be said to begin in earnest. All those represented are hardy, but if it is possible to plant them where there is hedge shelter from the north and east, there is less danger of the flowers being blighted by bitter winds.

1 FORSYTHIA, named after William Forsyth, a late 18th-century gardener at the Royal Gardens, Kensington. One species comes from Albania, the others, excepting the hybrids, from China. Forsythias flower, usually very freely, on the bare branches of the previous year's growth. One of the new varieties, great improvements on the older ones, should be grown. One of the latest and best is *F. x Beatrix Farrand* from the Arnold Arboretum of the U.S.A., which will make a 6–8 ft. shrub with large golden-yellow flowers up to 2 in. across and of exceptionally strong texture. Two other excellent shrubs, although with somewhat smaller flowers, are *F. x intermedia spectabilis* 'Lynwood', and the black-stemmed *F. suspensa atrocaulis* 'Nyman's Variety'. For trailing over an arch or pergola or up a tree the long whippy shoots of the old *F. suspensa* are particularly suitable. For small gardens the dwarf and compact *F. ovata*, though less showy, is very useful.

If forsythias fail to flower, the explanation may be that bullfinches and possibly tits have destroyed nearly all the buds before they opened. So in places where there are many bullfinches, some protection in early spring is necessary. Sun and a well-drained rich soil are desirable, and really old wood should be cut out immediately after flowering.

2 BERBERIS. There are about 170 species of berberis and many hybrids which are hardy and can be grown in England. Most of the species come from Asia, but a few from South America. They range in size from 1–12 ft.; some are deciduous and some evergreen; some flower early and some late. In general, the March to May flowering berberis are grown mainly for their flowers, and the June–July flowering species for their fruit (*see* p. 188).

B. darwinii from Chile and named after the famous Charles Darwin, is one of the best evergreen flowering shrubs; the pendant racemes of flower are well set off by the small holly-like leaves. The flowers are followed by blue berries which are rapidly devoured by birds. Its growth is compact and dense and it will make a good hedge. A newer plant from Chile with larger and even more brilliant flowers is *B. linearifolia*, but it has a somewhat ungainly growth. Its hybrid with *B. darwinii*, however, *B. x lologensis*, with pure apricot but rather smaller flowers, has a more compact habit of growth. An older *B. darwinii* hybrid, *B. x stenophylla*, has several varieties which are valuable when a slender shrub of pendant habit is desired. There are dwarf forms such as *B. x irwinii* which grow about 2 ft. tall.

3 OSMANTHUS DELAVAYI. This neat, free-flowering, small-leaved evergreen shrub from China was first introduced to France by the Abbé Delavay, though of the seeds he sent only one germinated. It is the only osmanthus worth the attention of the ordinary gardener. The rounded, spreading shrub grows up to 10 ft. high, and the flowers are fragrant. There is a variety with larger leaves, but as the flowers are no larger, it has no advantages over the type.

4 ULEX europaeus flore pleno (Gorse, Furze, or Whin). *U. europaeus* is the spring-flowering native gorse, while *U. minor* and *U. gallii* are autumn-flowering. The wild common gorse is no plant for the garden, but the double form is a first class plant, being more compact in habit and capable of being kept so by pruning. The mass of double flowers are a truly brilliant gold. It is a plant for a sunny position in poor dry soil; it grows too rank and flowers less in rich soil.

STACHYURUS praecox. *Stachys* = spike, *oura* = tail, because the spikes of flowers are like tails. This early-flowering shrub from Japan has long reddish-brown branches, leafless at flowering, which are hung with numerous racemes of pale yellow bell-shaped flowers. The racemes hang in a curious stiff fashion which is unique. *S. praecox* is a deciduous shrub growing 5–10 ft. tall, and the flowers begin to appear in February.

1 Forsythia x intermedia spectabilis
2 Berberis darwinii
3 Osmanthus delavayi
4 Ulex europaeus flore pleno

MARCH SHRUBS. 2

1 P R U N U S tenella (Dwarf Almond). The prunus genus includes plums, cherries, apricots, peaches, and almonds. Most of them are natives of temperate regions and several of Britain. *P. subhirtella autumnalis* flowers in the winter (*see* p. viii); some of the Japanese cherries (*P. serrulata*) flower in May (*see* p. 60); certain varieties of plums, peaches, apricots, and almonds are among the many March–April flowering shrubs. One variety of the almond tree, *P. communis praecox*, is in flower by February.

P. tenella, previously known as *P. nana* or *Amygdalus nana*, is a charming dwarf plant usually not more than 2 ft. tall and suitable, therefore, for the front of a shrub bed or border. It is inclined to sucker and form a dwarf thicket, if happy, and so is not really suitable for the rock garden. It comes from South Russia and South East Europe, and has been in cultivation for a very long time. There is a white form, but the best variety is *P. tenella gessleriana* or 'Firehill', introduced from Roumania. It has larger flowers of a much more vivid colour, as also are the buds. Like all almonds it is an excellent plant for a limy soil.

There are several varieties of *P. persica*, the ornamental peaches from China, which make small bushy trees and flower in April. *P. p. albo-plena* is a double pure white; 'Russell's Red' is a double crimson; and 'Clara Meyer' is a double rose-pink.

2 M A G N O L I A x soulangeana. This spreading shrub or tree, raised in the garden of M. Soulange-Bodin near Paris by crossing the white *M. denudata* with the rose-purple *M. liliiflora*, both from China and introduced to Britain from Japan, is one of the most successful of the many magnolias and will grow in any reasonable soil except one heavily charged with lime. There are a number of varieties arising either from seed or by back crossing the species on to the hybrid. The conspicuous large goblet-like flowers appear on the bare branches in April and continue into June as the leaves come. It is a good town tree and is often seen in old London gardens. The variety 'Brozzoni' is white with purple blotches at the base; 'Lennei' is rose-purple outside and paler within; *M. s. stricta* is a rare form with lilac flowers and more erect in habit; and *M. s. speciosa* is pure white with a purple eye.

M. stellata is the earliest magnolia to flower and also has the virtue that it starts to flower when the shrub-like tree is still young. It produces quantities of many petalled, fragrant, white flowers, about 2 ins. across, which become tinged with pink as they fade. (The variety *rosea* has pinker flowers.) *M. stellata*, like many magnolias, needs plenty of peat or leaf-mould in the soil.

Although the magnolias mentioned here are hardy, they are not plants for cold northern districts, as the flowers are blighted by severe frosts.

3 V I B U R N U M x burkwoodii. In 1902 the Korean *V. carlesii* was introduced from Japan, and its neat habit, slow growth, pink buds, and very fragrant pure white flowers soon made it popular in English gardens. Unfortunately it is difficult to propagate from

cuttings, and so it was grafted on the native *V. lantana* (Wayfaring Tree). The foliage being much alike, it was sometimes the more vigorous shoot from the stock which grew unnoticed, and the *V. carlesii* died out. Also this plant from the dry and cold Korean highlands did not flourish in the wetter parts of Britain and became subject to canker. In dry soils and dry areas it still remains the best viburnum, especially for the small garden. In 1924 the firm Burkwood and Skipwith produced the quick-growing, free-flowering, easily propagated *V. x burkwoodii* by crossing *V. carlesii* with the evergreen *V. utile*. This hybrid, although with less pink buds, less pure white flowers, and perfume not quite so sweet as in the original *V. carlesii*, is an excellent early-flowering plant. The hybrid nearest to *V. carlesii* is *V. x juddii*, a cross with the taller and more vigorous *V. bitchiuense*, which is a rapid grower. *V. x juddii* is deciduous, and apparently canker proof, therefore more suitable for wet areas. For later-flowering viburnums grown mainly for their decorative fruit, *see* p. 189. The earliest species is *V. fragrans* (*see* p. 3).

4 R I B E S sanguineum (Flowering Currant). This common cottage-garden shrub, introduced from Western North America in 1826, belongs to the same genus as the red, white, and black currants and gooseberries. Its early and regular flowering, its ease of cultivation, and its rosy-red flowers make it very popular. The original plant has been superseded by better forms with more brilliant colours, such as *atrorubens*, 'King Edward VII', and 'Pulborough Scarlet'. Of these, 'King Edward VII' is the dwarfest and 'Pulborough Scarlet' the most erect. There are also off-white and pale pink varieties, but they are not very effective. The only other species of ribes interesting to the ordinary gardener is *R. speciosum*, the Fuchsia-flowered currant from California, which has scarlet flowers which hang like tiny fuchsias in clusters from the underside of the long branches. This is a spiny shrub, like a gooseberry, and flowers in May or June.

K E R R I A japonica. The double form *flore pleno* is a useful early-flowering shrub, with its pom-pons of bright yellow growing in masses up the long canes. Kerria is often given a wall, but this is unnecessary as it is hardy and will grow almost anywhere. Although called 'japonica', it is a native of China, not Japan, but is commonly cultivated in Japan. It is named in honour of William Kerr of Kew, a collector of plants in China.

S P I R A E A. Many of the shrubby spiraeas are rather dull, but *S. thunbergii* and, even more, the hybrid *S. x arguta* are well worth growing. They make rounded bushes which reach 5–6 ft. tall, and the arching leafless branches of well-grown shrubs are smothered with clusters of white flowers. The flowers of the hybrid are rather larger and come a little later.

For the later-flowering white, pink, and crimson spiraeas, *see* p. 60.

1 Prunus tenella
3 Viburnum x burkwoodii
2 Magnolia x soulangeana
4 Ribes sanguineum

25

MARCH SHRUBS. 3

These early shrubs are mostly quite hardy, but the damaging cold winds which often occur in March and April may blight the flowers, and so it is advisable to plant them where some shelter is provided from the north and north-east. Except where stated, they will thrive in any reasonable soil in sun or half shade.

1 C O R Y L O P S I S (*korylus* = hazel, *opsis* = like). Hazel-like deciduous shrubs, with a slender twiggy growth, which are natives of Japan and China. *C. pauciflora*, the one illustrated, has the largest flowers in the genus but is the most tender, and is suitable only for mild areas or a very sheltered position. The early fragrant flowers of corylopsis are easily damaged by spring frosts, even of the more hardy species such as *C. spicata*. *C. pauciflora*, *C. spicata*, and *C. veitchiorum* (a hardy, primrose-yellow, April-flowering species) grow up to 6 ft. tall. *C. glabrescens* and *C. willmottiae*, both producing pale-yellow flowers in April, make small trees up to 12 ft. tall.

2 D A P H N E **odora variegata**. This somewhat spreading evergreen shrub with deliciously fragrant flowers is not a plant for cold gardens, and though this variegated form is regarded as hardier than the plain green one, it will not survive frosts of more than 20 degrees without protection. It is, however, an excellent plant for a cold or frost-free greenhouse. For out-of-doors, *D. mezereum* (*see* p. 3), is safer in all areas. *D. odora* was introduced in 1771 from China and Japan. For other daphnes, *see* pp. 12, 59, and 80.

3 C H A E N O M E L E S **lagenaria (Japonica)**. The Japanese Quince was, until recently, known as *Cydonia japonica*, and is still commonly called simply 'Japonica'. It is frequently grown on a wall, but this is not essential as all the varieties are quite hardy and make excellent 6 ft. shrubs in the open in any soil. They can be kept in shape by being pruned in the same way as an apple. Many varieties have been raised in Britain, France, and the U.S.A., and the following are excellent. *Alba* or *nivalis*, pure white; 'Aurora', deep salmon; 'Knaphill Scarlet', large orange-salmon, very good; *moerloesi* or 'Apple Blossom', white and pink apple-like flowers; 'Rowallane', orange-red, very good; 'Crimson and Gold', blood-red with bright yellow stamens; *umbilicata*, pink.

4-5 C A M E L L I A. Of recent years it has been realised that the varieties or hybrids of *C. japonica* are excellent hardy evergreen shrubs for lime-free soils, especially on shady walls protected from the north and east winds or in open woodland in the south, west, and midlands. In the north they need more sun to make them flower, though they do not like a dry, scorching place. Anywhere the open flowers may be destroyed by frost, but the unopened buds remain unharmed and develop as soon as the weather improves. In mild climates flowers may be appearing in January; further north they may continue till June. For cultivation out-of-doors the white varieties are the least satisfactory as rain and wind brown the petals. Also, the less formal, such as 'Lady Clare' (4), the one illustrated, are more satisfactory than the formal. Other good varieties of *C. japonica* are: 'Arejishi', turkey-red paeony-flowered; 'Elegans', rose-pink anemone-flowered; 'Gloire de Nantes', semi-double carmine-rose; 'Magnoliaeflora', pale shell-pink.

A number of hybrids of *C. japonica* have arisen by using other wild species recently introduced, particularly the Chinese *C. saluenensis* collected by George Forrest about 1917 in West China. This, crossed with the Chinese *C. cuspidata*, has given 'Cornish Snow' (5). Its buds are pink, and the flowers pink tinged and small compared with the *C. japonica* varieties, but the habit of the plant is light, and it flowers profusely. Other *C. cuspidata* hybrids are 'Michael', less pink but larger; 'Winton', carmine buds and almond-pink flowers.

R H O D O D E N D R O N. The earliest to flower of all the rhododendrons are *R. x praecox* and *R. mucronulatum* (*see* p. 2). Most rhododendrons flower in May and June (*see* p. 57), but there are several March–April-flowering species, in particular the hybrid 'Nobleanum' raised by crossing the dwarf, hardy *R. caucasicum* with the much larger, early-flowering but not so hardy *R. arboreum*. *R. x* 'Nobleanum' has scarlet-crimson flowers, and there are white, red, and pink varieties. *R. x shilsonii* (*R. thomsonii x R. barbatum*) has bright red flowers, dark green foliage, and attractive cinnamon-coloured bark. All rhododendrons require a neutral or slightly acid soil.

1 CORYLOPSIS PAUCIFLORA   2 DAPHNE ODORA   3 CHAENOMELES LAGENARIA
4 CAMELLIA JAPONICA   5 CAMELLIA X 'CORNISH SNOW'

TULIPS

The Near East is the home of many wild tulips, and, not surprisingly, the first garden tulips are recorded as being seen in the royal gardens in European Turkey in the 16th century. In fact, they must have been cultivated for many years before, as even at that time a great many varieties were known. Travellers soon began to bring bulbs back to Austria, Germany, and then to Holland where they have been cultivated on a large scale ever since. They came to Britain from Holland in 1578. In the 17th and early 18th centuries the raising of new tulips from seed became the rage, and there was much speculation on the value of new varieties. Bulbs changed hands at fantastic prices. This 'Tulipomania' raged in Holland especially between 1634 and 1637, and in the early 18th century there was a similar rage in Turkey. In Holland, tulips were raised not only for their spring flowers but also for their edible bulbs. Now tulips are also grown for the market on a large scale in Lincolnshire and near Wisbech in Cambridgeshire, in the Western United States and in British Columbia.

It is not known for certain whether the original garden tulip was developed from one species only, and if so which species, or by hybridization from more than one. The tulips first admired in Britain were May-flowering varieties with cup-shaped, self-coloured flowers, yellow or white at the base. These were known as 'breeders', and after a time a change called 'breaking' took place whereby the colour became streaked on a yellow or white background, the value of the tulip depending on the clarity of the colour and the regularity of the streaking. Though such varieties are still obtainable and are, indeed, attractive, particularly for indoor decoration, they are not now much grown.

In 1948, to avoid confusion, the many varieties of tulips were divided into fifteen classes. The following long-established classes are of most interest for garden purposes: Single Early (2), Double Early (3), Cottage, including Lily-flowered (6), Darwin (9), Parrot (14), and Late Doubles (15). Later developments are: Multi-flowered May tulips in which three or four flowers are carried on a branching stem and which are very effective in the border; Triumph (15), mid-season tulips obtained by crossing Single Earlies with Dutch Breeder, Cottage and Darwin types; and Mendel (4), obtained by crossing the very early-flowering Duc van Thol and Viridiflora group (1) with Darwins. Then various hybrids have been made using the species *T. fosteriana*, *T. greigii*, and *T. kaufmanniana* (*see* p. 31), introduced recently from Samarkand and Turkistan. These form a class 16. The figure following the name of the variety shows the class to which it belongs.

1 PARROT (14) 'Blue Parrot'. The parrot tulips are sports from various sections, all characterized by the heavily laciniated petals. They are May-flowering and are better as cut flowers than for garden decoration. There is a wide range of colours from 'Ivory Parrot' to 'Black Parrot', including pinks, lavenders, blues, oranges, scarlets, and crimsons.

2 COTTAGE (6) 'Picotee'. The lily-flowered Cottage tulips are May-flowering and are elegantly shaped with pointed reflexed petals. Other attractive varieties are the fragrant 'Ellen Willmot', soft primrose-yellow, and 'White Triumphator', and there are many in deeper and more vivid colours.

The ordinary Cottage tulips, so named because they have been grown in British and French cottage gardens for many years, are probably the descendants of the original Turkish tulips. They are hardy and need little attention and are the best for naturalizing in grass. Yellow, such as 'Inglescombe Yellow,' is a usual colour, but there are varieties in white, rose, salmon, and red.

3 DARWIN (9) 'Clara Butt'. These are tall, erect, strong, May–June-flowering tulips, coming originally from a collection imported from the north of France by Messrs. Krelage & Son of Haarlem. They range in colour from pure white to deep purple or violet-blue, and include the 'Black Tulip', which is so dark a maroon that in some lights it appears black.

4 EARLY SINGLE (2) 'Prince Carnival'. April-flowering tulips which are most commonly used for bedding, as their shorter stems stand up better to rough weather. They are also the best type to grow as a pot plant. Some, including the one illustrated, are scented.

5 EARLY DOUBLE (3) 'Dante'. Another good type of tulip for bedding and pot culture. They are not so elegant but they are longer lasting than the singles.

There are many varieties in different colours of all the classes of tulips, as well as the hybrids, and the choice depends mainly on an individual taste in colour. Therefore, in general, no attempt has been made to suggest named varieties.

1 Parrot tulip 'Blue Parrot'   2 Lily tulip 'Picotee'   3 Darwin tulip 'Clara Butt'
4 Early single tulip 'Prince Carnival'   5 Early double tulip 'Dante'

SUN-LOVING SPRING BULBS

Many spring bulbs enjoy or will tolerate shade, but there are also many which come from areas with hot, dry summers and which must have all the sun available if they are to thrive. They prefer a good soil, but even more important is a soil with very good drainage which will tend to dry out in the hot weather.

1 FRITILLARIA (*fritillus* = chess-board). The name has arisen because the flowers of some species, particularly the native *F. meleagris*, Snake's Head, have a chequered pattern. Fritillaries of various kinds are plentiful in Europe, particularly the southern countries, and in the Eastern Mediterranean, Central Asia, and North America. There is even one species in Japan. The well-known Crown Imperial, *F. imperialis*, with its many flowers grouped at the end of a 3–4 ft. stem, is a common wild plant in North India, Persia, and Afghanistan, and has crimson, red, bronze, and yellow garden forms. Most species of fritillary are plants for the expert grower, but the Siberian *F. pallidiflora* (1) is as easily grown as the Crown Imperial in good well-drained soil. It flowers in April and grows about 1 ft. tall. It varies somewhat in colour from pale greenish-yellow to pale canary, the chequering is slight, and the dying flowers assume a pink tinge. Strong plants may bear up to twelve flowers, but about six is more usual.

2-3 TULIPA (from the Turkish *tulbend* = turban). As well as the garden or Florists tulips (*see* p. 29), many wild tulips have been introduced to English gardens from Palestine, Turkey, and Persia. The greatest number, and the most magnificent, have come from Central Asia. It is from there that such species as *T. fosteriana, clusiana, greigii, kaufmanniana, linifolia, eichleri, praestans* and others were originally introduced by collectors for Messrs. van Tubergen of Haarlem. Most have brilliant scarlet and red flowers. They all need warm positions in the garden and protection from cold winds.

T. fosteriana (2), probably the finest of the wild tulips, comes from the Samarkand mountains of Central Asia. It can vary from 'Red Emperor' (20 ins. tall) to 'Princeps' and 'Rockery Beauty' (8 ins. tall), and it flowers early — often in March. None of the many hybrids recently raised excel the brilliance of the original vermilion scarlet with the black yellow-edged central star.

T. kaufmanniana (3), the Water Lily Tulip, so called because the white yellow-centred flowers of the original wild species from Turkestan resemble a water lily. There are now a great number of varieties in different colours of this dwarf, sturdy plant, usually not more than 4–8 ins. high and therefore better able to stand rough weather than *T. fosteriana*.

Other good species are *T. eichleri* and *T. e. excelsa*, crimson scarlet with central black star, and *T. praestans* which has several flowers on a stem and no star, and varies in the shade of red. Neither the bright scarlet *T. greigii* nor its golden-yellow form *aurea* are easy to grow or keep, but some of the selected seedlings or hybrids now developed are not too different and are easier to grow. Dwarf, as opposed to tall varieties, are likely to be more satisfactory. The variety 'Oratorio' is one of those with attractive brown markings on the leaves.

4 ANEMONE pavonina. This anemone, of which 'St. Bavo' is the best strain, is a widespread wild plant in Greece and Western Turkey and flowers in April–May. It has a wide range of colours — white, salmon, scarlet, crimson, and mauve, and is usually single with a greenish-black or white or yellow eye. The only double variety now available is known as *A. fulgens multipetala*. The 'St. Bavo' anemones will withstand considerable cold and do not need a very rich soil, but they should have a sheltered sunny position in well-drained loam. They seed freely, and if the ground is undisturbed, self-sown seedlings will appear and eventually flower.

The 'St. Brigid' anemones to be seen in the shops early in the year are the poppy anemones, *A. coronaria*, of which garden forms have been derived from several wild species of the Mediterranean and their hybrids. These are not satisfactory plants for cold gardens, though they will do well in the warm south and west. Even then, they need rich soil and are best renewed annually.

HYACINTHUS orientalis. The well-known common hyacinth, used for forcing in pots or for bedding out, has been derived from the wild *H. orientalis*, a graceful plant found from Italy and Southern France to Mesopotamia. Roman Hyacinths, so popular for forcing, come from *H. orientalis albulus*. There are now a great many varieties in different colours. They should be planted in moderately rich soil in October, and will usually come again for several years, but tend to produce fewer flowers on the spike.

1 FRITILLARIA PALLIDIFLORA   2 TULIPA FOSTERIANA
3 TULIPA KAUFMANNIANA   4 ANEMONE PAVONINA 'ST. BAVO'

BIENNIALS

A biennial is a plant that grows from seed one year and flowers, forms seed, and dies the next year. Some plants, such as Antirrhinums (*see* p. 126), can be grown either as annuals or biennials, and some plants best grown as biennials, if left in the ground, will flower for several years so long as they are not damaged by too severe winters (*see* Pansies, p. 55). Biennials should be sown in late May, June, or early July, in the open or in boxes, pricked out into a nursery bed 4 ins. or more apart when large enough to handle, and planted into their flowering positions in the autumn. They will thrive in most garden soils, but it is better to put them in not too exposed a position.

1 MYOSOTIS (**Forget-me-not**). This very well-known English garden flower has been developed from native wild species such as *M. alpestris*, *M. sylvatica*, and *M. scorpioides*. There are various shades of blue, white, pink, and even yellow species. In many places myosotis will seed itself from year to year.

2 MATTHIOLA **incana** (**Brompton Stock**). The garden stocks are mainly derived from this hardy native of Southern Europe, which is scented and usually has purple flowers. There are two main groups of garden stocks: the summer or 10-week stocks (*see* p. 127) and the spring-flowering or biennial stocks. The object with all stocks is to obtain double rather than single flowers. The double flowers do not produce seed, so doubles can be obtained only from strains of singles which tend to throw a large proportion, say 50% or more, of doubles. In general, the more vigorous seedlings produce the double flowers. Recently, Messrs. Hansen of Copenhagen, have evolved an 'All Double' race.

Brompton Stocks make sub-shrubby branching plants about 18 ins. high, which are very showy and last a long time. They are hardy and suffer more from excessive damp in the winter than cold. They can be wintered in a cold frame and planted out in March.

3-4 CHEIRANTHUS (**Wallflower**). *C. cheiri* (3) has been grown in English gardens for many centuries, and small-flowered yellow and bronze varieties became naturalized and persisted in old walls. The modern Giant-flowered strain produces bushy plants about 15–18 ins. tall in separate or mixed colours. The colour varieties include 'Blood Red', 'Fire King' (orange-red), 'Giant Ruby' (rich ruby-red), 'Golden Monarch', 'Primrose Monarch', 'Scarlet Emperor', and 'White Dame'. There is an early-flowering type, such as 'Early-flowering Phoenix', which in sheltered places in the south may be flowering by February.

Wallflowers need a sunny position and do better in a limy soil.

C. x allionii (4) (Siberian Wallflower) is a hybrid raised by John Marshall in 1846. It grows 12–15 ins. tall and is very free-flowering. It will persist to some extent as a perennial.

DIGITALIS (**Foxglove**). The ordinary foxglove, *D. purpurea*, and its varieties are biennials, though some species are perennial herbs. They flower rather later than most biennials (*see* p. 119).

CAMPANULA **medium** (**Canterbury Bell**). This native of Southern Europe has been grown in English gardens for over 300 years. As well as the common blue, there are now also different shades of blue, mauve, pink, and white. The variety *calycanthema* (Cup and Saucer) looks semi-double because the calyx has become coloured like the petals.

OENOTHERA **biennis** (**Evening Primrose**). This well-known tall plant from America, so called because the large yellow flowers open in the evening, is suitable for open places in a wild garden, where it will often sow itself. *O. grandiflora* is a like species, but with larger flowers and reddish stems.

5-6 BELLIS **perennis**. These are garden varieties of the common daisy. Although perennials, for garden purposes they are best treated as biennials, when they will generally seed themselves. Good ones, however, can be divided after flowering and so preserved. There are white, pink, and crimson colours in the large, double-flowered strains (6) growing 9–12 ins. tall, and in the new miniature strain (5) about 6 ins. tall. 'Dresden China', a dwarf variety with heads of deep pink quilled florets, is an attractive rock plant.

CYNOGLOSSUM **amabile** (**Hound's Tongue**). The name from *kynos* = dog, *glossa* = tongue, refers to the shape of the leaves. The plant grows 1–2 ft. tall, has grey-green downy foliage, and produces turquoise-blue, forget-me-not-like flowers later than most biennials — in July and August. There are also pink and white forms. Cynoglossum grows easily in any well-drained soil.

For other biennials, *see* Polyanthus (p. 15), Violas and Pansies (p. 55), Aquilegia (p. 39), Sweet William (p. 79).

1 Mysotis 'Carmine King' 2 Matthiola incana 3 Cheiranthus cheiri 'Giant Mixed'
4 Cheiranthus x allionii 5 Bellis perennis 'Miniature Mixed' 6 Bellis perennis 'Giant double'

DWARF MEADOW FLOWERS FOR SUNNY BEDS

1 IRIS **tectorum.** This is a Japanese iris which in Japan grows on thatched roofs — hence the name *tectorum* = 'of roofs'. In English gardens it needs a well-drained, sheltered, sunny spot, such as the base of a wall, where it will be out of the wind; and it begins to flower in May. It grows about a foot tall and is normally lilac-blue. *I. tectorum alba* is a white form.

For other dwarf irises, *see* pp. 5 and 11.

2 ASTER **alpinus.** A dwarf aster which makes a tufted clump and does well in most sunny places. The flower stems are about 9 ins. tall and should be cut down as soon as the flowers are dead. The plants tend to spread and are easily increased by division.

Good varieties are 'Beechwood', mauve-blue; 'Glory', amethyst-blue; 'Ideal', lavender-blue; and 'Wargrave', lilac-pink. There is a white form (*albus*) and a deep red one (*ruber*).

3 SISYRINCHIUM **(Pig Root** or **Blue-eyed Grass).** The name comes from *sus* = pig and *runchos* = snout, as pigs are said to dig up and eat the roots. Sisyrinchiums are natives of the Americas, and most of the hardy ones are easy to grow in any soil or position, flower from May to August, and often seed themselves about. Some very beautiful ones, however, such as *S. douglasii* (pale to dark purple), *S. filifolium* (white, lined purple), and the sweet-scented *S. odoratissimum*, need a light, well-drained soil.

As well as *S. bermudiana*, the species illustrated, there are bright blue, purple, yellow, and white species. Some grow only 6–8 ins. tall; others, such as the primrose-yellow *S. striatum*, grow up to 2 ft.

4 ALCHEMILLA **major (mollis) (Lady's Mantle).** This is a larger garden form of *A. vulgaris*, the species native to Britain. It will grow anywhere, in sun or shade, in walls, paving or flower beds, and its clouds of tiny pale-green flowers last many weeks. It seeds itself so generously that it is better to cut off the flowers before they have seeded.

The species *A. alpina* is a dwarf form, about 5 ins. tall, with silver-lined leaves, which is suitable for the rock garden.

THALICTRUM **alpinum (Alpine Meadow Rue).** This dwarf thalictrum, growing rarely more than 6 ins. tall, has greenish-yellow flowers with yellow tassels, on wiry stems, with dainty, attractive foliage. *See* also p. 149.

5 PULSATILLA **vulgaris (anemone pulsatilla).** Pasque Flowers grow wild on some chalk grasslands in Britain. According to tradition they grow well only in places where the Danes shed their blood, or along Roman roads. The dwarf wild form is a rich violet-blue; but there are garden forms in other colours, such as *P. caucasica* (pale yellow), and *P. v.* 'Red Clock' (pink, red, and crimson). They have very decorative seed-heads, and the seeds should be sown as soon as ripe. Chalky well-drained soil in an open position seems to suit them best, and they need very firm planting. They are usually in flower before the end of April.

6 GENTIANA **acaulis.** This very large family contains spring, summer (*see* p. 111), and autumn (*see* p. 177) flowering species. Many of them dislike lime, and some varieties are difficult to establish. *G. acaulis* from the European alps, is one of the easier gentians to grow successfully. It must have rich, firm, well-drained soil, and when well settled it will spread. *G. verna*, a small, vividly blue species, sometimes found wild in northern Britain, is a lovely spring-flowering rock plant. *G. septemfida* from Asia Minor and its varieties, with deep purplish-blue flowers with pale spots within, has a rather procumbent growth.

GEUM **montanum** is a low-growing plant with rough green leaves. The short-stemmed flowers, about 6 ins. tall, are golden and turn to fluffy silver seed-heads. It flowers earlier than the taller geums (*see* p. 107).

POTENTILLA. Some of the dwarf rock potentillas (*see* p. 107) flower in May or even earlier and sometimes go on flowering through the summer. *P. alba* is an early-flowering white species, and *P. verna* is yellow. Flowering in late May and onwards are the bright rich yellow *P. aurea* and *P. recta warrenii*.

1 Iris tectorum album   2 Aster alpinus   3 Sisyrinchium bermudiana

4 Alchemilla major   5 Anemone pulsatilla   6 Gentiana acaulis

35

EARLY BORDER FLOWERS. 1

1 MERTENSIA **virginica (Virginian Cowslip),** named after F. C. Mertens, a German Botanist. After flowering, in late June, the leaves turn yellow and die down, and reappear in April with their tightly-packed blue buds. The flower-stems are about 18 ins. tall, and need staking as both leaves and flowers are heavy. The plant does best in good rich soil, and grows well in partial shade. *M. ciliata* (bright blue with rose buds) grows up to 2 ft. More suited to a rock garden than a border is *M. alpina* from the Rocky Mts., which is about 6 ins. tall and has light blue, rather bell-shaped flowers, and *M. echioides* which grows up to 10–12 ins. tall and is dark blue.

2 DICENTRA **spectabilis,** from *di* = double and *kentron* = spur, because of the two spurs of the corolla. This typical cottage-garden plant is often called Bleeding Heart or Seál Flower. If planted in rich, moist but light soil in shade, it lasts in bloom for several weeks. Great care is needed in handling the roots, as they are as brittle as glass. *D. spectabilis* is hardy but the flowers are more likely to be cut by late spring frosts than the later flowering dicentras (*see* p. 119). It is 18–24 ins. tall. There is also a white form, *alba.*

3 POLEMONIUM, from *polemos* = war, for the discovery of this plant was said by Pliny to have led to war. *P. coeruleum*, the sky-blue Jacob's Ladder of cottage-gardens, has been greatly improved of recent years, with larger flowers and longer periods of flowering; it has a good pure white form, as well as blue. They grow easily in any soil or position so long as they are not either too wet or too dry. The varieties 'Blue Pearl' and 'Sapphire' are neat branched plants which make good edgings.

P. confertum, P. lanatum, and *P. reptans* are dwarf rock-garden species. *P. carneum*, which is flesh-pink, early-flowering, and grows 18 ins. or more tall, has also a blue form. *P. foliosissimum* (white or blue) flowers rather later and grows taller.

4-5 GERANIUM (Crane's-bill), from *geranos* = crane, the seed-heads resembling a crane's head and beak. The crane's-bills are a large group which furnish many good plants for border, shrub-garden, or woodland, and must not be confused with the pelargoniums, the greenhouse and bedding show geraniums (*see* p. 125). They grow well in sun or shade and are not particular as to soil. Some species start flowering in May and continue through the summer and into the autumn. They have decorative foliage which with many species colours well in the autumn.

Dwarf species such as the rose-pink, 6-in. *G. sanguineum lancastriense*, are excellent for the rock garden. Others, such as the pearly-grey *G. pratense* 'Silver Queen' and *G. sylvaticum album*, grow up to 3 ft. The claret-purple hybrid *G.* 'Russell Prichard' has a trailing form of growth. There is a wide range of colours from white to crimson, blue, and purple, and there are double forms of *G. pratense* and others.

Other attractive species are: *G. psilostemon*, magenta-red with black spots; *G. endressii* 'Wargrave', pale salmon-pink with grey foliage; and *G. ibericum*, violet-blue.

6 OROBUS **aureus** (Lathyrus *luteus aureus*) **(Bitter Vetch).** This plant has numerous clusters of vetch-like flowers and no tendrils to the leaves as the climbing peas usually have (*see* p. 163). Orobus grows easily in any ordinary garden soil and makes a bushy plant. *O. pannonicus varius* (*L. varius*) has rose and yellow flowers; and *O. vernus* (*L. vernus*) has pink and bright blue flowers, and there is also a white form.

AJUGA **reptans (Bugle).** This labiate, which flowers from late April to July, is a useful plant for carpeting, as it creeps quickly over the ground and will grow in moist and shady places and in odd corners. *A. reptans* is blue and grows 6 ins. tall. It has a white form (*alba*) and one with red leaves (*rubra*), and also a variegated form which has smaller tufts and grows more slowly. *A. pyramidalis* is a non-creeping dwarf species with brilliant deep-blue flowers, which makes good clumps in a damp, shady place.

INCARVILLEA **delavayi,** named after Pere d'Incarville, a French missionary in China and botanist. This hardy plant from China has tuberous roots and handsome, shiny, toothed leaves with exotic-looking, bright deep-rose trumpet flowers. It disappears completely after flowering. It needs rich well-drained soil (damp in winter may kill it), and grows 12–18 ins. tall.

I. delavayi 'Bees' Pink' is a pale pink variety. *I. grandiflora* is rather more dwarf and has large, deep rose-red flowers with yellow or orange tubes. Its variety *brevipes* has crimson flowers.

1 MERTENSIA VIRGINICA   2 DICENTRA SPECTABILIS   3 POLEMONIUM CARNEUM

4 GERANIUM MACRORRHIZUM   5 GERANIUM GRANDIFLORUM ALPINUM   6 OROBUS AUREUS

EARLY BORDER FLOWERS. 2

1 TROLLIUS (**Globe Flower**). *T. europaeus* is a not very common wild flower of Britain, the largest of the buttercups. It grows in damp meadows, and the garden varieties also need damp positions and are often planted beside streams or pools. Trollius will do quite well in an ordinary border if the soil is rich and damp: a heavy soil with plenty of humus is the best. The plants can be divided in the autumn. They grow 2–3 ft. tall.

The usual garden varieties are hybrids grouped under the name *T. x cultorum*. As well as the one illustrated, other good varieties are: 'Brilliant', fiery orange; 'Gold Quelle', butter yellow; 'Orange Queen', pale orange. The variety *T. europaeus superbus* is a pale lemon-yellow.

2 DORONICUM (**Leopard's Bane**), is one of the earliest flowers to open in the border, and its yellow daisy flowers on long stalks are excellent for cutting. It has good evergreen foliage and is not particular about soil or position. It is easily increased by division. It is a native of Europe and is found wild occasionally in Britain. As well as the variety 'Miss Mason', which is illustrated, other species are *D. austriacum*, large golden; *D. plantagineum excelsum* (Harpur Crewe), bright yellow; and *D. pardalianches* 'Bunch of Gold', canary yellow.

3 RANUNCULUS acris flore-pleno (**Bachelor's Buttons**). Although the ordinary wild meadow buttercup is a pernicious weed, the double forms make excellent May-flowering garden plants and do best in moist soil. There are also double forms of the bulbous buttercup, *R. bulbosus pleniflorus*, and of the creeping buttercup, *R. repens flore-pleno*, which are less tall.

For other garden ranunculus, *see* pp. 5 and 45.

4 AQUILEGIA, from the Latin *aquila* = eagle, because the flower resembles an eagle's foot. The Columbine of cottage gardens (*A. vulgaris*) grows equally well in sun or shade, and in addition to the dainty flowers in many delicate shades, has decorative glaucous foliage which lasts through the summer. It seeds itself freely. The modern garden varieties *A. x hybrida* have been produced by repeated crosses and have much larger flowers and a wide range of colours. The most popular are the long-spurred forms, in particular Mrs. Scott-Elliot's strain.

Other species and varieties include: *A. longissima*, pale yellow with very long spurs; *A. caerulea*, powder-blue and with other forms; *A. vulgaris nivea* (Munstead White); and the new *kana* Hybrids, large-flowered and mixed colours.

Dwarf aquilegias suitable for the rock garden include the tiny *A. bertolonii* (blue-violet), and the rather taller *A. glandulosa* (blue and white). The alpine aquilegias need sunny positions in well-drained loam with leaf-mould. Garden aquilegias can be grown satisfactorily as biennials.

5 LITHOSPERMUM (*lithos* =stone, *sperma* =seed, for the seeds are very hard). These members of the forget-me-not family provide some of the best blues of any garden flowers — in particular, *L. diffusum* (*prostratum*) 'Heavenly Blue'. But this species and some other lithospermums are lime-haters and will grow well only in sunny positions in well-drained sandy peat. Others, such as *L. fruticosum*, will tolerate lime; and there are several that will grow in any soil and are excellent plants for the front of shrubberies and for ground cover in shade. *L. doerfleri*, the species illustrated, can be used for this purpose, and also the purple-blue *L. purpureo-caeruleum*. These all grow about 12 ins. tall.

MECONOPSIS **cambrica** (**Welsh Poppy**), (*mekon* = poppy, *opsis* =like). This graceful yellow poppy-like plant is found wild in damp, rocky places in Wales and north-west England. It grows about 2 ft. tall, has grey-green foliage, and will seed itself freely in places where nothing else will grow, particularly in partial shade. It continues to flower through the summer. There is also a double orange form, *M. c. flore pleno*, which does not set seed.

The meconopsis genus contains the blue poppy. *M. betonicifolia* has sky-blue flowers on 4–5 ft. stems; *M. latifolia* has pale blue flowers on shorter stems. *M. nepaulensis*, reddish-purplish-blue, and *M. violacea*, violet-blue, are very tall, and *M. grandis*, deep blue, is suitable for the rock garden. *M. superba* is a very fine white poppy, about 3 ft. tall, and *M. paniculata* and *M. regia* are fine tall yellow poppies.

LYCHNIS (**Campion**). This member of the pink family is distributed over temperate regions of the Old World. The best of all is the brilliant scarlet *L. chalcedonica* which grows about 3 ft. tall and continues in flower for a long time. It does well in any good moist soil. *L. coronaria* (agrostemma) has woolly foliage and magenta, white, or pink flowers on 15–30-in. stems and sows itself freely. *L. viscaria splendens plena* (Viscaria viscosa) has double rose-crimson flowers on 12–18 in. stems, but is not a good perennial.

TELLIMA **grandiflora**. A member of the Saxifrage family, not unlike a heuchera (*see* p. 149) but less woody in growth. It makes a useful ground cover in sun or shade, and its beautifully etched leaves are pink in their early stages and turn crimson in autumn. The 2-ft. flower spikes, which appear in May, are hung with tiny green bells, which take on a pink tinge when they have been out about a week. *T. grandiflora purpurea* has bronzed-red leaves and yellow-green flowers, and grows rather less tall.

1 TROLLIUS 'ORANGE PRINCESS'　　2 DORONICUM 'MISS MASON'　　3 RANUNCULUS ACRIS FLORE-PLENO
4 AQUILEGIA, LONG-SPURRED　　5 LITHOSPERMUM DOERFLERI

TRAILERS FOR SUNNY ROCK GARDENS AND WALLS

These are plants which can be grown in a rock crevice or between stones in a dry wall with well-drained soil deep enough for their long roots; they may be grown on a fair-sized rock in the garden or hang over, or in, a dry wall. They flower the length of their trailing stems. Except for the lime-haters, such as some lithospermums, they will grow in any soil, preferably with some humus, but they dislike damp. They are most of them vigorous and need plenty of room.

1 SAPONARIA **ocymoides (Soapwort),** *sapo* = soap, for a soapy lather can be made from the leaves of *S. officinalis*. A hardy and vigorous trailer which will grow in any sunny place, though perhaps better in a lime-free soil, and quickly becomes covered with a mass of bright pink flowers. There is also a white variety (*albiflora*) and a deep rose (*rubra* or *splendens*). A more compact plant and better suited to small gardens is the excellent newer variety 'Bressingham Hybrid'.

There is also a hardy annual *S. calabrica* with white, pink, or red flowers, and a mat-forming hybrid *S. x olivana* with large deep-pink flowers.

2 VERONICA **armena.** This large family, which provides us with plants for almost every part of the garden (*see* pp. 81, 109, 161), has also many suitable rock plants. As well as *V. armena* from Armenia, and its pink variety, there is the evergreen shrubby *V. pectinata* which forms dense mats and will do well in shade. The variety rosea has deep pink, white-edged petals. *V. prostrata* (*rupestris*) produces a mass of brilliant blue, deeper blue ('Spode Blue'), or rich pink ('Mrs. Holt') spikes of flowers.

3 ARABIS. Many members of this genus are rather weedy plants very easy to grow, and some of them start flowering in early spring. *A. albida flore-pleno* is the well-known double-white arabis with greyish foliage and fragrant flowers. *A. aubrietioides* is a dwarfer species with pink-purple flowers, of which 'Fakenham Pink' and 'Rosabella' are attractive varieties.

4 AUBRIETIA, named after Claud Aubriet, a French botanical artist. A great many hybrids and varieties, both single and double, have been developed, most of them from *A. deltoidea*. In the case of aubrietia the hybrids are better garden plants than the species. Given sun and well-drained soil, they will quickly achieve a mass of colour in spring and early summer. The following is a selection of good varieties.

SINGLES: 'Dr. Mules', deep violet-purple;' Mrs. Rodewald, large rich crimson; 'Kelmscott Violet', rich bright mauve; 'King of the Blues', strong quick-growing lilac-blue.

DOUBLES: 'Barker's Double'; 'Bressingham Pink', deep silver-pink; 'Joan Allen', a very good large deep reddish-purple.

5 ALYSSUM **saxatile** (Madwort: the plant was said to cure the bite of a mad dog). There are many species of Alyssum, both perennial and annual (*see* p. 135), and the sub-shrubby varieties of *A. saxatile* are perhaps the most attractive. As well as the variety illustrated, there are *A. s. plenum* with bright gold double flowers, and the primrose-yellow *A. s. citrinum*. The yellow, dwarf, prostrate *A. serpyllifolium* is excellent for the miniature garden (*see* p. 194).

6 PHLOX **subulata (Moss Phlox).** Of the many species of phloxes from America suitable for the garden, *P. subulata*, with its large number of varieties, is a dwarf rock garden type. It is hardy, but may die off in damp winter weather. If never over-wet or dust-dry, it will produce a profusion of gay flowers. As well as 'Vivid', the one illustrated, 'G. F. Wilson' has clear lilac flowers and 'Temiscaming' has brilliant magenta-red flowers. The species *P. douglasii* is more compact and tufted and has many attractive forms such as 'May Snow', pure white; and 'Violet Queen', clear mauve. *P. subulata* is best propagated by cuttings taken in July.

For other phloxes, *see* pp. 143 and 157.

CALAMINTHA **alpina** (*kalos* = beautiful, *mintha* = mint). This thyme-like plant with purplish flowers flourishes in any ordinary soil in full sun and lasts in flower for several weeks. The form *grandiflora* is larger, finer, and more decumbent.

LITHOSPERMUM **diffusum** (*prostratum*). This member of the Forget-me-not family gives some of the best blue-coloured flowers of the garden, but it will not tolerate lime and needs a cool peaty soil. The variety 'Heavenly Blue' is the best known, but 'Grace Ward' has slightly larger flowers and an equally good blue. The species *L. oleifolium*, with silvery-grey leaves and powder-blue flowers, will tolerate lime but it needs a sunny dry position, such as a dry wall. (*See* also p. 39.)

1 Saponaria ocymoides rubra
2 Veronica armena
3 Arabis aubrietioides 'Fakenham Pink'
4 Aubrietia 'Barker's double'
5 Alyssum saxatile 'Dudley Neville'
6 Phlox subulata 'Vivid'

WALL AND ROCK CREVICE PLANTS

May and June are months when most rock gardens are at their best. On p. 41 are shown the plants which can be used to trail over rocks and hang over walls. On p. 45 are the plants which enjoy the light shade thrown by a rock or shrub. On p. 67 are the dwarf shrubs for the rockery. This page is concerned with the plants which, for the most part, like a sunny patch and which form tufts and rosettes. Their main requirements are an adequate depth of soil for their long roots and very good drainage, as damp is often their worst enemy.

1 SAXIFRAGA cotyledon 'Southside Seedling'. Saxifrages are among the most adaptable of rock garden plants and there is a wide variety. The early cushion-forming species are shown on p. 21. *S. cotyledon*, of which there are many varieties, form clumps of green broad-leaved rosettes, and in May throw up long arching plumes of white, spotted scarlet flowers, sometimes up to 2 ft. tall. They will flourish in a sunny or shady crevice. Another variety of *S. cotyledon*, *caterhamensis*, has white flowers spotted with red. *See* also p. 49.

2 GERANIUM cinereum subcaulescens. A recently introduced crane's-bill which quickly makes a spreading cushion and in June sends up brilliant dark-centred magenta flowers. It grows easily in any good garden loam in the sun. The variety *splendens* is brighter still and flowers for four months. A rose-pink form of the wild crane's-bill, *G. sanguineum lancastriense*, comes from Walney Island off the Lancashire coast. *G. wallichianum* 'Buxton's Blue' makes large loose clumps of trailing stems. The large clear violet-blue flowers, up to 1½ ins. across, appear rather later than *G. cinereum*, usually not until August, and do better in a sheltered spot. Another good rock geranium and also later flowering is *G. dalmaticum*, which has a number of clear salmon-pink flowers on short stems in July. It flowers more freely if frequently divided. *See* also p. 37.

3 HELICHRYSUM virgineum (Everlasting Flower). This grey woolly-leaved plant from Mt. Athos in Greece is hardy so long as it has a sunny position with very good drainage, preferably in a wall. It will soon succumb to damp. The flower stems, which grow about 6 ins. tall, can be successfully dried (p. 191). Another rock helichrysum is *H. milfordae* which makes a silvery mat with tiny crimson buds and ivory flowers (p. 91). *H. selago* is a stiff shrub about 9 ins. tall, very suitable for a miniature or trough garden (*see* p. 194).

4 AETHIONEMA coridifolium 'Warley Rose'. A shrubby long-lived little plant, 4–6 ins. tall, with flowers resembling a miniature daphne *cneorum* (*see* p. 58). It grows well on a dry wall in full sun, and is easily propagated by cuttings of new shoots taken after flowering. *A. grandiflorum* is the largest species, with brilliant pink flowers on 12-inch stems.

5 ERINUS alpinus 'Dr. Hanele'. *E. alpinus* makes 2–3-inch rosettes of dark-green leaves with spikes of lilac-pink flowers some 3 ins. high. 'Dr. Hanele' is a deeper pink, 'Mrs. C. Boyle' is salmon-pink, and there is a white form, *alba*. Erinus seeds freely, but the plants do not always come true from seed.

6 ARENARIA montana. Arenaria is a large genus of plants native to temperate or cold areas, most of which are creeping and mat-forming, with white flowers. *A. montana* is found wild in woods and heaths in France and Spain. *A. tetraquetra*, from S. W. Europe, is a smaller plant making a dense grey-green mat with white, almost stemless flowers. *A. purpurascens* makes a green mat covered with purplish flowers. *A. balearica* is useful for covering the shady side of rocks, the green carpet being covered with tiny starlike flowers.

7 ASPERULA arcadiensis. There are native British asperulas, Squinancy wort and Woodruff. *A. arcadiensis* comes from Greece and is not difficult to grow if planted in a sunny crevice and, like most of the plants on this page, kept dry in winter. *A. lilaciflora caespitosa* has fine shiny green foliage and deeper pink flowers and is more prostrate and much less fastidious. *A gussonii* from Sicily forms dark green cushions studded with shell-pink flowers. For the annual asperula, *see* p. 135.

LINUM. Many of the hardy perennial linums are good rock plants, easy to grow in dry soil. The shrubby *L. arboreum* from Crete grows 1–2 ft. tall with large golden-yellow flowers. *L. flavum* is similar and 'Gemmel's Hybrid', with rich yellow flowers on 6-inch stems, is one of the best new rock plants of recent years. *L. narbonense*, up to 2 ft. tall and the shorter and very hardy *L. perenne* have large blue flowers and are suitable for a border. For annual linums, *see* p. 133.

LEONTOPODIUM (*leon* =lion, *pous* =foot) (Edelweiss). The common edelweiss of the Alps, *L. alpinus*, is neither so rare nor so difficult to grow as is generally believed. It is best raised from seed and grown on a light, well-drained soil in full sun. *L. stracheyii* is the larger Himalayan form, which has large felt-like flowers on 12-inch stems, and there are many others with similar characters.

1 SAXIFRAGA COTYLEDON 'SOUTHSIDE SEEDLING' 2 GERANIUM CINEREUM SUBCAULESCENS

3 HELICHRYSUM VIRGINEUM 4 AETHIONEMA 'WARLEY ROSE'

5 ERINUS ALPINUS 'DR. HANELE' 6 ARENARIA MONTANA 43

7 ASPERULA ARCADIENSIS

ROCK PLANTS FOR LIGHT SHADE

In contrast to the plants shown on pp. 41 and 43, the plants on this page for the most part prefer a moist and fairly shady situation, some of them preferring a crevice facing north rather than south. Most of them do better in fairly rich soil with plenty of humus.

1 DODECATHEON meadia (American Cowslip). These members of the Primrose family, natives of North America, are sometimes called 'Flowers of the Twelve Gods' (*dodeka* =twelve, *theoi* =gods). Another name is 'Shooting Star Flower'. They are easily raised from seed or propagated by division in spring after flowering. Their position in the garden needs to be marked as they do not appear above ground until late spring and many disappear again fairly soon after flowering. *D. meadia* is the most vigorous, growing up to 18 ins. high. *D. pauciflorum* and 'Red Wings', a very good new variety, grow 8–12 ins. tall and are more suitable for a small garden. There are colour varieties from white and pale lilac to crimson.

PRIMULA. Most of the best rock garden primulas flower earlier in the season (*see* p. 15), but there are several May–June flowering species, such as *P. alpicola* (white, yellow, and violet) and *P. japonica* (purplish-red), which do well in moist and shady places. *See* also p. 75.

2 RANUNCULUS amplexicaulis. Growing to a height of about 9 ins., this plant from the European mountains forms clumps of blue-grey foliage from which spring slightly-branched stems of large buttercup flowers. It blooms rather earlier than most plants on this page; and earlier still and also smaller are the snow-white *R. alpestris* with dark-green foliage, and the white-flushed pink *R. calandrinioides*, growing about 4 ins. tall. *R. gramineus* flowers rather later and has golden flowers on 9-inch stems and silver leaves. *See* also pp. 5 and 39.

3 OXALIS enneaphylla (*oxys* =acid — the sap tastes acid). A very hardy plant from the Falkland Is., which spreads rapidly in moist soils. Some species, such as the British wood-sorrel, *O. acetosella*, can become tiresome weeds. *O. enneaphylla* has fragrant white flowers; the one illustrated is the variety *rosea*. An autumn-flowering species, *O. lobata*, has golden flowers.

4 HABERLEA ferdinandi-coburgi. Haberlea, a native of the Balkans, is named in honour of the botanist Professor Haberle of Budapest. In fact, the true species *H. ferdinandi-coburgi*, may not be growing in England at all, and this is a variety of *H. rhodopensis*, with larger flowers and more oblong leaves. Haberlea flowers have three large lobes and two small, sometimes giving them a lip-like expression, though there is really no lip. They are best propagated by division of the rosettes after flowering. There is also a beautiful white variety, *virginalis*.

5 CORYDALIS cashmeriana. The yellow fumitory, *C. lutea*, and the whitish climbing *C. claviculata* are found wild in Britain. This gentian-blue species, one of the best blue-flowered rock plants there are, is rather rare and has been often coddled in frames or glasshouses where the conditions are too dry for it. Treated as a primrose and planted rather shallow in a cool peaty and leaf-mouldy soil in a north aspect, it will flourish.

HYLOMECON japonicum (*hyle* =wood, *mekon* = poppy). Another plant requiring cool, shady conditions, which is much more rare than it should be. This Asiatic poppy, growing up to 12 ins. tall, has large golden flowers carried well above the foliage. It can be propagated by seed or division.

6 LEWISIA cotyledon. A Western American plant named after the American explorer Captain Lewis. Lewisias are the only plants on this page which prefer a sunny, well-drained position: for example, they grow well in a niche in the south side of a dry wall in light, gritty soil. *L. cotyledon* is white, veined pink, and the variety illustrated is a hybrid. Other good species are *L. heckneri* with rose flowers, *L. howellii* with striped orange flowers, and *L. tweedyi* with large, broad-petalled, pale apricot flowers on short stems.

7 RAMONDA myconi, named after a French botanist, L. R. Ramond. These are alpine plants, closely related to haberlea and enjoying the same conditions— a crevice in a north-facing wall, for example, with some limestone grit mixed with the loam and leaf-mould. The flowers are deep mauve or rose-pink (*rosea*) or white (*alba*). They can be propagated by division, leaf-cuttings, or seed. Plants from seed take about three years before large enough to flower.

1 Dodecatheon meadia 'Red Wings'
2 Ranunculus amplexicaulis
3 Oxalis enneaphylla rosea
4 Haberlea ferdinandi-coburgi
5 Corydalis cashmeriana
6 Lewisia cotyledon hybrid
7 Ramonda myconi

BEARDED IRISES

The 200 or so species of iris comprise many sections, separated from each other by distinct botanical characteristics. There are two distinct types: those that grow from more or less stout rhizomes, and those that have bulbs (*see* pp. 11 and 71). They are distributed throughout the northern hemisphere, and their flowering period extends from winter (*see* p. 5) to June and July (*see* p. 75). The bearded iris or pogoniris, with which this page is concerned and which have stout rhizomes, come from Europe and Asia.

Bearded irises, because they are easy to grow and their rhizomatous roots are easy to transport, have been cultivated for many centuries, and it is not possible to say from which wild species the garden varieties originally arose. They used to be called German irises, but in fact *I. germanica* was neither a wild species nor came from Germany. Breeding new varieties became active in Britain in the late 19th century and soon extended to North America. Both countries soon produced so many varieties that some sort of classification became necessary. The only practical classification appeared to be by colour, so now they are divided into colour classes. These include flowers with white standards and coloured falls; those with standards of a lighter and falls of a darker shade of the same colour; those with yellow as the base and a combination of several other colours; those with white or yellow petals stippled or feathered round the edges with blue, pink, red, or brown; those with standards and falls of the same colour (self); and those with standards in yellow, gold, or orange and falls in a contrasting colour (the variegata group).

Some of the very lovely new iris are not good British garden plants, particularly some of the American ones, because they find the climate too damp and sunless. With the rapid introduction of new varieties others soon become superseded, but some of the older ones are still grown because of a colour or garden quality which has not been improved upon. 'Wild Fire' (1) and 'Flaming Sword' (2) are examples of older ones, while newer ones are 'Red Torch', with gold-bronze standards and velvety-red falls, and 'High Command', with butter-yellow standards and velvety-crimson falls. These two belong to the 'Variegata' group, descended mainly from a wild species, *I. variegata*, from south-east Europe.

Other good tall bearded iris are 'Aline', azure-blue and scented; 'Amigo', lavender standards, pansy-purple falls; 'Berkeley Gold', deep yellow; 'Cotillon', white; 'Great Lakes', pure blue; 'Katy', creamy-yellow; 'Master Charles', mulberry-purple; 'Mulberry Rose'; 'Pale Primrose'; 'Sable', blackish-violet; and 'Vice Regal', bronzy-purple. These grow from 3 to 4 ft. tall.

The disadvantage of bearded iris for small gardens is that they occupy a good deal of space and have a rather short flowering season. For such gardens it is better to grow the dwarf species or hybrids between these and the taller ones, such as 'Pearly Dawn' (3) which is $1\frac{1}{2}$ ft. tall. The dwarf *I. pumila*, with practically stemless purple, yellow, or cream flowers, is a native of Austria to South Russia and the Caucasus, and has a pale yellow form (*attica*) to be found in Greece. *I. mellita* from the Balkans is similar but is usually a curious brown-purple and rarely yellow. *I. chamaeiris* from south Europe usually has a rather longer stem. From these are being bred many varieties. Forms of *I. pumila* are 'Blue Lagoon'; 'Burgundy', claret-purple and rather tall; 'The Bride', white; and 'Path of Gold', golden-yellow. Others, about 8 ins. tall, are 'Blazon', deep maroon with gold beard; 'Cup and Saucer', red-purple; 'Green Spot', white with green spot on each fall; 'Little Elsa', white standards, lemon-yellow falls; 'Moongleam', pure yellow; and 'Stylish', petunia-purple. The dwarf iris usually flower in late April or May.

Bearded iris are easy to cultivate if certain simple requirements are provided. They must have full sun and a well-drained soil, neutral or preferably limy. On heavy soils, as well as adding sand, grit, or ashes, it is better to raise the beds a few inches above ground level. At planting time, unless the soil is already rich, a sprinkling of bone meal or hoof and horn may be dug in. In March, and again after blooming, superphosphate should be sprinkled round, but not on the rhizomes.

Iris should be planted or divided in August just as the new roots are starting. It is very important not to bury the whole of the rhizome. It is desirable to tie the growth to a stick to prevent the plant rocking until the new roots have a hold on the ground. The clumps should be divided every 3 or 4 years according to the vigour of their growth. The best pieces to plant are the rhizomes on the outside of the mass, and these should be planted singly — that is, with one tuft of leaves to each division.

1 Iris 'Wild Fire'   2 Iris 'Flaming Sword'   3 Iris 'Pearly Dawn'

SMALL SUMMER FLOWERS FOR SHADY PLACES

Nearly every garden has its shady corners or borders and, if these are not dried out by the roots or overhanging branches of trees, they can also be made attractive with shade-loving plants. Epimediums, tiarellas, and other woodland plants can give very attractive foliage effects in varying shades of green and gold, even at times when there are no flowers. Pages 13 and 17 give some of the earlier flowering species. This page makes suggestions for summer plants coming after the spring burst of colour is over.

1 CHIASTOPHYLLUM oppositifolium (Cotyledon *simplicifolia*). A vigorous plant with wide-spreading mats of shiny green leaves, from which in summer come erect stems of small bright yellow flowers. It will grow in almost any situation in the rock garden, but in a sunny place the leaves turn a good bronze-red in autumn. Cuttings, taken after the plant has flowered, root quickly.

2 ROSCOEA humeana. This showy iris-like plant from the Himalayas and China is hardy and easy to grow if given cool conditions in light rich loam. *R. humeana* is the most striking of the genus and grows about 8 ins. tall. *R. purpurea* flowers later, with smaller flowers on longer stems. *R. cautleoides* is yellow and variable, some forms being larger than others. Roscoea can be increased by division after flowering.

3 SAXIFRAGA primuloides (Elliott's Variety). A variety of *S. umbrosa*, the well-known 'London Pride', but much shorter, about 6 ins. tall, and with deep crimson flowers instead of pink. It is an easy plant to grow in a cool position, making a good border to a shady bed, as its neat dark-green rosettes of leaves are attractive all the year round. The 'Ingwersen's variety' is still smaller, and the leaves often bronze. The plants can be divided at almost any time of year.

4 EPIMEDIUM x warleyense. A very good hybrid epimedium which starts flowering as early as April.

The vigorous young foliage, one of the attractions of the plant, does not come until the flowers are over. It is best to remove last year's leaves in January so that the flowers can show better in the spring. Varieties of *E. grandiflorum* and *E. x youngianum* in white, rose, violet, and purple, are all easy to establish in a shady garden.

5 SANGUINARIA canadensis (Bloodroot) (*sanguis* = blood, for the sap is orange-red). A North American member of the poppy family, which flowers in the spring and has very decorative, glaucous, blue-grey foliage which opens out fully after the flowers are over. Sanguinaria dislikes being disturbed, but the roots can be divided carefully about August. *S. canadensis flore plena* is a very beautiful double form said to have been found wild in north-eastern America.

6 TIARELLA wherryi. A typical plant of cool woodland conditions, where it grows easily and soon provides good ground cover. The red-veined leaves are also decorative and turn a reddish-bronze in autumn. The varieties of *T. cordifolia*, the Foamflower, especially *purpurea* with bronzy-purple leaves and rose flowers, are also useful plants for shady places.

All but one of the tiarellas come from North America. They belong to the saxifrage family and much resemble the heucheras. A cross between *T. cordifolia* and *H. x brizoides* has produced heucherella (*see* p. 149).

1 Chiastophyllum oppositifolium   2 Roscoea humeana   3 Saxifraga umbrosa primuloides

4 Epimedium x warleyense   5 Sanguinaria canadensis   6 Tiarella cordifolia wherryi

LILY OF THE VALLEY AND RELATIVES FOR SHADY PLACES

These flowers of the Lily family have creeping rootstocks and so most of them spread freely and are suitable for naturalizing in light woodland. They are easy to grow in shade so long as there is enough reasonably moist leaf-mouldy soil.

1 DANAE racemosa (Ruscus racemosus) (Alexandrian Laurel). An attractive evergreen plant not often seen in British gardens. Its habit is like that of a bamboo, 3–4 ft. tall, the green stems bearing what appear to be shining green leaves but which are really flattened evergreen branches. The flowers are small, yellowish, and inconspicuous, but the red berries are attractive, though not borne freely in Britain. The bamboo-like sprays are excellent, especially in winter, for foliage decoration. Danae comes from Turkey and Persia and has been in cultivation for over 250 years.

RUSCUS aculeatus (Butcher's Broom). A closely related plant which provides good evergreen under-growth in shady places. The hermaphrodite form bears large red berries freely, but the plants are usually male and bear no berries. The name Butcher's Broom has arisen because in the past the very hard flattened green stems were used for cleaning the butcher's chopping block.

2 POLYGONATUM multiflorum (Solomon's Seal). A native of Northern Europe, including Britain, and Asia. It varies considerably in height, sometimes growing as tall as 4 ft., and also in size and number of flowers. Apart from this type, the most usual variety available is one with attractive white-striped leaves, which is not so strong a grower. Another species, *P. officinale*, has one or two larger and whiter flowers in each leaf axil and is a native of limestone country. The giant American *P. commutatum* (*giganteum*) may grow up to 7 ft. high, with three to eight large white flowers from each leaf axil. The miniature *P. falcatum* is only about 6 ins. tall. All these plants run at the roots and are therefore very suitable for naturalizing.

3 SMILACINA racemosa (False Spikenard or False Solomon's Seal). A North American plant growing about the same height as Solomon's Seal but with dense spikes about 4 ins. long of small star-like flowers and attractive veined and marbled purplish berries. It may be used both in a shady border or the woodland. There is a miniature species, *S. stellata*, which has short spikes of flower on 6-inch stems, and spreads modestly in any shady place.

MAIANTHEMUM bifolium (*maios* =May, *anthemon* =blossom). A plant somewhat like *Smilacina stellata*, requiring similar conditions, and also found wild in Britain. The flower stalk, with its fluffy head of small star-like white flowers, rises about 6 ins. high between two bright green leaves. It is mat-making and, like most of these plants, has a creeping rootstock. The Western American variety may grow up to 1 ft. high.

4-5 CONVALLARIA majalis (Lily of the Valley). This is native to most parts of the Northern Hemisphere and has long been treasured in gardens for its charming white bells and exquisite perfume. 'Fortin's Variety', also known as *grandiflora*, is very large, and the variety 'Everest' perhaps larger still. These larger forms require good cultivation if they are to retain their character. There is also a rare variety with double flowers and another with yellow striped leaves. *C. majalis rosea* is of interest as a colour break but is not to be compared in beauty with the wild species, which is the best for woodland planting and an excellent smotherer of weeds. *C. majalis* is a limestone plant.

UVULARIA grandiflora (*Uva* =bunch of grapes, because the flowers and then the fruit hang like a bunch of grapes). The little forest of erect stems, clothed with clasping leaves, grow about 1 ft. tall, with one to three fairly large pale-yellow flowers hanging at the top of each stem. Uvularia comes from North America.

TRICYRTIS (Toad Lily). This is closely related to Uvularia but flowers in the autumn, and comes from the Himalayas and Japan. The upstanding flowers are usually white with few or many purple spots. *T. macrantha*, however, has hanging primrose bells, spotted within. They need a sheltered position so that the early autumn frosts do not spoil the flowers.

DISPORUM smithii. A dwarf relative of tricyrtis, about 6 ins. tall, with relatively large whitish flowers rather hidden by the leaves. These are followed by attractive large orange berries. Other species of disporum, such as *D. pullum* with white to deep purple, nodding, bell-shaped flowers, grow 1–2 ft. tall.

1 Danae racemosa   2 Polygonatum multiflorum   3 Smilacina racemosa
4 Convallaria majalis   5 Convallaria majalis rosea

PAEONIES

The plant is named after Paeon, an ancient Greek physician who first used the paeony for medical purposes. Paeonies belong to the Buttercup family and are natives of temperate regions, some in Europe, some in north-west America, and others in the Far East. Some have foliage which colours attractively in the autumn, and the large seed-heads of some are ornamental.

Paeonies are hardy, but they dislike being disturbed once they are established. Most of them prefer partial shade and shelter from east winds. They need a deep, rich, well-drained soil, with plenty of humus to prevent drying out in the summer. They grow into bulky plants so they need plenty of room. They should be planted in September or October when they are dormant, and the brittle 'eyes' should be at least 2 ins. below the surface. Once planted, they need little more attention except some support for the heavy heads of double varieties, the removal of dead heads, and a mulch of manure or dressing of bone meal each year.

Paeonies vary from the shrubby species (tree paeonies) up to 5–6 ft. tall to the dwarf rockery herbs only 1–2 ft. tall. They vary in colour from yellow, white, and magenta to all shades of pink and red.

1-2 HERBACEOUS PAEONIES. The old, May-flowering cottage-garden paeony is *P. officinalis*, a species found wild in many parts of Europe, with red flowers. There are many varieties, including double forms in white, pink, and crimson, and also a crimson and yellow anemone-flowered form.

A great many of the garden paeonies are varieties of *P. lactiflora*, known as Chinese paeonies. They flower for the most part in June, and grow about 3–3½ ft. tall. These are single-flowered, double-flowered, and Japanese or anemone-flowered varieties. Only an arbitrary selection can be given here.

SINGLE-FLOWERED PAEONIES: 'Soshi' (1); 'Emma', large carmine-pink with silver reverse and golden centre; 'Jan van Leeuwen', large white with golden centre; 'Pink Delight', dog-rose pink with orange stamens; 'The Moor', deep maroon-crimson.

DOUBLE-FLOWERED PAEONIES: 'Mons. Jules Elie' (2), early-flowering and excellent for cutting; 'Alice Harding', very large creamy-white and tall; 'Kelway's Glorious', large white, well-shaped, rather late-flowering; 'Bowl of Beauty', bright rose with centre of pale yellow, early-flowering; 'Adolphe Rousseau', dark crimson-red; 'Karl Rosenfield', wine-crimson, tall, and early-flowering; 'Sarah Bernhardt', apple-blossom pink, perfect shape, free-flowering, and excellent for cutting; 'Peter Brand', bright red.

JAPANESE PAEONIES: 'Globe of Light', deep rose-pink with yellow centre; 'Isani Gidui', pure white with large golden centre; 'Seioba', clear pink with creamy-white centre; 'Mikado', bright red with golden centre; 'Fuyajo', velvety maroon-red with red and gold centre.

DWARF SPECIES: *P. veitchii woodwardii*, 1 ft., rose-pink, June; *P. tenuifolia*, 12–18 ins., deep-red, both single and double forms, May; *P. broteri*, 16–20 ins., rose, May; *P. mlokosewitschi*, 18–24 ins., yellow with bronzy foliage, early May.

3-4 TREE PAEONIES. The wild tree paeonies from Asia, mainly China, such as *P. delavayi* (4), *P. lutea ludlowii* (3), and the white, maroon-centred *P. suffruticosa*, make shrubs up to 5–6 ft. high. The flowers of some forms are rather small in proportion to the size of the plant, but they are free-flowering, hardy, and have decorative foliage.

Garden varieties are derived from *P. suffruticosa* or its varieties crossed with *P. lutea*. They are very hardy, but, since they flower early, the young foliage and buds may be damaged by late spring frosts. Some protection, therefore, in early spring is desirable, and it is better to place them where the sun does not shine on them too early in the day. They have very large flowers and, though they grow slowly, they start flowering when still small. They will grow in any well-drained soil in sun or shade.

VARIETIES: There are a great number, and this is an arbitrary selection. 'Bijou de Chusan', double white, shaded pink; 'Hakugan', single or semi-double white; 'Chromatella', double sulphur-yellow; 'L'Esperance', large semi-double prim-rose, blotched crimson; 'Souvenir de Maxime Cornu', double golden-yellow, fragrant; 'Souvenir d'Etienne Mechin', double rose, fragrant; 'Fragrans maxima plena', double salmon-pink, fragrant; 'Madame Louis Henry', single carmine-shaded copper; 'Mme. Stuart Low', double bright salmon-red.

1 Paeonia 'Soshi'
3 Paeonia lutea ludlowii
2 Paeonia 'M. Jules Elie'
4 Paeonia delavayi

VIOLAS AND PANSIES

Botanically speaking, the genus *Viola* includes violas, pansies, and violets (*see* p. 4). Pansies, therefore, are violas. But gardeners distinguish between them because they have been developed by different crosses from wild species. Violas have a rather more compact growth and in favourable situations may survive for several years. Both are most satisfactorily treated as hardy biennials (*see* p. 33) or in very cold districts as annuals started under glass. If grown as biennials, the seed should be sown at the end of June or early July, preferably in boxes in a frame or cold greenhouse, though often successfully in a prepared seed-bed out of doors. They should be pricked out as soon as they are large enough to handle, and planted into flowering positions in the autumn. They must not be allowed to get dry. Named varieties can also be propagated by cuttings which usually root easily.

Both pansies and violas are easy to grow and adaptable. They do not like a very heavy or a very dry soil, and do best in a good loam with plenty of humus, which does not dry out. They will grow in a sunny position, but will also thrive in light shade.

2 PANSIES (**V. x wittrockiana**). These were first developed, mainly from the native *V. tricolor*, in 1810 by the gardener T. Thomson, and by 1835 there were as many as 400 varieties with a wide range of colours and very large 'faces'. These are called 'show' and 'fancy' pansies, and these old-fashioned 'faced' pansies have remained very popular ever since. It is probably best to grow a good mixture, such as Sutton's 'Giant Fancy' (2) or 'Englemann's Giant'. After a mild winter these will begin to flower in late April and continue flowering for a long time, especially if the dead flowers are removed. Another good strain of mixed pansies is 'Perfection Mixed'. These are rather smaller on shorter stems, but have more regular markings and are very good for an edging. Separate self colours in very many shades can also be easily obtained true from seed.

There are winter-flowering strains of pansies, both mixed or in separate colours, such as 'North Pole' (white) or 'Winter Sun' (golden with black blotch). These are very hardy and will flower in sheltered positions in the mild periods during winter and early spring.

1, VIOLAS (**V. x williamsii**). These were developed by
5-6 a Scottish gardener, James Grieve, in 1863 by crossing the tufted Pyrenees species *V. cornuta* (1) with varieties of garden pansies. The flowers are rather smaller and more usually self-coloured, though there are strains of 'faced' flowers, such as the hybrid strain 'Sutton's Fancy' (5). Their compact tufted habit of growth makes them very suitable for bedding, serving as a carpet for taller plants (*see* p. 125).

3-4 VIOLETTAS (**V. x visseriana**). These miniature or tufted violas, developed by Dr. Charles Stuart about 1887, are suitable for rock gardens or for edgings. The first form was a compact little plant with small white flowers. There are now many varieties but mostly self-coloured. 'Buttercup' is deep yellow; 'Lorna' is deep lavender-blue; 'Tom Tit' is purplish-blue; 'Picotee' is white edged violet; and 'Jackanapes' is yellow and chocolate.

1 VIOLA CORNUTA 'BAMBI' 2 VIOLA TRICOLOR 'GIANT FANCY' 3 VIOLA 'BOWLES BLACK'
4 VIOLA BOSNIACA 5 VIOLA HYBRIDS 'SUTTON'S FANCY' 6 VIOLA 'PERFECTION'

ERICACEOUS SHRUBS

Ericaceous plants are, with a few exceptions, plants which will not tolerate limy or chalky soils. A neutral or slightly acid well-drained loam or sand with plenty of humus suits them best. As they make a mass of small fibrous roots near the surface, they must not be in a position where the soil gets hot and dry; on the other hand, few like deep shade where they tend to get leggy and flower less freely. The right position to choose depends on the natural moisture of the soil or the possibility of artificial watering in times of drought.

1-3 RHODODENDRON (*rhodon* = rose, *dendron* = tree). There are not less than some 500 species of rhododendrons, including azaleas, the greater number coming from alpine moorlands and temperate woodland in China, Tibet, and the Himalayas. Some, mainly azaleas, come from North America. One or two come from the European Alps, in particular, *R. ferrugineum*, the well-known Alpine Rose. True rhododendrons are evergreen, but the American and Japanese azaleas are mostly deciduous. The hardiness of rhododendrons and azaleas varies from very hardy indeed to species which need greenhouse protection. They also vary in height from trees up to 40 ft. or more to rock garden shrubs. We are concerned here only with the more dwarf species and hybrids suitable for the ordinary garden. The main flowering time is May and June, though *R. x praecox* and *R. mucronulatum* (*see* p. 2) are winter-flowering and several others flower in March and April (*see* p. 26).

The larger rhododendrons need shade, but the dwarfer types described here will tolerate more sun: in fact, if planted in too much shade they become drawn and leggy. The deciduous azaleas need sunny positions, though even then they wilt in too strong sun unless there is ample moisture.

R. x 'Blue Diamond' (1) is a hybrid between the tall blue *R. augustini* and the dwarf hybrid *x intrifast* (*R. fastigiatum x intricatum*). In all these dwarf hybrids the forms vary and it is important to obtain only good ones. Other good hybrids are *R. x impeanum* (cobalt violet) and the bright yellow 'Yellow Hammer' (*R. sulfuream x flavidum*). Among the many species the following are good hardy dwarf plants: *R. calostrotum* (magenta crimson, very dwarf), *R. cephalanthum* (pink daphne-like flowers), *R. pemakoense* (mauve-pink, 2 ft. tall), *R. racemosum* (pure pink dwarf variety), *R. russatum* (deep blue-purple), and *R. sargentianum* (pale yellow). All these flower about May and give odd flowers in the autumn.

Rhododendron luteum (2). Often called *Azalea pontica*, this is a very hardy native of East Europe and Turkey with bright yellow, fragrant flowers and deciduous coloured autumn foliage. It is one of the species used in developing the first 'Ghent' azaleas, raised by M. Mortier, a baker of Ghent. These are very hardy, will stand sun and wind, range in colour from cream to red, and some are sweet scented. Good varieties are 'Altaclarense Sunbeam' (bright yellow), 'Bouquet de Flore' (pink, white, and yellow), 'Coccinea Speciosa' (brilliant orange-red) and 'daviesii' (white with yellow centre).

Rhododendron 'Fedora' (3). An example of the semi-evergreen azaleas obtained by crossing the mauve *R. 'malvaticum'* with the very hardy salmon-red Japanese *R. kaempferi*. These newer hybrids are very hardy, have large flowers, and grow up to 10 ft. tall, with beautifully coloured autumn foliage. As well as 'Fedora', good varieties are 'Addy Wery' (vermilion-red), 'John Cairns' (orange-red), 'Palestrina' (white), and 'Willy' (pink).

4 VACCINIUM virgatum. This is the genus to which bilberries, cranberries, and blueberries belong. For the garden the value of vacciniums lies chiefly in the brilliant colours of their autumn foliage. *V. virgatum* from the Eastern United States is the best for autumn colour and grows about 2–2½ ft. tall. Other good species are the tall *V. corymbosum*, *V. erythrocarpum*, and *V. ovalifolium*, as well as the smaller *V. angustifolium* (*pennsylvanicum*), about 18 ins. tall. The fruits of these vacciniums are black or blue-black, often with a grape-like bloom.

5-6 KALMIA, after Peter Kalm, a pupil of Linnaeus. *K. latifolia* (5) is the Calico Bush or Mountain Laurel of the U.S.A., and the most lovely of American evergreen shrubs. It was introduced to Britain in 1734, and was very popular until the many new flowering shrubs from China to some extent superseded it. The flowers, which appear in June, vary very much from almost white to deep pink. The shrub needs plenty of room, when in time it will make a large evergreen mound 8–10 ft. high. It needs more sun than do rhododendrons and the same kind of soil.

Kalmia angustifolia rubra (6) is, in effect, a miniature *K. latifolia*, and in the eastern states of the U.S.A., from which both come, it is called 'Sheep Laurel', and said to be poisonous to animals. It grows only about 2 ft. high and is proportionally smaller in all its parts. As well as the rose form, there is a very beautiful but rare white form.

MENZIESIA purpurea. A shrub of medium growth from Japan, with drooping bell-shaped flowers of a rich wine-red, and foliage which colours well in the autumn. It does best in light shade.

PIERIS formosa. The best variety is *forrestii*, in particular the Wakehurst variety. Pieris has the unusual quality among ericaceous shrubs of producing colour in spring. The spring foliage is fiery-red, followed by massive panicles of urn-shaped white flowers in April-May. A native of China, it must be planted in a sheltered position to prevent spring frosts destroying the young foliage. Once established, it will make a large shrub.

1 RHODODENDRON DWARF HYBRID 'BLUE DIAMOND' 2 RHODODENDRON LUTEUM 3 RHODODENDRON 'FEDORA'
4 VACCINIUM VIRGATUM 5 KALMIA LATIFOLIA 6 KALMIA ANGUSTIFOLIA RUBRA

EARLY SUMMER LARGER SHRUBS

1-2 CYTISUS scoparius (Broom). The British wild Common Broom, *Cytisus scoparius*, is well known for its golden yellow flowers. In 1884, a sport, with the wings of a rich brownish-crimson and the standards lined with the same colour, was found in Normandy by M. Andre and named *C. scoparius andreanus*. A sulphur-yellow sport has also occurred more than once. From these, by seedling selection and hybridization with other species, a series of garden cytisus have been raised, with colours varying from sulphur to various orange-reds and crimsons, the wings and standards often being of contrasting colours. The introduction of *Cytisus albus*, the white Spanish Broom from Spain and Portugal, has given rise to colours of lilac, rose, and claret-red, such as 'Minstead' (fuchsia-purple and white), 'Burkwoodii' (cerise and maroon-red), and 'Enchantress' (rose-pink and carmine).

Cytisus grows best in acid sandy soils, but can be grown in other soils if plenty of peat or leaf-mould is incorporated. They should be pruned every year immediately after flowering; otherwise they become lanky and liable to be blown down by the wind. *See also p. 67 for dwarf species.*

3 SYRINGA sweginzowii (from *syrinx*, a pipe or tube). The common Lilac (*S. vulgaris*), a native of eastern Europe, has been long grown in British gardens, but during the last 50 years many natives of China have been introduced, some of them differing from the common lilacs by a more graceful habit and looser panicles of flower. *S. sweginzowii* will grow up to 12 ft., and the fragrance of the flowers differs from that of the ordinary lilacs. In the variety *superba* the handsome panicles of flower are very large. Among other species *S. reflexa* is worth mentioning because of its unusual drooping panicles of white and pink flowers and handsome foliage. Ii general, however, the hybrids are more worth growing than the species. There are many varieties developed from *S. vulgaris*, both double and single, and ranging in colour from pure white and cream to mauve, lilac-pink, carmine-rose, and dark reddish-purple. They grow easily in most soils, but prefer a moist rich soil with lime. They sucker rather easily and the suckers should be removed; the flower-heads, also, when dead, should be cut off. The varieties are usually propagated by grafting on *S. vulgaris* stock.

The shrub often known as syringa is Philadelphus *coronarius*, the Mock Orange (*see p. 61*).

4 DEUTZIA x rosea, named after Johann van de Deutz. The deutzias are a large family of deciduous shrubs from China, Japan, the Himalayas, etc. Considerable hybridization has been done, and the hybrids, of which this is one (*D. gracilis* x *D. purpurascens*), are more frequently grown than the species, although many of the latter are valuable garden plants, and make bushy shrubs 6 ft. tall or rather more. There are two varieties of *D. x rosea*, *campanulata* (pure white) and *grandiflora* (white-flushed pink). Another attractive hybrid is *D. x kalmiiflora* (*D. purpurascens* x *parviflora*) which has drooping branches covered with pink flowers rather like kalmias (*see p. 57*). Deutzias grow in any good garden soil and flower on the previous season's growth. They will tolerate light shade.

5 WEIGELA florida foliis purpureis. Weigela was introduced from North China over 100 years ago. It is deciduous and may grow 6–7 ft. high. It seems prone to leaf variation for, as well as the purple-leaved form, there is a variety with the leaves edged pale yellow, one with a silver edge, a rather rare one with silver veining, a dwarfer one with creamy-white edging, and a wholly yellow-leafed one called *D. looymansi aurea*. For garden purposes some of the many hybrids which have been raised are superior. A good selection is 'Conquete' (soft salmon-pink), 'Bristol Ruby' (large-flowered ruby-crimson), 'Newport Red' (deep red), 'Le Printemps' (pink), 'La Perle' (creamy-white, pink outside), and 'Feerie' (shell pink). They all flower on the previous year's wood.

6 DAPHNE x burkwoodii. A cross between the tall white-flowered *D. caucasica* and the dwarf, evergreen, pink-flowered *D. cneorum* has produced two excellent, easily grown plants — the one illustrated and the very similar *D. x 'Somerset'*. Both retain the perfume of the parents, and both grow about 4 ft. and do well in limy soils, as do most daphnes. The dwarf *D. cneorum* itself is a very popular plant, easy to grow and tolerant of lime if mixed with leaf-mould. An older hybrid of slower and more compact growth is *D. hybrida* (*D. collina* x *odora*), 3–4 ft. tall with fragrant, pinkish-purple flowers. The hybrid is quite hardy and continues to produce flowers through a large part of the year. For early-flowering daphnes, *see pp. 3 and 12.*

ESCALLONIA. These South American shrubs have both later flowering (*see p. 159*) and earlier flowering species. Many of the most attractive evergreen species and hybrids are not hardy in all areas, but they are wind-resistant and good seaside shrubs. The hardiest species is the deciduous *E. virgata*, with white flowers and growing about 4–6 ft. tall. The most reliable hybrids have *E. virgata* blood. *E. x 'Apple Blossom'* has large soft pink flowers on dwarf bushes; *E. x 'langleyensis'* is semi-evergreen and has rose-pink flowers on arching branches; the Donard hybrids grow about 6 ft. tall and include 'Donard Brilliance' (large deep-crimson), 'Slieve Donard' (large pink), and 'Donard Radiance' (dark pink).

DIPELTA floribunda. A very much neglected shrub flowering at this time. It is deciduous with curious peeling bark and can grow as tall as 10 ft. The sprays of fragrant flowers are like those of weigela but larger and pale pink with a striking yellow throat. For good flowering it must have plenty of sun.

1 CYTISUS 'DIANA'   2 CYTISUS FULGENS   3 SYRINGA SWEGINZOWII
4 DEUTZIA GRACILIS ROSEA   5 WEIGELA FLORIDA FOLIIS PURPUREIS   6 DAPHNE X BURKWOODII

EARLY SUMMER SHRUBS

1 **KOLKWITZIA amabilis.** An excellent shrub from China, named after Professor Kolkwitz, which is far too seldom grown. It is related to and resembles abelia (*see* p. 171), though it flowers earlier, and if given room and a sunny position, may grow up to 7–8 ft. tall and produce an abundance of flowers. Like all shrubs which flower on the previous year's growth, it should have the older stems removed each year after flowering.

2 **GENISTA aethnensis,** the Mt. Etna Broom, is a native of Sicily. It flowers later than the other plants on this page — not usually before July in most parts of the country; in fact, this later flowering is one of its advantages (*see* p. 158). It is a graceful plant with green rush-like pendant branches, the leaves being so small as to be of no account. It can grow as tall as 15–20 ft., when it needs some support, but it is better to prune it back carefully immediately after flowering, and so keep it more bush-like, though not too short to show its graceful habit. It is an excellent shrub for dry limy soils in the sun.

Two other genistas closely allied to *G. aethnensis* but flowering in June, are *G. cinerea* from Spain and *G. virgata* from Madeira. These reach about 10 ft., and the leaves, which are covered with silky hairs, give the plants a silver-grey appearance.

3 **GENISTA lydia** from the Balkans is a dwarf shrub about 2 ft. tall. It forms a hummocky mass of pendulous shoots and is most suitable for a bank or the top of a retaining wall. It is not as much grown as it should be, for it blooms with the greatest freedom in full sun.

4 **LONICERA chaetocarpa.** The shrubby loniceras as opposed to the climbers (*see* p. 63) are not frequently grown, because few are sufficiently attractive. *L. chaetocarpa* has the largest flowers of the shrubby kinds, and these hang in pairs beneath the leaves; but it is really a collector's plant and not as attractive as the Chinese *L. syringantha*, with very fragrant rosy-lilac flowers. This makes a spreading shrub about 6 ft. tall. The fruits are bright red.

5 **PHILADELPHUS x lemoinei 'Manteau d'Hermine'.** The Mock Oranges (sometimes called syringa) are among the most popular June shrubs because they are very free flowering and also most of them very fragrant. For garden purposes one of the hybrids is now usually grown, although the old European *P. coronarius* may be grown for its very rich scent. They vary from 3-ft. dwarfs, such as the one illustrated, a hybrid between *P. coronarius* and *P. microphyllus* (a species noted for its pineapple scent), to plants 8–10 ft. high. Good modern hybrids are: 'Beauclerk' (very large white, 6–8 ft.), 'Belle Etoile' (white flushed maroon at the centre, 4–5 ft.), P. x 'burfordensis' (large cup-shaped flowers with conspicuous yellow stamens, 8–10 ft.), 'Sybille' (white with purple stain, 6–8 ft.), and 'Velleda' with crimped petals. These are all single. Perhaps the best fragrant double hybrid is 'Virginal',

8–10 ft. 'Boule d'Argent' is a more dwarf double, 4–5 ft.

SPIRAEA. There are two types of spiraea from the gardener's point of view: the early-flowering white spiraeas such as *S. thunbergii* (*see* p. 24) which flower on last season's growth; and the later-flowering white, pink, or crimson spiraeas which flower on the current season's growth. All like a sunny position and should be pruned according to their type.

Good June-flowering species of the first type are *S. canescens*, bearing bunches of white flowers on the upper side of arching shoots; *S. nipponica* from Japan; and *S. trichocarpa* from Korea, all growing about 6 ft. tall. Those of the second type flower from June to September. June-flowering species include *S. japonica*, 3–5 ft. tall with rosy-red flattish panicles of flowers, and its varieties, especially the brilliant carmine dwarf 'Anthony Waterer'; and the rather taller hybrid *S. x billiardii*, which bears pyramidal panicles of bright rose flowers. *S. bullata* is a dwarf, rather later-flowering species, with a mass of scarlet-rose flowers, very good for the rock garden.

STAPHYLEA. A small group of May-flowering shrubs, of which *S. pinnata*, the Bladder nut, with its pale-green bladder-like seed pods, is naturalized in Britain. The best choice for the garden is *S. colchica* with creamy-white flowers in erect panicles, or the rarer *S. x elegans* with larger drooping panicles. More striking but less easy to obtain is *S. holocarpa rosea*, an erect growing plant up to 12 ft., bearing numerous drooping panicles of rose-pink blooms.

EXOCHORDA racemosa (Pearl Bush). This is another May-flowering shrub from China. It bears masses of white flowers all along the branches, the unopened buds having a pearl-like appearance. It makes a rounded bush up to about 10 ft. tall and grows easily in any sunny position.

PRUNUS serrulata. The majority of Japanese cherries are over by the end of April, but *P. serrulata*, a parent of the ornamental Japanese cherries, is rather later flowering, and the latest to flower is the variety 'Shimidsu-Sakura' (*P. serrulata longipes*). The large flowers are pink in bud and open to pure white. They hang in particularly long-stalked clusters among the young foliage. It is of outstanding beauty, but is a small tree rather than a shrub. The improved form of the native Bird Cherry, *P. padus watereri* or *grandiflora* is another May-flowering small tree, with 8-in. racemes of scented white flowers.

ROBINIA kelseyi. A very beautiful shrub or small tree of the Pea family from North America, which bears clusters of bright rose-pink, pea-shaped flowers and very attractive foliage. This plant, however, must have a position well protected from wind, for the wood is extremely brittle and easily broken. It must also have full sun and does better on a dry and not too rich soil.

1 Kolkwitzia amabilis   2 Genista aethnensis   3 Genista lydia
4 Lonicera chaetocarpa   5 Philadelphus 'Manteau d'Hermine'

WOODY JUNE CLIMBERS

1 WISTARIA sinensis. Wistaria is named after Professor Wistar of Philadelphia. It is best grown in a sunny position and does well on a south wall or balcony. It can also be grown up a tree (but should not be planted too near the trunk), or even trained to make a small tree. Plants grown in a restricted space have to be pruned hard in the late winter with a second pruning in August. Wistaria will grow in any soil but usually takes a year or so to become established. In very hot weather growth can be encouraged by syringing the foliage from time to time. Wistaria *sinensis* will climb up to 100 ft. and make a trunk up to 5 ft. in girth. The racemes of fragrant flowers are up to a foot long. There is also a white and a double mauve form.

Other good species are the Japanese *W. floribunda macrobotrys* (*multijuga*) which climbs about 30 ft. and has enormous racemes of lavender flowers up to 3 ft. or more long. *W. venusta* is a downy species with shorter racemes of large white scented flowers.

2 AKEBIA quinata. A Chinese and Japanese twining plant, evergreen in warm localities, which is hardy but does best on a south wall. It can be grown effectively on pillars, when the flowers can be seen against sunlight, or near other wall shrubs that flower earlier or later, when its strong shoots will work their way through them. It has separate male and female flowers on the same plant, the female being the larger and more showy, and both are scented. It forms fat, plum-like, greyish-lilac seed-pods, lined with white down and containing black seeds. The species *A. lobata* is deciduous and grows in the same way, up to 30 ft. long, with dark-purple flowers.

3 CLEMATIS montana. There is a great variety of clematis flowering from early spring (the cream-coloured *C. cirrhosa*) to autumn (*C. orientalis* p. 165). Most are climbers, but some, such as *C. heracleifolia* (*see* p. 171) are shrubby herbaceous plants. Many will make their first flowering in May or June and then flower again or even a third time. Some, such as *C. montana* and *C. armandii*, flower on last year's growth and so must be pruned after flowering in the late summer or autumn; the later flowering kinds such as *C. x jackmannii*, which flower on the current year's growth, should be cut back in early spring. They are hardy plants and can be grown on walls with trellis work or wire netting to climb on, or over fences and sheds and through trees and shrubs.

Clematis need a deep, well-drained soil with plenty of compost and old manure mixed well into the soil below the roots. When planting, sifted soil and leaf-mould should be packed firmly among the roots, and the crowns should be about 2 ins. below the surface. New plants should be cut down the first spring to within 6–12 ins. of the ground. Some protection, such as large stones, is desirable to keep the roots cool, and a bushy herbaceous plant or small shrub planted in front protects the main stem from direct sun. The shoots need careful guiding and tying up.

MAY–JUNE FLOWERING VARIETIES. Among the early-summer flowering species are *C. alpina* and *C. armandii* (April–May) and *C. macropetala* and *montana* (May–June). All have many varieties in a wide range of colours — white, pink, and various shades of blue and red and purple.

Good varieties of *C. alpina* are 'Columbine', soft lavender-blue; 'Pamela Jackman', Oxford-blue; *alpina siberica*, white; and a.s. 'Ruby', rosy-red. Varieties of *C. montana* include *montana rubens*, rosy-red; *montana wilsonii*, white with twisted petals (late flowering). *C. macropetala* includes 'Markham's Pink'; 'Lagoon', semi-double deep lavender; and 'Maidwell Hall', semi-double blue. *C. spooneri* has large white flowers.

Many of the large-flowered varieties, such as the *C. x jackmanii* group, flower in the late summer and autumn; but some, such as the *C. patens* varieties, flower in spring and early summer. These include 'Nelly Moser', pale mauve-pink with a red bar; 'Barbara Jackman', soft petunia with plum-coloured bar and cream stamens; 'Fair Rosamond', white with pale wine-red bar; and many others.

4 LONICERA brownii fuchsioides (Scarlet Trumpet Honeysuckle). This is a hybrid of the similar but tender *L. sempervirens* and the more hardy *L. hirsuta*, both from North America. It has no scent, but flowers from June to September, and as a rule does best grown up a wall.

Other vigorous climbing lonicera are the fragrant *L. japonica* (white tinged purple) and *L. tellmanniana* (yellow flushed red) which is without scent. There are several varieties of *L. japonica*, including *L. j. brachypoda* with flowers and leaves tinted crimson, and 'halliana', white and yellow. A strong-growing hybrid is *L. x americana*, which has large panicles of fragrant creamy-yellow flowers, tinged pink. There is a dark red-purple variety, *atrosanguinea*.

For winter-flowering lonicera, *see L. x purpusii* p. viii, and for shrubby loniceras, *see* p. 61.

1 WISTARIA SINENSIS
3 CLEMATIS MONTANA 'PINK PERFECTION'

2 AKEBIA QUINATA
4 LONICERA BROWNII FUCHSIOIDES

SMALL SHRUBS FOR DRY SOILS

Apart from gardens in the drier eastern counties, there are places in many gardens where the soil remains dry or relatively so for long periods — on banks, for example, and near or in front of trees. As most herbaceous plants are unsuitable for such positions, we need to fall back upon dwarf shrubs. Fortunately there are many available — plants from drier and hotter climates which in Britain are frequently longer lived and happier in such positions.

1 FABIANA imbricata prostrata. The tall heath-like *F. imbricata* with masses of white tubular flowers is suitable for mild areas only, as it is not very hardy. *F. violacea* of more spreading habit and mauve blossom is somewhat hardier, and this dwarf form of *F. imbricata* with bluish flowers is hardier still. Even this, however, needs a sheltered sunny position in light soil, and is not really suitable to cold districts. All are. natives of Chile.

2 HELICHRYSUM plicatum (*helios* =sun, *chrysos* = golden). In this large genus there are annuals, perennials, and shrubs of various sizes, most of them half-hardy from Australia and South Africa and a few hardy ones from south-east Europe, of which this is one. The characteristic dry and hard bracts of the flowers which retain both colour and shape when dried has led to the name 'Everlasting Flowers', applied mostly to the annual *H. bracteatum* (*see* p. 191). Helichrysums also often have leaves and stems downy with white hairs. Both these characters are associated with the capability for withstanding long periods of drought. *H. orientale* is a similar plant but with paler straw-coloured flower heads. For rock garden helichrysums, *see* pp. 43 and 91.

3 HYPERICUM olympicum citrinum. There are free-flowering hypericums, or St. John's Worts, varying in height from 6 ft. to a few inches, the latter being excellent plants for the rock garden. They continue to flower for a very long period. Procumbent species such as *H. fragile*, *H. polyphyllum*, and *H. rhodopeum* are excellent for dry sunny positions. Hypericums are usually gold, but there are pale yellow variants which are most attractive. *H. olympicum* is a summer-flowering shrub about 1½ ft. high, coming from south-east Europe, Syria, and Turkey. The variety *citrinum* is a beautiful plant with larger flowers on stems seldom more than 1 ft. long. *See* also p. 161.

4 HELIANTHEMUM (**Rock Rose** or **Sun Rose**), *helios* =sun, *anthemon* =flower. The common rock rose (*H. nummularium*), a very attractive dwarf spreading shrub with clear yellow flowers, is native to Britain, as are also *H. canum*, yellow and *H. appenninum*, white. The garden plants have all been derived from the green-leaved *H. nummularium* and the grey-leaved *H. glaucum* of south Europe, also yellow. It is remarkable that the many coloured varieties now available — white, pale yellow, pink, orange, red, and crimson — should all have arisen from two yellow wild plants, only one known to have produced a pink variant in the wild. There are doubles as well as singles, the flowers of the doubles lasting longer than the day or half day of the singles. Probably a good mixture is the best to grow, though for small areas the dwarfer Ben series or the clear orange 'Amy Baring' is more suitable. The plants should be cut over with shears immediately the main flowering is over to prevent their becoming straggly and to encourage them to form a flowering evergreen carpet.

5-7 CISTUS. Cistuses in general are not as hardy as helianthemums for, being natives of the Mediterranean region, they need more sun and heat than Britain can usually provide. The really hardy varieties *C. laurifolius* and *C. populifolius* and the moderately hardy *C. x cyprius* are too tall for our purpose. The beautiful hybrid *C. x 'Silver Pink'* and the white natural hybrid *C. x corbariensis* are the most hardy dwarf varieties. The natural hybrid *C..x skanbergii* (5) from Greece cannot be relied upon to withstand cold winters, and it is safer to keep a few young plants in a cold frame. All cistuses need full sun, do not mind lime, and their flowers last less than a day, longer on dull days than sunny ones.

Halimiocistus x wintonensis (6), a hybrid of *Halimium formosum* and *C. salvifolius*, sometimes listed as a cistus but generally under the name halimiocistus, is an extraordinary and very beautiful hybrid which is, unfortunately, neither very hardy nor easy to grow. It needs a very hot sheltered situation in the driest place possible.

Cistus crispus (7) from south-west Europe is one of the group with reddish flowers. A hybrid grown from it, called 'Sunset', is more vivid in colour, but neither it nor the species is very hardy.

ANTHYLLIS hermanniae. A twiggy gorse-like plant with yellow, sometimes orange-tinged, pea-shaped flowers, which should be grown in dry positions more often than it is. Although a native of the Mediterranean, it grows high up and is reasonably hardy, making a shrub about 3 ft. tall and flowering earlier than the other plants on this page.

MOLTKIA petraea from Greece, has deep violet-blue forget-me-not-like flowers, and will in time make a bush 1 ft. tall and as much through. It is suitable for rock gardens and is hardy and easy to grow.

1 Fabiana imbricata prostrata   2 Helichrysum plicatum   3 Hypericum olympicum citrinum
4 Helianthemum hybrids   5 Cistus x skanbergii   6 Halimiocistus x wintonensis
7 Cistus crispus

DWARF SHRUBS FOR THE ROCK GARDEN

There are many naturally dwarf shrubs or dwarf forms of larger shrubs which are suitable for sunny positions in the rock garden. They are widespread on low hills and mountain sides, where they are exposed to sun and wind in rock crevices or in stony soil, and often receive only a low rainfall. Such areas occur in South Europe, in the Near East, North America, New Zealand, and other places. These, and some of the larger plants shown on p. 65, are also suitable for the front of a shrub border. Most can be propagated most easily from cuttings taken after flowering.

1 CYTISUS **hirsutus demissus (Broom).** As well as the taller brooms shown on p. 59, there are several dwarf species which, like all of them, need a light soil and full sun. The species illustrated is one of the most prostrate, its slow-growing spreading shoots being only about 3 ins. high. In May the whole plant is covered with flowers very large for its size.

C. *ardoinii* makes an upright bushy little shrub about 6 ins. tall with golden flowers. C. *kewensis* is prostrate but larger in growth, too large for a small rock garden. It bears freely creamy-white flowers.

ERINACEA **pungens (Hedgehog Broom).** A very much branched and spiny, broom-like plant from Spain which makes mounds up to a foot high, with insignificant leaves and pale lavender pea-shaped flowers. Some plants are more free-flowering than others. It requires a poor dry soil, and should be more often grown than it is. It is not easy to propagate, as cuttings do not root easily and seed seldom sets in Britain. It is now usually listed as an anthyllis.

2 ALYSSUM **spinosum roseum.** A spiny little shrub up to a foot high, with small, grey, thyme-like foliage and dense clusters of small pink flowers in May and June. It is a plant which does best in a very hot dry position. For other alyssums, *see* pp. 41 and 135.

3 PENSTEMON **newberryi humilior.** Penstemon is a very variable group of plants from North America which includes many tall herbaceous species (*see* p. 169), most of which flower later in the summer. The penstemon illustrated is a dwarf form of a shrubby species, which, though only 6–8 ins. tall, can spread twice that length along the ground or over a rock.

Also suitable for the rock garden are *P. scouleri albus* which has white flowers on a taller plant; *P. pinifolius* which has scarlet flowers and very small leaves (*see* p. 91); and *P. aridus*, very dwarf, with rosettes of leaves and 6 in. spikes of small brilliant blue flowers. All these need very well-drained soil in full sun, the very dwarf ones being best grown in a scree or dry wall.

HEBE x **'Carl Teschner'.** This belongs to the same family as the Veronicas. It is a recent introduction and natural hybrid from the New Zealand Alps, and grows quite easily in British gardens if given a sunny open position. It is a slow-growing shrublet with small dark green leaves, black stems, and deep violet-blue flowers. *H. pagei* is rather larger-growing and has silver-blue leaves and pale blue-white flowers.

4 RHODOTHAMNUS **chamaecistus.** A slow-growing ericaceous shrub from limestone ranges of the European Alps, especially the Dolomites. In contrast to most plants on this page, it prefers a semi-shady position in a peaty leafy soil. In early summer its large pink flowers almost hide the small leaves.

5 EURYOPS **evansii.** A recently introduced plant of the Daisy family from the Drakensberg mountains in South Africa. Although from Africa, it has proved quite hardy, but dislikes a close damp atmosphere. All winter it is a delightful rounded silver-green shrub about 9–12 ins. high, and in May or June it becomes covered with flowers. It needs very well-drained light soil and an open position, and cuttings root easily.

DAPHNE **cneorum eximea (Garland Flower).** There are several evergreen, sweet-scented, free-flowering, procumbent dwarf daphnes which are among the best rock-garden shrubs. If they establish themselves, they will flourish, though it is not always easy to discover what suits them. They need a peaty, leafy, well-drained soil and full sun, except for *D. blagayana*, an early-flowering creamy-white daphne which prefers half shade. *D. cneorum eximea* is an improved form of *D. cneorum*, with large deep-pink flowers. The plant should be top-dressed yearly with gritty soil.

Other good May-June-flowering rock-garden daphnes are *D. arbuscula* from Hungary, which is easily grown and has deep rose flowers and shiny deep-green leaves; and *D. petraea*, the smallest, very slow-growing, and rather more difficult, but perhaps the most beautiful. It grows in rock crevices in limestone cliffs above L. Garda in Italy and has intensely fragrant waxy rose-pink flowers. *D. retusa* is a larger upright species, the easiest of all to grow, and bearing clusters of purplish flowers tinged pink within. *See* also pp. 3, 27, and 59.

1 CYTISUS HIRSUTUS DEMISSUS   2 ALYSSUM SPINOSUM ROSEUM   3 PENSTEMON NEWBERRYI HUMILIOR

4 RHODOTHAMNUS CHAMAECISTUS   5 EURYOPS EVANSII

EARLY LILIES

The bulbous lilies which may be grown out of doors are all natives of the northern hemisphere; species are found in Europe, many parts of Asia including Siberia, Korea, Japan, and China, and the Western and Eastern States of North America. Naturally European lilies were the earliest to be brought into cultivation, and the frequent portrayal of *L. candidum* (the Madonna Lily) in mediaeval religious paintings indicates that it was a common plant even then. It is not known for certain from where this lily first came, but it may be a Balkan lily and an escape from cultivation in other places where it appears wild.

By the end of the 16th century, *L. bulbiferum* with erect wide-open orange-red flowers, the light orange variety *croceum*, the brilliant red-orange *L. chalcedonicum*, and the purplish-pink Turk's Caps Lily *L. martagon* were being grown in English gardens. By the early 17th century *L. pomponium*, a sealing-wax-red, and *L. pyrenaicum*, yellow or greenish-yellow, both of the martagon type, and the lovely American *L. canadense* with nodding, yellow, spotted, bell-shaped flowers were also to be found. Although other American and Asiatic lilies were from time to time introduced, it was the European ones which persisted.

When, in 1862, the magnificent late-flowering *L. auratum* was introduced from Japan, there was a short 'lily rage', but through lack of success, partly due to faulty methods of cultivation, the enthusiasm soon declined, and was not reawakened until the white, yellow-throated *L. regale* from Szechwan in China was discovered and introduced by E. H. Wilson in 1903. Wilson led gardeners to understand that wild lilies live under spartan conditions and that therefore under cultivation they do not need, in fact resent, a highly fertile and moist soil. The easily-grown trumpet *L. regale* proved very successful. Wilson also introduced the white-trumpeted *L. sargentiae* and the orange martagon type *L. davidii*, and these, with the yellow late-flowering *L. henryi* already introduced, from China, re-stimulated lily culture and revived interest in older introductions such as the orange-yellow *L. hansonii*, and the canary-yellow, black-spotted *L. szovitzianum*, as well as some later-flowering species (*see* p. 192).

In the early 20th century, R. Farrer introduced the beautiful fragrant, white, pale-yellow throated, brown-streaked *L. leucanthum centifolium* — not an easy plant to maintain but very important in hybridization. Before this there were already several groups of easily-grown hybrids, such as the Backhouse hybrids, crosses of varieties of *L. martagon* with *L. hansonii*. Also Dutch gardeners had produced *L. x hollandicum*, yellow and orange upright lilies often known as *L. umbellatum;* and in Japan many varieties of *L. x maculatum* (*L. dauricum* x *L. concolor*) were developed. The great interest in lily breeding was stimulated from America by an accidental cross between *L. x imperiale* (*L. leucanthum centifolium* x *L. regale*) and the Bellingham hybrids, combinations of the native July-flowering *L. pardalinum*, *L. parryi*, and *L. humboldtii ocellatum*, which turned difficult species into easy plants, without affecting their decorative value.

Recently many new hybrids and seedling selections suitable for English gardens have come from America, and some also from Australia and New Zealand. In fact, there are only about a dozen species of lilies easy to cultivate, and most of the best lilies for English gardens are hybrids — old or new. The lilies illustrated here show two hybrids and one well-established species.

1 **MID-CENTURY HYBRIDS (L. tigrinum x L. x hollandicum).** This is a selected seedling strain raised by the firm of Jan de Graaff of Oregon, U.S.A. They are very vigorous and should be divided when they become too crowded. They vary in colour from yellow to orange and various shades of orange-red, and grow 3–5 ft. tall.

2 **FIESTA HYBRIDS.** Another de Graaff strain of open martagon shape developed from the crosses made by Dr. Abel of New York, using *L. amabile* and the variety *luteum*, *L. davidii*, and others. They vary from pale straw-yellow, orange, red, and maroon-red, and grow up to 6 ft. tall.

3 **L. HANSONII.** A lily from an island off Korea and introduced as long ago as 1871. It was found growing in thicket and open forest and will grow in Britain in open woodland and among shrubs, in fact it does better not in full sun. It is a parent of numerous hybrids which, like itself, are hardy and easily-grown.

CULTIVATION OF LILIES. Most lilies require full sun and a well-drained loamy soil, best obtained by raising the beds. In hot areas they prefer some shade at the roots, but in most parts of Britain this is not necessary, particularly with American strains. Some dislike lime; some produce feeding roots from the stem and therefore should be planted deeper than those which do not. There are specialist books on lilies which give details about the great number of species and varieties, and also of cultivation, which is not the same for all.

1 MID-CENTURY HYBRID LILY   2 FIESTA HYBRID LILY   3 LILIUM HANSONII

BULBOUS SUMMER FLOWERS

Although, with few exceptions, the spring bulbs are well known, it is not always realised that the alliums, camassias, some iris, brodiaeas, gladioli (*see* p. 117), ornithogalums, and others may carry the display on into the summer.

1 CAMASSIA. These are North American plants which may be white, cream, blue, or purple and vary in height from 1–3 ft. or more. They are best planted close together in a moist soil, even heavy clay, in sun or partial shade. If conditions are right, they will in time make a beautiful mass of colour from self-sown seed. The species illustrated, *C. cusickii*, flowers in June. It has an enormous bulb from which the 3-ft. stems arise. The bulbs of this and *C. quamash* are said to be edible, and to be enjoyed by the Indians. The finest variety is *C. leichtlinii atrocaerulea*, with long spikes of deep purple-blue flowers on 4-ft. stems.

2-3 ALLIUM. These very valuable garden plants are strangely neglected, possibly because most of them have a strong onion or garlic smell, which is particularly strong in *A. siculum* (2). Onions, garlic, leeks, and shallots all belong to this genus, but there are also many beautiful flowering plants and some pernicious weeds, such as the crow garlic (*A. vineale*). *A. siculum* from Sicily and south France is a graceful plant about 3 ft. tall, and somewhat variable in colour. It has the curious habit that the hanging flowers become erect as the seeds form. *A. giganteum* from Central Asia and Iran is 4 ft. or more high and has a round ball of lilac flowers. *A. rosenbachianum*, about 2 ft. tall, has round purplish-violet heads. Even brighter in colour and rather taller is *A. aflatuense*, and *A. sphaerocephalum*, a native of Europe and Turkey, has round, small, tight balls of dark red-purple.

Allium albopilosum (3), a native of Turkestan, is an extraordinary looking plant, with heads about a foot across on 2-ft. stems. These heads can be dried successfully for winter decoration (*see* p. 191). On a smaller scale is the round-headed *A. karataviense* with starry whitish flowers on a 6-in. stem, and very decorative broad glaucous green, red-edged leaves. *A. caeruleum (azureum)* also from Turkestan, has small balls of sky-blue flowers on 12–18 in. stems. As well as the alliums of the Old World there are several good species in North America, such as the rose-purple *A. acuminatum* and the rose *A. unifolium*, which can be raised from seed.

ORNITHOGALUM. Some of these white or yellow relatives of the alliums are greenhouse plants from South Africa; some flower in the early spring; but others are useful plants in May to July. *O. pyramidale* has loose racemes of 20–50 white flowers with a green keel on the back, on stalks 18–24 ins. long. *O. narbonense* is similar. *O. umbellatum* (Star of Bethlehem), a native of Britain, is a tiresome garden weed. The large, drooping flowers of *O. nutans* are so green at the back that the general impression is of soft jade green. It grows 1½ ft. tall and does well in semi-shade. *O. thyrsoides* is more tender, suitable only for a

greenhouse; it has white to golden-yellow flowers, which are long-lasting, and are often sent by sea from South Africa to British flower markets.

4 IRIS, Spanish, Dutch, and English. The Spanish Iris, *I. xiphium*, grows 1–2 ft. tall and is white, yellow, or blue with a yellow-orange patch on the blade. The rather tender North African *I. tingitana* is lilac-purple, and the rather hardier variety *fontanesii* is deep violet-blue with an orange blotch. The English iris, *I. xiphioides*, a native of damp meadows in the Pyrenees, is the latest of the bulbous iris to flower, June-July. Its colours are blues and lavenders with also a white form. Today, the newer race, the Dutch iris, obtained by crossing varieties of the Spanish and North African species, shows signs of superseding the others. They bloom about 2 weeks before the Spanish iris and are of stronger growth. They range in colour from white and cream through yellow and orange to mauve and blue, and are excellent for cutting. All these hardy bulbous iris are easy to grow in any good soil in the sun, though the English ones prefer a dampish soil.

5 BRODIAEA laxa lilacina (Ithuriel's Spear), named after James Brodie, a Scottish naturalist. The brodiaeas all come from western North America and the hardy species have white, pinky-mauve, or pale or dark blue flowers, except for *B. ixioides* which is pale yellow, or the variety *splendens*, bright yellow. The shape of the blossoms varies from the cup shape of *B. lactea* to the tubular shape of *B. laxa* and *B. coronaria*, and the flowers may be in loose or tight heads. They vary in height from the 2-in. *B. minor* to about 1 ft. or over, and they grow much taller in their native habitats. At present those available in Britain mostly come from nurseries in Holland. As well as the one illustrated, good ones to grow are *B. bridgesii*, pink-violet; *B. grandiflora*, deep purple; and the pale blue hybrid *B. x tubergenii*. All need full sun and a light, well-drained soil.

LAPEYROUSIA cruenta. A dwarf bulb with bright scarlet-crimson flowers on 6-in. stems, which flowers freely, and in suitable conditions spreads quickly by seed. It is not entirely hardy in cold areas, but will usually survive, even in the north, in a sheltered position.

SCILLA peruviana. There are several scillas that bloom in May and June, the most striking being *S. peruviana* with a rosette of broad leaves and a huge head, 6 ins. across, of deep violet stars. There is also a white variety. Another good late-flowering species is *S. pratensis* which has a dense head of violet-blue stars which, in the variety *amethystina*, are bigger and brighter.

1 Camassia cusickii   2 Allium siculum   3 Allium albopilosum
4 Iris, dutch 'Yellow Queen'   5 Brodiaea laxa lilacina

71

LILY FAMILY BORDER PLANTS

The lily family contains about 200 genera. Although based on the true lilies, all the members do not possess bulbs, but may have corms, fleshy roots, or rhizomes. Most are herbaceous perennials; a few are annuals; and one or two are woody shrubs. Apart from the true lilies (*see* pp. 69, 192), some of the best-known members of the family are: Erythronium (Dog's Tooth Violet) (p. 7); Chionodoxa, Hyacinthus, Puschkinia, and Scilla (Squill) (p. 9); Tulipa (pp. 29, 31); Fritillaria (p. 31); Convallaria (Lily of the Valley) and Polygonatum (Solomon's Seal) (p. 51); Camassia (p. 71); Kniphofia (Red-hot Poker) (p. 173); Agapanthus (p. 175); and Colchicum (p. 183); together with the plants shown on this page. Members of the family may be found in almost all parts of the world, but the main garden plants come from the northern hemisphere, including some native to Britain.

1-2 HOSTA. The hostas, funkias, or plantain lilies are natives of China and Japan and have been cultivated in Japan for many years. As a result, the true origin of many garden varieties is not known. They are grown more for their handsome foliage than for their flowers which are not particularly effective. They will grow in almost any position, but if in full sun they need water in dry periods. For foliage effect they are best grown in half shade in the spaces between shrubs, and they are excellent ground cover to keep down weeds.

H. sieboldiana elegans (*H. glauca*) (1) is the best of those with blue-green leaves, and is often confused with forms of *H. fortunei* which has distinctly less blue leaves. *H. fortunei albo-picta* has bright yellow young spring leaves with an edging of pale green. In the course of a month or two the yellow has changed to green and the effect is less striking. *H. undulata* (2) is one of the smaller leaved and variegated forms which make attractive plants in half shade. Another good small variety is *H. albo-marginata* in which the green leaves have a white border. A larger plant with waved leaves edged with a broad band of white is *H. crispula*. A good late-flowering hosta is *H. plantaginea*, with particularly elegant, bright, shining leaves and pure white, sweet-scented flowers in September or October. Because of its late flowering it should be planted in a sheltered position. Also for a sheltered position is the late-flowering miniature *H. tardiflora*, with lilac flowers, which will grow larger in a very wet spot than a dry one, but will grow well in either.

3 ASPHODELINE lutea (Asphodelus luteus) King's Spear. A native of the Mediterranean regions and therefore will do well in a very hot dry position. This and its fragrance are its claims to a position in the garden for it does not produce much effect, so few flowers being open at one time. It grows 3–4 ft. tall.

4-5 HEMEROCALLIS (*hemera*=day, *kallos*=beauty). The name Day Lily is given because the flowers last only for a day, but a succession is produced over a long period, often into the autumn. *H. flava*, lemon-yellow and scented, and *H. fulva*, orange-red, have been cultivated in British gardens since the 16th century, and the latter has become naturalized in the eastern states of the U.S.A., where masses can be seen by the road-side in July. As it sets no seed, how it became so widely distributed is rather mysterious. The pure orange *H. aurantiaca*, *H. dumortieri*, and *H. middendorfiana* were later introductions, and later still were several others from China and Japan, tall and dwarf, in various shades of yellow. In more recent years improved varieties, such as those illustrated, have begun to appear in nurseries, especially after the introduction of the pink *H. fulva rosea* had added to the limited colour range. Today there is a remarkable range of colours from pale yellow, orange, salmon, pink, red, to maroon, some being self coloured, others having contrasting stripes down each petal, and others a contrasting throat. Because of their long flowering and ease of cultivation they have become increasingly popular, particularly in the U.S.A. where there is a society devoted to these plants only and many outstanding varieties have been raised there. They are excellent for naturalizing in rough grass, and withstand heat and drought well.

EREMURUS (*eremos*=solitary, *oura*=tail). These stately plants from Central Asia have long spikes of star-shaped flowers on stems 4–10 ft. high. The roots are fleshy and like a huge star-fish and must be handled very carefully. Full sun, perfect drainage, and preferably a limy soil are what they want, with plenty of room for the large leaves. *E. bungei* is a yellow plant, 4 ft. or less tall; *himalaicus* is 6 ft. tall with white flowers; and *E. robustus* is flesh coloured and 8–9 ft. tall. In general, it is probably best to grow the 'Shelford hybrids' in shades of pink, coppery-yellow, orange, and so on, and of moderate size. These were raised in the village of Shelford near Cambridge.

1 Hosta sieboldiana   2 Hosta undulata   3 Asphodeline lutea
4 Hemerocallis 'Tejas'   5 Hemerocallis 'Pink Lady'

BOG AND WATERSIDE PLANTS

Though all the moisture-loving plants do best in a really damp position, some of them, such as the astilbes, can be grown in an ordinary bed if the soil is rich and deep, there is light shade, and they are watered in dry weather. They should never be attempted in sunny positions in poor dry soil.

1 ASTILBE X arendsii 'Red Sentinel', *a*=without, *stilbe*=brilliance. These members of the Saxifrage family vary from the dwarf *A. chinensis pumila, A. crispa*, and *A. simplicifolia*, only about 6 ins. tall and suitable for the rock garden, to the 4-ft. or more *A. davidii* and *A. palmata* with lilac or pink flowers. The hybrid astilbes, first developed by Herr Arends of Ronsdorf, and the *A. x rosea* hybrids are in general the best garden varieties. They range from white and cream to pinks, crimsons, and garnet reds. The rust red of 'Red Sentinel' is a distinct colour break. It grows about 2½ ft. tall. Some astilbes, particularly the variety 'Fanal', have attractive dark foliage. 'Etna' (crimson), 'Gertrude Brix' (rose-red), and 'Gloria' (shaded pink) are all about 1½ ft., and of the taller varieties 'Prof. Van der Weilan' is white and 'Salland' rose-red.

2 PRIMULA florindae. A late-flowering primula with a strong scent. It has handsome rounded dark green leaves with reddish stems. It is a robust plant growing 2–3 ft. tall in a moist position, and will even succeed in shallow water. In July and August this giant cowslip with its hanging bells scents the air over a wide area. There is a range of coloured forms of *Florindae* hybrids, including many shades from tawny orange to apricot.

3 IRIS siberica 'Caesar'. With their graceful narrow foliage and delicate flowers on stiff stems, the Siberian irises are useful border or waterside plants. Although they like damp conditions, they will tolerate almost any position in the garden. They flower in June and July, grow 2–3 ft. tall, and are excellent flowers for cutting. The variety 'Caesar', grows up to 3 ft.; 'Emperor' is dark blue with rust-red winter foliage; 'Papillon' is blue, feathered white; Perry's Blue' is sky-blue; and 'Snow Queen' is creamy white. Two other irises of the same type, which also prefer moist or even wet conditions, both from Japan, are *I. kaempferi*, which has many colour varieties and large flowers, and the closely related clear blue *I. laevigata*. There is a charming but rather expensive variety of *I. laevigata*, 'Rose Queen', which is pink.

4 RODGERSIA pinnata superba. This, like astilbe, is a member of the Saxifrage family. It was named after Commodore Rodgers of the US Navy, who commanded the expedition on which the pale buff-yellow species *R. podophylla* was discovered. Rodgersias have fluffy heads of flowers and large, handsome, glossy leaves, heavily veined and crinkled, and in some species bronze in colour. They will grow in sun or shade and do best in a deep peaty soil, but they need shelter from wind. They are easily increased by cutting up the woody root stock. As well as the species illustrated and the buff-yellow *R. podophylla*, which grow 3–4 ft. tall, there are white species — the 4-ft. tall *R. aesculifolia*, and the shorter *R. sambucifolia*, 2–3 ft. tall.

5 MIMULUS (Monkey Flower), *mimus*=mimic. Its names have arisen because its flowers resemble a mask or a monkey's face. Mimulus produces a succession of brilliant flowers over a long period; but some need a rich, moist soil to succeed, and some are not completely hardy in all districts and need some protection through the winter. Most species grow about 12–18 ins. tall.

The variety *M. cupreus* 'Monarch Strain' has large flowers in various brilliant colours, all beautifully spotted and blotched. The hardy *M. cardinalis* has scarlet flowers and is rather tall; *M. luteus* is bright yellow and also hardy; and *M. luteus* 'A. T. Johnson's variety' is yellow spotted with mahogany and is dwarf. Other dwarf varieties suitable for the rock garden are 'Cerise Queen', deep pink; 'Nasturtium', scarlet; and the yellow miniature *primuloides*.

Mimulus can be grown very satisfactorily from seed as a half-hardy annual, and one of the hybrid forms such as 'Giant Hybrid' or 'Queen's Prize', sown in March under glass, produce flowers in June or July.

CALTHA palustris plena (Marsh Marigold). A double garden form of the native 'Kingcup', with large golden-yellow flowers. It must have a rich moist soil and does best growing on the margin of water. It flowers in May, rather earlier than most of the plants on this page.

1 ASTILBE X ARENDSII 'RED SENTINEL'   2 PRIMULA FLORINDAE   3 IRIS SIBERICA 'CAESAR'
4 RODGERSIA PINNATA SUPERBA   5 MIMULUS CUPREUS 'MONARCH STRAIN'

BORDER PEAFLOWERS

Lupins and the other peaflowers closely related to them mostly come from Western North America, though *Lupinus luteus*, a fragrant yellow lupin about 2 ft. tall, is a native of Mediterranean regions. They are hardy plants and will grow in any moderate soil, preferably sandy, though some dislike lime and too much winter wet. The name Lupinus is said to come from the Latin *lupus*='wolf' because lupins were thought to destroy the fertility of the soil. As a matter of fact lupins, like other leguminous plants, are valuable nitrogen fertilizers, and farmers grow crops of *L. luteus* to plough into sandy soil as a green manure.

1-2 LUPINUS arboreus (Tree Lupin). These grow to about 5 ft. and make big bushes after a year or two. They do particularly well by the sea, and most of them are sweetly scented. They can be used in shrub beds or in mixed borders, and with their informal manner of growth can even be used to clothe rough banks. *L. arboreus* is bright yellow but varies to blue or lilac. As well as the rosy-mauve 'Mauve Queen', there is a deep yellow variety 'Golden Spire' and a pure white one 'Snow Queen'.

3 RUSSELL LUPINS. The herbaceous perennial lupins have been improved out of all knowledge in recent years by cross breeding and selection, mainly from *L. arboreus* and *L. polyphyllus*. There is now a wide range of colours, especially in the strain raised by George Russell. They will grow in sun or shade in any well-drained soil, and do not need manure or lime. In heavy clay soils they are best treated as biennials. In light soils they should be planted in October or November, and in February or March in heavy soils. As they make plants 3 ft. in diameter they need plenty of space. If the seedpods are removed after flowering, they will often produce a second crop of flowers, but the plants should not be cut to the ground until the autumn.

VARIETIES: Russell Lupin 'Royal Parade', violet and white; 'Bonington Lass', pink and white; 'Canary Bird', yellow; 'City of York', red and crimson; 'Fireglow', salmon orange; 'George Russell', pink with white eye; 'Heather Glow', wine purple; 'Venus', salmon and crimson.

There are also hardy annual lupins which, if sown in April or May in the place where they are to flower, give a good display in the late summer. *L. hartwegii*, blue and white, and *L. tricolor*, white turning pink, are 1½–2 ft. tall; *L. sub-carnosus* is a dwarf rich blue species; and *L. mutabilis* is much taller and is white and blue with pink and yellow markings.

4 BAPTISIA australis. This native of North America makes good clumps 3–5 ft. high in a sunny position, the brilliant blue flowers showing up against the glaucous leaves. There is also a white form, not often seen.

THERMOPSIS montana. A bright yellow lupin-like plant with bluish foliage and long slender spikes of flowers about 3 ft. high. Though it will grow in shade, it flowers best in sun. It has tough roots, which resent disturbance, so is best increased from seed.

GALEGA (Goat's Rue), *gala*=milk, for it was thought that the plant encouraged the production of milk in herds. These plants from South Europe and Asia Minor make large informal clumps about 4 ft. tall, and the blue and white flowers last for many weeks. They will grow in almost any soil, but do much better in a rich deep soil in the sun.

1 LUPINUS ARBOREUS 'MAUVE QUEEN'   2 LUPINUS ARBOREUS
3 RUSSELL LUPIN 'ROYAL PARADE'   4 BAPTISIA AUSTRALIS

PINKS AND CARNATIONS (DIANTHUS)

The word 'dianthus' comes from *dios*='divine' and *anthos*='flower'. It is a very large group of both annual and perennial flowers, many of which are natives of Europe and one or two of Britain. It includes the Pinks, Carnations, and Sweet Williams, as well as many dwarf dianthus suitable for rock gardens.

Pinks and carnations are some of the oldest flowers to be cultivated. They were known in Britain by the 14th century, for Chaucer mentions them. The garden pinks were derived from the single South-east European *D. plumarius*, and carnations from the larger red *D. caryophyllus*. By the 16th century double pinks were being mentioned, and in Elizabeth I's reign there were various colour combinations. 'Flake' pinks with two distinct colours and 'Bizarre' pinks with more than two were very popular — as they still are today. In the 18th century the Lancashire weavers and later the Paisley weavers near Glasgow took up their culture seriously and produced a strain of laced pinks which had something of the same oriental charm as their Paisley shawls and fancy muslins.

In the early 19th century the florist Thomas Hogg was famous for his pinks and carnations, and as a result of crossing carnations and pinks many 'border pinks' appeared. Mrs. Sinkins of Slough had already raised the very well-known and popular double-white fragrant pink named after her. At the end of the century a deep rose-pink carnation, Mrs. T. W. Lawson, was produced in Massachusetts, U.S.A., and this has been used a good deal in developing the perpetual-flowering carnations for the garden or market.

The garden pinks and carnations are easy to grow in fairly light, well-drained limy soil. Sticky clay soils need to be lightened with humus and sharp sand; sour soils need a dressing of chalk. The plants are better renewed every 2 or 3 years either by cuttings taken in June or by plants raised from seed — though the latter may not come true. Carnations can be propagated by layering the side shoots in July, after flowering.

1 BORDER CARNATION 'Edenside Fairy'. There are 'self' types, one colour only; 'fancy', two or more colours; and 'picotee', light ground colour with darker edging. There is a wide range of colours in each type, and the stronger varieties do well in clumps in the flower border. In heavy soils they do best in a special raised bed.

2-6 GARDEN PINKS. A race of perpetual-flowering pinks have been raised by Allwood of Wivelsfield, resulting from crossing the old fringed white pink with the perpetual-flowering carnation. There are many varieties, both single and double. In the main *D. x allwoodii* and other garden pinks make tufts of glaucous bluish-green foliage. They are usually very easy to propagate by pulling clumps to pieces and planting the pieces, which soon root.

7-8 DWARF PINKS 'Vanity' and 'Damask Superb'. These are good varieties for growing to hang over on a dry wall or from a rock crevice. *See also* p. 90.

9- LACED PINKS 'Dad's Favourite' and 'Belle of
10 Ware'. These are some of the oldest types of pink. The white or pink ground is 'laced' with markings in ruby-red, crimson, purple, or nearly black. They can be grown effectively on a bank.

11- ALPINE PINKS. *D. alpinus* has large flowers on
12 3-ins stems and dark glistening foliage. *D. caesius plenus* is a double form of the Cheddar pink, still sometimes to be found on the cliffs of the Cheddar gorge. *D. allwoodii alpinus* is a race developed by crossing *D. x allwoodii* with these alpine species. There is a wide range of colours of dwarf plants, 4–6 ins. high, sweetly scented and with silvery foliage.

DIANTHUS barbatus (Sweet William). A long-grown British garden flower. The wild plant has light or dark red flowers, often striped and with white spots. There are good mixed garden strains or strains of separate colours such as 'Pink Beauty' or 'Scarlet Beauty'. Though perennials, they are best grown as biennials (*see* p. 32). The race of hybrids developed by crossing *D. barbatus* with *D. x allwoodii*, is called 'Sweet Wivelsfield', a plant best grown as a half-hardy annual, and with a long flowering season (*see also* p. 127). For annual pinks, *D. chinensis*, see p. 141.

1 BORDER CARNATION 'EDENSIDE FAIRY' 2 GARDEN PINK 'ALLWOODII THOMAS'
3 GARDEN PINK 'C. T. MUSGRAVE' 4 GARDEN PINK 'MARGARET CURTIS'
5 DIANTHUS SUNDERMANNII 6 DWARF PINK 'BRYMPTON RED'
7 DWARF PINK 'VANITY' 8 DWARF PINK 'DAMASK SUPERB'
9 LACED PINK 'DAD'S FAVOURITE' 10 LACED PINK 'BELLE OF WARE'
11 DIANTHUS ALPINUS 12 DIANTHUS CAESIUS PLENUS

SUN-LOVING PLANTS FOR ROCK GARDEN OR BORDER

All the plants on this page are plants of the sun. Armeria *caespitosa*, Campanula *raineri*, Delphinium *nudicaule*, and the Globularias are suitable for the rock garden only; the others may be grown either in the rock garden or the front of a sunny border.

1 PRUNELLA **grandiflora 'Loveliness' (Self-heal)**. A useful later-flowering plant easy to grow in any soil. It produces the best effect if planted in large groups in the sun. It is wise to divide the plants in the spring every two years as the younger plants produce finer flowers. The varieties of *grandiflora*, *alba* and *rosea*, are also popular.

2 ARMERIA **maritima 'Bloodstone' (Thrift)**. Thrifts or Sea Pinks are very well known, very amenable plants which will thrive in almost any position. Many good garden varieties from white to crimson have been developed from the native *A. maritima*. *A. corsica* has unusual brick-red flowers on rather longer stems. *A. caespitosa* from Spain has almost stemless large pink flowers on light green cushions of foliage. The variety 'Six Hills' has particularly large flowers, and is well worth growing.

3 DELPHINIUM **chinensis 'Blue Butterfly' (Larkspur)**. The taller perennial delphiniums are shown on p. 85, and the annual larkspurs on p. 87. As well, there are dwarf perennial species which are excellent rock garden plants and easy to grow, but must be protected from slugs in the spring. 'Blue Butterfly' or the paler 'Azure Fairy' grow about 12 ins. tall, carrying their flowers above the foliage. *D. tatsienense* has deep blue flowers and can be grown easily from seed or from cuttings taken from well-established plants. *D. nudicaule* from California has scarlet flowers and can be grown only from seed.

4 VERBENA **peruviana (chamaedrifolia)**. A lovely creeping plant from South America which continues to give a wealth of dazzling flowers from early summer onwards; but it is not entirely hardy and needs a warm situation with very good drainage. It is best propagated from cuttings taken in late summer, and it is safer to overwinter these in a cold frame. For annual verbenas, *see* p. 141.

5 VERONICA **spicata 'Heidekind'**. Most varieties of *V. spicata* are more suited to the herbaceous border (*see* p. 108), but this new variety is dwarfer and makes a sturdy plant useful for either rock garden or border. Any ordinary garden soil and open position suits it, and it is easily increased from cuttings taken in late autumn. For other dwarf veronicas, *see* p. 41.

6 CAMPANULA **raineri**. This is a beautiful plant but is difficult to grow. It needs a position wedged between stones in full sun, and it must be protected from slugs. It can be propagated by seed or by division. Nearly as lovely and easier to cultivate are the forms of *C. carpatica* or of *C. turbinata*. For taller herbaceous campanulas, *see* pp. 111 and 157.

JASIONE (**Sheep's-bit**). A member of the Campanula family though it looks more like a small scabious (*see* p. 89). *J. montana* is a British wild plant of dry banks and heaths. *J. jankae* and *J. perennis* have bright blue pincushion flowers, about 10–12 ins. tall, on erect stems. They are easy to cultivate.

7 TANACETUM **densum amami**. This recent introduction from Turkey provides one of the best silver-foliaged carpeting plants for the rock garden or border and needs a dry position in full sun. It has somewhat inconspicuous flowers and is grown for its silvery foliage. It is easy to propagate from cuttings taken any time from spring to autumn. There is some confusion over its name, and it is often listed as *Chrysanthemum haradjani* or under other names.

GLOBULARIA **bellidifolia**. Globularias are natives of the Mediterranean region. This species bears small blue powder-puff flowers on 2-in. stems from tufted foliage. The sub-shrubby *G. cordifolia* has white and pink as well as blue forms, and several are suitable for the miniature garden. Globularias like a sunny dry place in a light limy soil.

1 PRUNELLA GRANDIFLORA 'LOVELINESS'   2 ARMERIA MARITIMA 'BLOODSTONE'
3 DELPHINIUM CHINENSIS 'BLUE BUTTERFLY'   4 VERBENA PERUVIANA
5 VERONICA SPICATA   6 CAMPANULA RAINERI
               7 TANACETUM DENSUM AMAMI

ANNUAL POPPIES

Many members of the Poppy family are short-lived perennials, but most are better treated as annuals or some of them as biennials. They can be grown easily from seed and do well in any well-drained soil in an open sunny position. Many poppies, such as the Shirley and Iceland poppies, make good cut flowers and will last for several days if cut when just opening, and the stems dipped into boiling water or charred in an open flame to coagulate the sticky juice and enable them to draw up water.

1 E S C H S C H O L Z I A **californica (Californian Poppy).** These are natives of dry sunny places in California. They have glaucous foliage and stout fleshy tap roots. From the original bright yellow have arisen orange, bronze and orange, crimson, and pink varieties and a semi-double orange form. Two recent varieties are 'Aurora', a creamy-pink, and 'Fireglow', a brilliant orange, both with large, beautifully-shaped flowers. Although they may survive from year to year, eschscholzias are best grown as hardy annuals sown in March or April, and do particularly well on a dry sunny bank.

There is a dwarf species, *E. caespitosa*, with more finely cut foliage and tiny yellow or primrose flowers, 6–8 ins. tall, very suitable for pockets in a rock garden. *E. maritima* has a low spreading habit, bright blue-grey foliage, and yellow flowers with an orange base.

2 A R G E M O N E **mexicana (Prickly Mexican Poppy).** A hardy annual with lemon-yellow or white flowers and prickly foliage; it grows about 2 ft. tall. *A. grandiflora* has large glistening white flowers and bluish foliage without spines. Argemone needs a hot, sunny situation.

G L A U C I U M **flavum (Horned Poppy).** A very handsome poppy which grows wild on sea coasts in Britain and is suitable for a semi-wild garden. It grows 2–3 ft. tall and has attractive glaucous grey-green foliage and yellow or sometimes orange-red flowers. It will thrive on poor sandy soil but also responds to better soil. It is best treated as a biennial, the seed being sown in June.

3 P A P A V E R **rhoeas (Shirley Poppy).** About 1880, the Rev. W. Wilks, Secretary to the Royal Horticultural Society, noticed in a cornfield near his house a scarlet poppy plant with a white edge to the petals and a white instead of black base. From this poppy Wilks gradually evolved many of the present colours — white, shades of pink and salmon, slatey blue, and many with picotee edging, as well as doubles. Shirley poppies are hardy annuals or can be sown in September to flower in May. They do not transplant easily, so are best sown where they will flower.

P A P A V E R **somniferum (Opium Poppy).** Native of Greece and the East, the cultivated opium poppies make rather stout showy plants, 2 ft. or more high, with smooth blue-green glaucous foliage, and large fully-double flowers in white, lilac, salmon-pink, scarlet, and purple. They are best treated as annuals.

P A P A V E R **nudicaule (Iceland Poppy).** A poppy from northern sub-arctic regions, best grown as a hardy biennial, sown in June-July to flower from May onwards the next year. It can also be sown under glass in the spring to flower the same year. Iceland poppies form tufted plants with light green foliage, from which arise many dainty flowers on 12–18-in. stems, in a wide range of colours, some with attractive picotee edging.

P A P A V E R **alpinum (Alpine Poppy).** A tiny poppy, 6–8 ins. high, with masses of flowers in pale pastel shades. It is a hardy annual or short-lived perennial suitable for a sunny dry place in the rock garden.

4 H U N N E M A N N I A **fumariifolia (Mexican Tulip Poppy).** It is rather like eschscholzia in growth and foliage, and the cup-shaped yellow flowers have long stems. If grown as a hardy annual, it flowers in late summer, from July to September; or it can be grown as a biennial, sown in a cold frame in August and planted out in the spring.

5 P A P A V E R **glaucum (Tulip Poppy).** A hardy annual poppy from Asia Minor, with glaucous green foliage and large flowers on long stems. A characteristic is the attractive pointed blue-green buds.

1 Eschscholzia californica 2 Argemone mexicana 3 Papaver rhoeas
4 Hunnemannia fumariifolia 5 Papaver glaucum

ANCHUSAS AND DELPHINIUMS

These are among the most important herbaceous border plants for June and July. They are easy to grow but need a fair amount of attention. Though perennials, they deteriorate in course of time and should be divided every few years or replaced with new plants grown from seed. They do best in a sunny border, and delphiniums particularly need deep rich soil with plenty of humus and manure. As both anchusas and delphiniums carry tall heavy trusses of flowers, they must be carefully staked. With tall varieties, especially if grown in exposed situations, it is better to stake each spike with a separate bamboo.

1 ANCHUSAS. These members of the forget-me-not family are closely related to the Common Borage and *Brunnera macrophylla* (*see* p. 17). Anchusa can be used in salads and, like borage, sprays are put into claret or other 'cups'. The garden anchusas are mainly derived from the tall-growing *A. azurea*, with varieties ranging from pale blue to deep purple-blue and from 2–4 ft. or more in height. They are easy to grow in any good soil, but not so long-lived in heavy wet soils. *A. capensis* is an annual species from South Africa. The variety 'Blue Bird' makes a compact, free-flowering plant, 15–18 ins. high. The perennial varieties of *A. azurea* can also be grown successfully as biennials, the seed being sown in April and the plants put into flowering position in the autumn.

VARIETIES: 'Loddon Royalist', 2 ft.; 'Royal Blue', 2½ ft. with a bushy habit; 'Morning Glory', deep gentian-blue with white centre; and 'Opal', pale sky-blue with dark foliage — both 4 ft. tall.

2-4 DELPHINIUMS (*delphis*=dolphin, because the flower spur is said to resemble a dolphin's head). Delphiniums have been so much developed in recent years that there are now a great many varieties, single and double, in white and shades of mauve, pink, blue, and purple. The sky-blues and gentian-blues are particularly satisfactory. There are several very good strains of tall large-flowered delphiniums, such as the Pacific Giants from America, best grown as annuals, and the Blackmore and Langdon's Exhibition strain (3).

The tall border delphiniums are mainly hybrids of *D. elatum*. The belladonna delphiniums are shorter with more bushy growth and branching habit, and consequently, more suited to small gardens and exposed borders. *D. belladonna semiplena* (2) is an example of the semi-double type and grows some 3 ft. tall. 'Pink

Sensation' (4) is a belladonna type raised by crossing the tall *D. elatum* with the dwarf *D. nudicaule* (*D. x ruysii*). It starts flowering in June and, if fed well and the dead heads removed, will usually flower freely again in September.

The best time for planting or dividing delphiniums is in the spring, though plants can be divided in the summer after the first flowering. As they start growing early in the spring, they should have been planted by the third week in March, in ground which has been well dug and manured. The young growth usually needs protecting from slugs. Unless the soil is very deep and rich, delphiniums need to be watered in dry summers. In a drought their leaves may suffer from mildew, and this can be checked by a dusting of green sulphur when the dew is on the leaves, or a spraying with lime-sulphur.

If the central spike is cut off as soon as it has finished flowering, the side shoots will flower. Then, later, if the plant is cut down to the ground, fed with manure or manure water, and in dry weather mulched with well-rotted manure, there will be a fresh growth which will produce late-summer flowers.

Perennial delphiniums can be treated as biennials, or even as annuals sown in gentle heat in February to flower in August and September. There are also several annual species (Larkspurs) which are described on p. 87.

VARIETIES: There are good mixed strains, such as those mentioned. The following give a range of colours, though there are many others just as good: *D. hybridum* 'Sutton's White', single; 'Lady Eleanor', double, pale blue and lilac; 'C. F. Langdon', semi-double, pure blue with black eye; 'Nell Gwynne', semi-double, mauve; 'Purple Prince', semi-double, violet-purple, with white eye — all 4–5 ft. *Belladonna Type:* 'Blue Bees', single, pale blue with white eye; 'Isis', single, mauve; 'Naples', single, gentian-blue with deep blue eye; 'Lamartine', single, dark blue — all 3 ft.

1 ANCHUSA 'LODDON ROYALIST'   2 DELPHINIUM BELLADONNA SEMIPLENA
3 DELPHINIUM 'SWAN LAKE'   4 DELPHINIUM 'PINK SENSATION'

CORNFIELD ANNUALS

These are all hardy plants which in their native habitat sow themselves in waste land or among cereal crops. They need sunny open situations, and most of them are not fastidious as to soil so long as it is well-drained.

1 DELPHINIUM ajacis (Larkspur). The garden larkspur comes from two species, both wild in Southern Europe: *D. ajacis*, with blue, pink, or white flowers and growing about 18 ins. tall, and *D. consolida*, which is rather taller with mainly blue flowers. The variety illustrated, 'Waldenbury Blue', is the most like the wild *D. ajacis*. It first appeared in the garden of Waldenbury, Hertfordshire, and was preserved because of its excellent colour.

Garden larkspurs of the *D. ajacis* group, called Rocket or Hyacinth-flowered larkspurs, produce single spikes of double flowers about 3 ft. tall in mixed colours. There is a dwarf variety about 1 ft. tall. Larkspurs of the *D. consolida* group, called Stock-flowered or Imperial larkspurs, are the more commonly grown. They form tall, branching plants, 3–5 ft. high, usually in mixed colours, though separate colours are available.

If sown in August or September in the place where they are to flower, larkspurs survive most winters and are in flower by the end of June. If sown in March or April, they flower in mid-July.

For perennial delphiniums, *see* pp. 85 and 81.

2 AGROSTEMMA githago 'Milas' (Corncockle). This form of the British wild corncockle was found near the town of Milas in Turkey. It grows 2–3 ft. tall, with flowers 2–3 ins. across. In spite of its slender appearance it stands up well to wind and wet, and is a useful flower for cutting. It is best to sow agrostemma where it is to flower, either in the autumn or the spring.

3 CENTAUREA cyanus (Cornflower). A well-known British cornfield weed which, since it has been introduced into gardens, has been improved from selected natural variations and sports until it has become a very different plant. The flowers are larger, the plant taller and more robust, and the colour range now includes not only the original bright blue but also white, pink, maroon, and purple. In most parts of the country seed sown in August to October, and thinned to 12 ins. apart in the spring, will produce bushy plants 3–4 ft. high and covered with flower in June and July. They can also be sown in spring as soon as the weather allows. Cornflowers often need to be sprayed to kill aphis.

4 CENTAUREA moschata (Sweet Sultan). A close relative of cornflowers from the Eastern Mediterranean, long-known in English gardens. The strain known as Imperialis or Giant Hybrids produces branching plants, 3 ft. or more tall, with large heads on long stems in colours ranging from white, pink, and mauve to purple and also yellow (though smaller flowers). Sweet Sultan is usually best sown in April and will flower all summer, though in favourable situations in warmer districts seed sown in September will make stronger plants flowering earlier.

For perennial centaureas, *see* p. 115.

5 CHRYSANTHEMUM carinatum (Annual Chrysanthemum). This native of Morocco was introduced to English gardens about 150 years ago and was often called *C. tricolor* because of the white petals with yellow base and dark chocolate centres. There are now several varieties. The variety 'Burridgeanum' was the first to show crimson colouring, and an even deeper coloured form 'Atrococcineum' is now available, as well as double forms. A cross between *C. carinatum* and the South European Crown Daisy (*C. coronarium*) has produced *C. x spectabilis*, tall vigorous, branched plants bearing throughout the summer many white, yellow, and primrose flowers, both double and single. Although the first cross was made in the early 1920's, seeds only became generally available in 1956.

CHRYSANTHEM segetum (Corn Marigold). A garden daisy developed from the well-known cornfield weed. Varieties such as 'Morning Star' and 'Evening Star' are in shades of yellow and ivory-white, and 'Eastern Star' has primrose flowers with chocolate-coloured centres. Corn Marigolds grow about 18 ins. tall.

6 SCABIOSA atropurpurea (Sweet Scabious). The original dull purplish-crimson Scabious, a native of Southern Europe, has been grown in English gardens for some 300 years. It was often used in funeral wreaths and so was called Mournful Widow. In the last 20 or 30 years, however, by careful selection, scabious with larger flowers, longer and stronger stems, and a wide range of colours have appeared. A well-grown plant may be 3–4 ft. tall and bear fifty or more flowers. There is also a dwarf strain of bushy plants 12–15 ins. tall.

Sweet Scabious may be sown out-of-doors about April or in a cold frame in the autumn. The autumn-sown plants make the strongest plants but they must have winter protection. They do best in a well-worked soil with some lime.

For perennial Scabious, *see* p. 155, and for dwarf rock garden species, *see* p. 89.

1 DELPHINIUM AJACIS   2 AGROSTEMMA GITHAGO   3 CENTAUREA CYANUS

4 CENTAUREA MOSCHATA   5 CHRYSANTHEMUM CARINATUM   6 SCABIOSA ATROPURPUREA

CARPETING ROCK PLANTS

Compact perennial plants forming carpets of attractive foliage are most useful in the rock garden. Thymes, for example, make delightful aromatic pathways and alpine lawns. The lines of paving stones can be broken by occasional carpeters, which can also be used to cover the ground beneath small shrubs and in difficult corners, and so save weeding. Another place where creepers are useful is in the inevitable blank space after bulbs have finished flowering.

Most carpeters are sunlovers and appreciate a good well-drained soil, though some will tolerate or even prefer some shade. Between paving stones the soil is often poor and shallow, so it is necessary to add a pocket of good earth if the plants are to flourish. They spread for the most part by rooting stems, and can easily be propagated by dividing the plants in autumn or early spring.

1 FRANKENIA laevis (Sea Heath). The soft, evergreen, heather-like foliage is grey-green in summer and touched with orange in autumn. The plant spreads by rooting stems. It prefers sandy soil and a sunny position, flowers in July-August, and is about 2 ins. tall.

F. thymifolia, which is not seen in gardens as much as it should be, has larger rose-pink flowers, borne more freely, and starts flowering rather earlier.

2 THYMUS serpyllum. This is a mat-forming kind of Thyme, which spreads very quickly by rooting stems. There are many varieties which hybridize very easily, and the colours range from white to pink ('Pink Chintz'), mauve, and crimson (*coccineus*).

T. lanuginosus, closely related to *T. serpyllum*, is a grey, woolly-leaved plant with lilac-pink flowers which clings closely to the ground. *T. herba-barona* is a highly aromatic, caraway-scented, early-flowering thyme from Corsica where it grows wild. It has fine leaves and lilac-pink flowers, and grows a little taller than *T. serpyllum. See* also p. 104.

3 ACAENA microphylla (New Zealand Burr). *Akaina* means 'thorn', for most species have hooked calyces or fruit. It is a useful neat carpeting plant about an inch high, and will grow in shady places and even poor soil. The spines or burrs on the fruit become red as the seeds ripen and last for many weeks.

A. novae-zealandiae is a larger, more spiny variety, which makes a quick-spreading ground cover on poor soil. But it will quickly smother other rock plants if allowed to.

4 NIEREMBERGIA repens (rivularis). This is the most hardy species, a native of South America. It is a delightful carpeter, creeping and rooting in all directions on a well-drained soil, and growing about 3 ins. tall. It prefers some shade and moisture.

N. caerulea is a slightly tender plant from the Argentine, with branched stems carrying many deep violet flowers. It is attractive to grow in protected places but is not a carpeter, its much branched stems being 6–10 ins. tall.

5 MAZUS reptans. This plant from the Himalayas needs more moisture and is not so easy to grow as the Thymes. It will do well, however, in protected semi-shady positions in the rockery. Its slender leafy stems are 1–2 ins. high.

6 SCABIOSA pterocephala (Pterocephalus parnassi). A tuft-forming rather than a true carpeting plant, which forms mounds of attractive grey foliage. It comes from Greece, and grows well on sunny dry walls, flowering in June with flower stems 2–6 ins. tall.

7 MENTHA requienii. This relative of the culinary Mint is minute — a mere film of bright green foliage smelling strongly of peppermint when bruised. It comes from Corsica and is not completely hardy in this country.

ANTENNARIA dioica 'Nyewood'. A silvery-leaved carpeter, with fuzzy deep pink daisy-like flowers which appear in June or earlier. It likes a light, well-drained soil and will make a silver-grey mat in the poorish spots in the rock garden.

COTULA squalida. Another mat-forming plant with dark, fern-like leaves on slender, branched, hairy stems, and yellow daisy-like flowers. It makes a good carpet over bulbs and grows vigorously, in fact, sometimes spreads too much. It comes from New Zealand. *See* also p. 140 for the annual cotula.

1 FRANKENIA LAEVIS   2 THYMUS SERPYLLUM (*a*) COCCINEUS
3 ACAENA MICROPHYLLA   (*b*) 'PINK CHINTZ'
4 NIEREMBERGIA REPENS   5 MAZUS REPTANS
6 SCABIOSA PTEROCEPHALA   7 MENTHA REQUIENII

DRY WALL-TOP PLANTS

Plants for this position are those which do not need a great deal of moisture from the soil — in fact, as a rule dislike damp. Sedums and sempervivums are ideal plants for dry walls because they store moisture in their fleshy foliage and so can endure long dry periods. Others, such as the helichrysums, form woolly tufts which enable them to resist drought. They prefer a light sandy soil.

1-3 SEDUM (Stonecrop), *sedo*=sit, referring to the manner in which sedums attach themselves to rocks and walls. This is a very large group of mainly dwarf plants, several of them natives of Britain. Nearly all of them are easy to grow (some species spread too easily), and do best in sunny situations in a rock crevice in a poor soil.

S. anacampseros (1), from Central Europe, has thick trailing stems, often quite bare except for the tips. *S. middendorfianum* (2), from Manchuria, forms a clump of narrow, bronze-green leaves. The yellow flowers appear in clusters during July and are sometimes followed by bright red seed pods. *S. spathulifolium purpureum* is one of the best wall-top plants and comes from North-west America. It forms large clumps of deep plum-red rosettes which, especially in the variety 'Capa Blanca', are heavily powdered with mealy white farina. For autumn-flowering sedums, *see* p. 177.

4-5 SEMPERVIVUM (House Leek), *semper*=for ever, *vivo*=to live. These hardy plants from Central and South Europe are called house leeks because of a very old custom of growing them on the roof of the house to keep away illness. They produce neat mounds of fleshy rosettes, often brightly coloured, and with some varieties cobwebbed with silvery hairs. All the smaller kinds are most suitable for filling crevices in a wall or between cracks in rock work.

S. grandiflorum (4) is an early-flowering species from the Alps, and the cluster of large yellow flowers are on stems 6–10 ins. tall. *S. arachnoideum* (*arakhnoeides*=cobwebby) is one of the best and comes from alpine regions (5). Its rosettes are small and heavily covered with 'cobwebs' of silvery hairs. The variety 'stansfieldii' has larger rosettes which turn deep crimson in winter.

6 PENSTEMON pinifolius. One of the most persistent of the North American dwarf shrubby penstemons. Many of these tend to die in the winter, especially in wet seasons; so it is wise to keep a stock of young plants. They are easy to propagate from cuttings in June.

P. rupicola is much more prostrate and has large crimson tubular flowers. *P. scouleri* is rather taller and pale lilac; and *P. crandilla* grows only about an inch tall and has deep sky blue flowers. For the more shrubby rock garden penstemon, *see* p. 67.

7 ANACYCLUS atlanticus vestitus. This member of the Daisy family from the Atlas Mountains in North Africa is quite hardy in Britain if given a sunny position and not allowed to suffer from damp in the winter. Although a perennial, it is sometimes short-lived, and can be grown from seed.

8 HELICHRYSUM milfordae (marginatum). An everlasting flower from Basutoland which forms in time large mounds of intensely silvery rosettes. In June, or sometimes earlier, they are covered with attractive red buds which open into large, almost stemless, typical everlasting flowers. It flowers best if grown in poor dry soil in full sun. Like other plants on this page, it needs winter protection from damp in wet districts — best by being covered with a pane of glass.

H. bellidioides is a vigorous trailer with small grey-green leaves and innumerable small white flowers which last for many weeks. *H. virgineum* is shrubby, forming silver-grey mounds of foliage up to a foot high, and producing peach-pink buds which open into sprays of creamy-white flowers (p. 43). For other shrubby perennial helichrysums, *see* p. 65.

DIANTHUS deltoides (Maiden Pink). Many species of pinks (*see* p. 79) are suitable for dry walls, and form loose mats of foliage. They flower from June to the autumn. *D. deltoides* is native to Britain, and there are varieties with white, bright rose, crimson, or purplish-red flowers.

TEUCRIUM polium. An evergreen procumbent shrublet of the labiate family, which has charming silvery-grey foliage and yellowish flowers. It grows about 6 ins. tall and does well in sandy soil.

1 SEDUM ANACAMPSEROS
2 SEDUM MIDDENDORFIANUM
3 SEDUM SPATHULIFOLIUM PURPUREUM
4 SEMPERVIVUM GRANDIFLORUM
5 SEMPERVIVUM ARACHNOIDEUM 'STANSFIELDII'
6 PENSTEMON PINIFOLIUS
7 ANACYCLUS ATLANTICUS VESTITUS
8 HELICHRYSUM MILFORDAE

ROSE SPECIES

This term is used for the wild roses which are found in every country of the northern hemisphere. They include British briars as well as the dwarf alpine rose and the tall luxuriant climbers of the Indian and Chinese jungle woodlands. Although many are too big and untidy to be grown in the garden, the choicer rose species are some of the most attractive shrubs, both in flower and in fruit (*see* p. 187). They are all easy to grow in any soil that will support shrubs, and require little pruning apart from an occasional thinning out.

1 R O S A **farreri persetosa**. The 'threepenny-bit' rose is a pretty Chinese June-flowering bush under 5 ft. high. Of the many other pink wild briars, none is more pleasant than the wild sweet briar *R. eglanteria*, a moderate twiggy bush which can be clipped into a hedge. Though not of outstanding beauty, its foliage after rain has a delicious scent. More than most roses, the sweet briar tolerates a poor chalky soil.

R O S A **pendulina**. The alpine rose is a sturdy little bush about 3 ft. high, with few thorns. Its flowers are large and a rather deep pink, and are followed by handsome scarlet spindle-shaped hips.

R O S A **moyesii**. A tall rather sparse Chinese briar growing to 8 or 10 ft. It has splendid deep crimson flowers, followed by long scarlet urn-shaped fruit in September (*see* p. 187). *R. moyesii* 'Nevada' is a garden hybrid with big, single, creamy-white flowers, and flowers in June and again in autumn. It will often grow 7 ft. high and as much across, bearing hundreds of flowers, but it is sterile and sets no fruit.

R O S A **rubrifolia**. A Hungarian briar with unusual plum-coloured glaucous foliage. Its smallish, bright carmine-pink flowers are followed by heavy clusters of dark red fruit.

R O S A **complicata**. A hybrid of unknown parentage, with large single rich-pink flowers. A tall shrub of 6 ft. or more, it will often climb into a tree if it has the chance.

R O S A **macrantha** 'Raubritter'. A low trailing shrub, not over 2 ft. high, with greyish foliage and clusters of deep pink, semi-double flowers of an unusual globular shape.

R O S A **nitida**. An American species, somewhat like the Scotch rose in growth, spreading by means of underground shoots, and never much over 2 ft. in height. It has deep pink flowers, red fruit, and small shiny foliage which turns vivid scarlet in the autumn.

2 R O S A **spinosissima** 'King William IV'. A rare old double crimson-purple Scotch Rose. The wild Scotch

Rose is a suckering plant, not more than 2 ft. high but often 10 ft. across, thriving in the poorest sandy soils where no other rose except *R. rugosa* will grow. This suckering habit makes it useful for holding banks and dunes. Normally it has a single white flower, but it is also found in shades of pink, purple, and pale yellow, both with single and double flowers. The single forms have round black fruit. The modern 'Fruhlingsgold' is a hybrid of *R. spinosissima*, but unlike its parent, it is a vigorous tall bush, up to 8 ft., with saucer-sized primrose-yellow flowers in May.

3 R O S A **xanthina**. This is an old Chinese garden rose, a shrub of 5–6 ft., flowering in late May. There is also a wild form, *R. xanthina* 'Canary Bird', with single deep yellow flowers.

R O S A **hugonis**. A tall arching bush of 8 ft., with single pale yellow flowers set an inch or two apart all along the stems. It is one of the best taller shrubs, beautiful either at the back of a border or as a specimen bush grown in grass.

R O S A **primula**. A smaller and slighter species, a graceful bush, also with pale yellow flowers, but distinguished by the remarkable and delicious incense-like fragrance of its leaves.

R O S A **foetida**. The so-called Austrian briar has rich yellow flowers and, though probably a Persian plant, it seems to like cool soils and thrive best in the north. A remarkable variety, *R. foetida bicolor*, or 'Austrian Copper', is the brightest of all roses, a vivid orange-scarlet with a yellow reverse, growing about 4 ft. tall.

4 R O S A **rugosa** 'Frau Dagmar Hastrup'. One of the Japanese Roses which are all slow-growing bushy shrubs with few thorns and thick, dark green, deeply-wrinkled foliage, which is remarkably disease-free. Natives of sandy soils, they thrive in the poorest soils. Besides this single pale pink form, there are single white and purple varieties — all bearing large, round, red, tomato-like fruit.

Of the double forms, the white 'Blanc Double de Coubert' and the purple 'Roseraie de l'Häy' have a rich delicious scent. Though scentless, the little double 'Grootendorst Pink', with flowers fringed like a carnation, is also worth growing. *See* also p. 187.

1 ROSA FARRERI PERSETOSA   2 ROSA SPINOSISSIMA
3 ROSA XANTHINA   4 ROSA RUGOSA 'FRAU DAGMAR HASTRUP'

OLD GARDEN ROSES

Under this heading are grouped the double-flowered roses descended from *R. gallica* and other species which have been grown in gardens since classical times. They are mostly hardy, long-lived shrubs, with flowers in various shades of pink, purple, crimson, and white. Except for a few groups of more recent introduction which are bred from the repeat-flowering China rose, they flower but once, at mid-summer.

Most gardeners prefer the more brightly-coloured and perpetual-flowering modern roses, floribundas and hybrid-teas (*see* pp. 99, 101), but these old roses possess a charm and character of their own, and most interesting gardens contain at least a few. They look their best as specimen bushes allowed to grow up to 5 or 6 feet high and as much across. They should be planted not among modern roses but separately or with shrubs and herbaceous plants, where their quiet colours are in place.

Their cultivation is simple. They mostly like a fairly rich soil, but once planted need little attention apart from annual autumn pruning to remove the spent flowering wood.

1 ROSA **chinensis** 'Perle d'Or'. This is one of the miniature China rose hybrids, a pretty upright bush, flowering over many months. 'Cécile Brunner' is similar in character, with small pale pink flowers. The ordinary China roses are slender bushes up to 5–6 ft. high, flowering over 6 months, the best known of which are 'Hermosa' and 'Old Blush', with double soft-pink flowers, and 'Mutabilis', with single flowers which change from bright red to apricot and finally crimson. Also in this group belongs the strange little green rose, *R. viridiflora*. These are all shrubs of moderate growth suitable for small gardens.

2 HYBRID MUSK ROSES. This group, of which 'Callisto' is one, are perpetual flowering shrubs, varying in height from 4–6 ft., mostly with double softly-coloured flowers. 'Callisto' is not much over 4 ft., but 'Buff Beauty', with amber-yellow flowers, and 'Penelope', with pale cream-pink flowers, grow to 6 ft. or more. These are all rather broad-spreading shrubs, handsome as bushes or trained into an informal hedge.

ROSA **alba**. One of the most ancient roses, a tall, very hardy shrub, with greyish foliage, bearing double flattened flowers in June. *R. alba* 'Celestial' has beautifully-shaped clear pink flowers; *R. alba* 'Maiden's Blush' is palest pink. Smaller and somewhat different in growth is *R. alba* 'Queen of Denmark' which has deep pink flowers.

ROSA **centifolia** (Cabbage Rose). Another ancient rose, a tall slender bush, with huge, rounded, double-pink flowers with a characteristic hollow centre. Many mutations and seedlings have been raised from the original form, best known of which are 'White Provence'; 'Tour de Malakoff', a deep smoky purple colour; 'de Meaux', a miniature, not much over 2 ft. with double pink flowers; and 'Fantin Latour', a splendid modern hybrid with large, flattened, shell-pink flowers.

The Moss roses, *R. centifolia muscosa*, originated as a sport from the cabbage rose. There are many varieties, with white, pink, and crimson flowers, all of which have curious mossy, balsam-scented calyces, and were highly prized in Victorian times.

3 ROSA **gallica versicolor**. The most frequently grown of the large *gallica* group. The species itself is an Eastern plant now established in Europe, hence its name. It is a low, spreading bush of suckering habit, with dull-green leaves and single deep rose-purple flowers. There are many colour variants, such as 'Tuscany', a deep maroon; 'Président de Sèze', a vivid rose-pink; and 'Charles de Mills', an extra fully double crimson-purple flower with a delicious scent.

ROSA **damascena**. This is the rose grown for attar of roses in the Near East. A double deep pink variety, known as 'Kazanlik', is called after the district in which it is grown. Other worthwhile varieties are 'Mme Hardy', double white, and 'Omar Khayyam', double pink and named after the poet on whose grave it was found. There is also a striped form of the Damask rose, known as the 'York and Lancaster Rose'. 'Hebe's Lip', a pretty semi-double, blush-rose with a crimson petal edge, also belongs to this group.

4 ROSA **bourboniana** 'Boule de Neige'. A fine upright shrub with full fragrant flowers. The Noisette (p. 97) and the Bourbon roses, first raised in the late 18th century, were the first modern roses, and many are still well worth growing. Of the bush and shrubby kinds, 'La Reine Victoria', a pale pink flower with a lovely rounded shape; 'Mme Lauriol de Barny', deep pink; 'Souvenir de la Malmaison', shell-pink; and 'Coupe d'Hébé', rose-pink, are all beautiful shrubs.

The thornless roses, 'Zephirine Drouhin', deep pink, and 'Kathleen Harrop', shell-pink, are either tall bushes or short climbers. These all flower intermittently through the summer.

1 ROSA CHINENSIS 'PERLE D'OR'　　2 MUSK ROSE HYBRID 'CALLISTO'
3 ROSA GALLICA VERSICOLOR　　　4 ROSA BOURBONIANA 'BOULE DE NEIGE'

95

CLIMBING AND RAMBLING ROSES

The distinction between climbers and ramblers is somewhat artificial, but it is useful to the gardener. Ramblers have soft flexible shoots which are easily trained over arches and fences. Climbers, on the other hand, are stiffer, growing long erect shoots which may be bent but do not lend themselves so readily to being trained. As in the other roses, pruning should be directed to the older shoots that have flowered, leaving the young strong shoots to flower next season.

Most climbing and rambler roses flower well on shady walls, the chief exceptions being the tender sun-loving Banksian and Tea roses. The more rampant rambler roses, such as the white-flowered species *R. moschata*, *R. filipes*, and *R. brunonii*, are only suitable for growing over trees, as they make too much growth to be satisfactorily trained over a building.

CLIMBING ROSES. The wild large-flowered climbing tea rose, *R. odorata* (*indica odoratissima*), is one parent of nearly all the modern Hybrid Tea roses, a vigorous leafy plant, flowering over a long period, with big pale pink or yellow blossoms deliciously scented like freshly-crushed tea-leaves. Its influence is perhaps most clearly seen in its offspring 'Maréchal Niel', a lovely rose for the cool greenhouse with beautifully shaped, strongly scented, soft-yellow flowers. The oldest climbing garden roses are the Bourbon (*see* p. 94), the Noisette, and the Tea roses. Most of these flower twice in the summer.

Noisettes. These include the creamy-pink 'Gloire de Dijon' and the white 'Mme. Alfred Carrière', two of the best roses for a north wall. 'Alister Stella Gray' and 'William Allen Richardson' are apricot-yellow Noisettes which need a south wall.

Tea-rose Climbers. 'Lady Hillingdon' (1) is typical of the Tea-roses, a slender rose for sunny walls, with purple-tinted foliage. The modern Hybrid Tea climbers are mostly climbing mutations of bush roses. They are all vigorous upright climbers ideal for house walls; but if pruned too hard when young they may revert to bush form. Not all climbing sports flower freely, but the better kinds produce hundreds of flowers and are often more vigorous than their parent variety. Best known are the deep red climbers, such as 'Etoile de Hollande' and 'Crimson Glory'; the pinks, such as 'Caroline Testout' and 'Shot Silk'; and the yellows, such as 'Speks Yellow' and 'Golden Dawn'. 'Lemon Pillar', a large double cream; 'Mme. Gregoire Staechelin', pink; 'Elegance', yellow; and 'Guinée', a dark red, are originally climbers and not sports of bush varieties.

One of the most distinct climbers is the lovely single yellow 'Mermaid', which flowers all the summer. It is particularly disease-free, and is suitable for any aspect.

The small cluster-flowered Banksian Yellow is a vigorous climber, easy to train for it has no thorns, and happily free from mildew, black-spot, and greenfly; but it needs a sunny wall.

Modern perpetual-flowered climbers. These are somewhat intermediate between climbers and ramblers, deriving from parents in both groups. Their most valuable characteristic is their long-flowering season, lasting over several summer months. Mostly of fairly short stature with plenty of flexible stems, they are equally suitable for arches, fences, pillars, and the walls of the smaller house, in sun and shade. 'Golden Showers' (2) is the best yellow in this group; 'Coral Dawn' (3) is one of the several pinks; 'Morning Dawn' is somewhat lighter; and 'Parade' a deep rose-pink. In scarlets there is 'Danse du Feu', and for deeper reds the climbing floribunda 'Frensham' is admirable.

Though not strictly belonging here, this is the best place to mention the other floribunda rose mutations, such as the climbing forms of 'Allgold', 'Masquerade', 'Korona', and 'Orange Triumph', all of which have the good qualities of the dwarf forms.

RAMBLING ROSES. The true ramblers derive from several white clustered roses: *R. semperflorens*, *R. multiflora*, *R. moschata*, and *R. wichuraiana*. The oldest ramblers are white, two of which, 'The Garland' and 'Little White Pet', are still among the most charming ramblers we have.

Later, brighter colours were bred in from other roses, resulting in the so-called wichuraiana ramblers, with small flowers in cluster. These include deep reds, such as 'Crimson Shower' and 'Excelsa'; pinks, such as 'Dorothy Perkins' and 'Lady Godiva'; and whites, such as 'Sanders White'. These flower but once, in July. 'Phyllis Bide' (4) is rather unusual in this group, having pinkish-yellow flowers borne over a long period.

There are finally the hybrid wichuraianas, with larger flowers than the last group, big, strong-growing plants with shiny foliage and long, rather arching canes. Best known is the lovely salmon-pink 'Albertine', but there are also yellows such as 'Emily Gray' and 'Easlea's Golden'; reds such as 'Paul's Scarlet' and 'Crimson Conquest'; and creamy-whites such as 'Alberic Barbier'. In contrast to the wichuraiana roses these are mildew-resistant, but they also mostly flower but once. 'New Dawn' (5) is alone in this respect, flowering on and off the whole summer. It arose as a mutation of the otherwise identical 'Dr. Van Fleet'.

1 Climbing rose 'Lady Hillingdon'   2 Climbing rose 'Golden Showers'   3 Climbing rose 'Coral Dawn'
4 Rambling rose 'Phyllis Bide'   5 Rambling rose 'New Dawn'

POLYANTHA AND FLORIBUNDA ROSES

The original polyantha roses were little, much-branched bushes with small flowers in clusters. The floribunda roses, which have in part descended from them, are taller, more vigorous bushes with larger flowers in a wider variety of colours, inheriting their good qualities of longevity and hardiness from several different varieties. As a group, they are perhaps the most valuable decorative plants in the modern outdoor garden, providing a bright show of blossom throughout the summer with the minimum of trouble and expense. They are as a rule much hardier and more disease resistant than the Hybrid Teas.

Although they benefit by regular and fairly hard pruning to keep them healthy and compact, many of the more spreading varieties, especially those descended from the Hybrid Musk roses, can be allowed to grow into large bushes 5–6 ft. high without their becoming unmanageable.

VERMILION, SALMON, AND ORANGE ROSES. A brilliant vermilion-scarlet is a very popular colour, especially in drab surroundings. The first large-flowered rose of this colour was 'Independence', but it has now been superseded by a score of more brilliant varieties. The tallest are 'Friedrich Heyer' and 'Korona'; somewhat shorter are 'Dickson's Flame' and 'Highlight' and the singles 'Orangeade' and 'Sarabande'; 'Meteor' is the dwarfest, being only 18 ins. high.

In 'Anna Wheatcroft' (1) and 'Vilia' the vermilion is softened by a salmon tint. 'Border Coral', 'Spartan', and 'Jiminy Cricket' are all double salmon-pink varieties of medium height; 'Cri Cri' is a similar colour but very dwarf. 'Fashion' is salmon-orange, a lovely bright colour but one of the few floribundas which sometimes prove difficult to grow.

SALMON AND PINK ROSES. The single-flowered varieties 'Charming Maid' and 'Clair Matin' are salmon-orange in bud but pink in flower; the first is a tall erect bush, the second spreading in habit. 'Chanelle' and the older varieties 'Pinnochio' and 'Ma Perkins' are a pale shell-pink with orange tints. These are all nicely-shaped little double flowers.

In shades of true pink there are many good varieties. The tallest and most vigorous is the 'Queen Elizabeth Rose', which will grow to a height of 7 ft. if lightly pruned, making a good hedge. At the other end of the scale are 'Posy' and 'Jean Mermoz', which do not exceed 18 ins. There are also several good varieties with single flowers, such as 'Dainty Maid' and 'Silberlachs' which have superseded the old 'Else Poulsen'.

CRIMSON, RED, AND SCARLET ROSES. The darker crimson-reds range in size and form from the well-known 'Frensham', which will make a tall hedge, to the neat dwarf bedding varieties 'Lilli Marlene', 'Red Favourite', and 'Moulin Rouge'. 'Dusky Maiden' (2) is the best dwarf single crimson variety, and 'Henry Morse' is a much taller bush. 'Concerto' is a rather lighter scarlet but otherwise very similar to 'Moulin Rouge'; both last remarkably well as cut-flowers.

The vivid colouring of such varieties as 'Firecracker', 'Jane Lazenby' and 'Sea of Fire' is cherry-red or rose-cerise. Even more intense are 'Red Wonder' and 'Rosemary Rose'; both these have coppery-crimson foliage which sets off the brilliant flowers most effectively. 'Garnette', a pretty small double variety now widely grown as a pot-plant on account of its long-lasting qualities, is of the same colouring.

WHITE ROSES. Of the white varieties the new tall variety 'Iceberg' is the finest and most graceful. There is also the old 'Yvonne Rabier', a compact bush with double flowers, and 'Irene of Denmark' of similar dwarf growth with pearly-white flowers.

YELLOW AND GOLD ROSES. Among the true yellows 'Allgold' is supreme, a fine deep double yellow flower, of dwarf habit when pruned hard, but capable of making a shrub 5 ft. high if allowed to. Of paler colouring are the single varieties 'Danish Gold' and 'Sandringham', both of which are primrose-yellow. 'Clare Grammerstorf' and 'Golden Fleece' are a deeper shade of honey-yellow.

In 'Circus' (3) the golden colour is blended with pink and apricot. 'Rumba' (4) is a newer variety in which the contrasted yellow and red colouring is more pronounced. 'Masquerade', a taller variety, also has similar colouring. 'Shepherd's Delight', 'Tambourine', and the single variety 'First Choice' also offer a contrast of red and yellow, the yellow being on the reverse of the petal.

MAUVE AND LILAC ROSES. There are many good mauve or lavender-coloured varieties. The earliest is 'Lavender Pinnochio', a dwarf variety with mauve flowers tinted with tan. 'Lavender Girl' is a better shaped flower, of purer colour. 'Magenta' is a taller bush with flattened double flowers of a deep rosy-lilac. Also tall is 'Lavender Lassie', with double flowers of a bright and pleasing lilac. 'Overture' is a dwarf with deeper cyclamen-pink colourings.

Finally there is 'Café', a most unusual and pleasing rose when grown on its own, with double flowers of a distinct soft coffee-brown.

1 FLORIBUNDA ROSE 'ANNA WHEATCROFT'   2 HYBRID POLYANTHA ROSE 'DUSKY MAIDEN'
3 FLORIBUNDA ROSE 'CIRCUS'   4 FLORIBUNDA ROSE 'RUMBA'

HYBRID TEA ROSES

To most people these are the best-known roses. Their scent, their vivid colours, and their beautifully-formed flowers are the result of generations of deliberate hybridization to combine the most desirable characteristics of many species in a single plant. Through careful breeding, modern varieties tend to be more vigorous and disease-resistant than their predecessors, but they need good soil and regular protection against disease. The most suitable soil is a retentive one, with sufficient potash, phosphate, and other essential elements, but not too much lime. Heavy clay soils can be lightened by adding peat, leaf-mould, and sand, while dry sandy soils can be made cooler by mixing in plenty of humus and cow manure when planting. It is generally most satisfactory to grow them in beds on their own so that they can be sprayed without interference.

While wild roses, most older kinds, and climbers can be grown on their own roots, the hybrid tea roses are budded or grafted on to a vigorous root stock, usually that of the dog-rose *R. canina* or its near relatives. Suckers from this wild rose root invariably appear and have to be removed as soon as they show; otherwise they will kill the grafted or budded rose. The main point in pruning hybrid tea roses is to encourage the production of young vigorous flowering shoots and to remove older shoots. During the dormant season in winter or early spring, all thin twiggy wood should be cut out, leaving only the stout young shoots, and these should be shortened by half or two-thirds to encourage more shoots from dormant buds.

When deciding what to grow, the choice often has to be made between scent and colour. As a rule, deep crimson-reds and rose-pinks, which are descended from the Damask rose (p. 95), have a richer scent than the newer vivid pinks, salmon, orange, and yellow colours; but some of the apricot-yellow and buff roses have a delicious tea-scent inherited from *R. indica* (p. 97).

1 CRIMSON AND RED ROSES. 'Mme Louis Laperrière' (1) is one of the best dark red varieties. The once popular 'Étoile de Hollande' has now been superseded by this and many other newer sorts which do not suffer from the faults of the red varieties — a weak stem and a tendency to turn purple as they age. For scent, 'Brilliant', 'Chrysler Imperial', and 'Crimson Glory' are good choices; while for magnificent flowers, 'Charles Mallerin', 'Josephine Bruce', and 'Christian Dior' are favourites, though the best free-flowering garden bush is 'Ena Harkness'.

A new brick-red or vermilion colouring has recently been introduced into the hybrid tea roses. Best is 'Super Star', a pure light-vermilion colour of unusual brightness, and 'Baccara', 'Lady Zia', and 'Lucy Cramphorn' are also good darker varieties.

ROSE-PINK AND PINK ROSES. Rose-pinks are nearly all richly scented, especially 'Wendy Cussons'. Somewhat lighter are 'Eden Rose', 'Prima Ballerina', and 'Sarah Arnot', all large fragrant varieties.

Lighter in colour again are 'Picture', 'Silver Lining', 'Margaret', and 'Monique', usually described as bright pink. Of the pale pink varieties the old 'Madam Butterfly' is still a favourite. There is also 'First Love', a newer kind with a similar slender bud formation.

SALMON - PINK AND BICOLOR ROSES. Between pale pink and salmon come such lovely varieties as 'Helen Traubel', 'Michèle Meilland', and 'Serenade', all free-flowering roses with slender buds. Deeper coppery-pink or salmon-orange are 'Mrs. Sam McGredy' and 'Mary Wheatcroft', both of which have unusual crimson-tinted foliage.

The bicolor varieties are red with a white or yellow petal back. 'Westminster', 'Tzigane', and 'Sultane' are scarlet with a yellow petal back; 'Fortyniner' is a deeper purple tint with a straw-coloured petal back.

YELLOW ROSES. Of all the yellows the pink-tinted variety 'Peace' is the most vigorous. Its thick shiny foliage and strong growth, up to 6 ft., are always easily recognisable. 'Tahiti' and 'Grandmère Jenny' are similar roses but more noticeably scented. 'Perfecta' is of similar vigorous growth to 'Peace', but of a creamy-pink colouring.

'Spek's Yellow', 'Buccaneer', and 'Golden Giant' are the best bright yellow roses. They are all fairly tall and slender in growth, with dark foliage. 'McGredy's Yellow' and 'Diamond Jubilee' are primrose-yellows; 'Belle Blonde' and 'Beauté' are an orange-yellow, and 'Lady Belper', 'André le Troquet', and 'Thais' are a deeper apricot-yellow. These lovely orange-coloured varieties are, unfortunately, some of the least hardy. In 'Sutter's Gold' and 'President Hoover' the yellow colouring is mixed with pink and red tints. Both are tall-growing roses with a strong scent.

2 LILAC, GREY, AND WHITE ROSES. 'Sterling Silver' (2) is perhaps the best of the grey and lilac roses. 'Prelude' is a warmer tint with some brown shadings and 'Grey Pearl' is nearer to grey. Of the pure white roses the best are 'Virgo' and the greenish-white 'Message'.

3 SINGLE HYBRID TEA ROSES. Few of these possess the vigour of the double varieties, nor are ever likely to be as popular, but they flower very freely, and some people prefer them. 'White Wings' (?) is one of the loveliest, but there is also 'Golden Wings', lemon-yellow, and the pink varieties 'Dairty Bess' and 'Ellen Willmott'.

1 HYBRID TEA ROSE 'MME LOUISE LAPERRIERE'   2 HYBRID TEA ROSE 'STERLING SILVER'
3 HYBRID TEA ROSE 'WHITE WINGS'

TALL HALF-HARDY SHRUBS FOR SUNNY WALLS

A shrub's hardiness means its capacity to resist frost, and this depends on what may be called its 'constitution'. Shrubs from the tropics and warm temperate zones succumb to a degree or two of frost; others from climates rather warmer than Britain will stand a certain amount of frost depending largely on the conditions under which they are grown. Shrubs grown in a climate and position in which the wood is able to 'ripen' properly are hardier, for ripened wood can withstand much more cold than unripened. Most shrubs which are half-hardy in Britain are evergreen. In frozen ground evergreens may die of drought, for water continues to pass out of the leaves, particularly if there are cold drying winds. In very severe frosts the sap may freeze and burst the plant tissues, in which case death is certain. If the plant is at all resistant, it will survive short cold spells, but fall victim to continued low temperatures. In general more than 10 degrees fahrenheit of frost will seriously damage or kill the plants shown here.

The stones and bricks of a wall warm up slowly in the sun and give out this heat equally slowly at night, so that shrubs grown against a wall are kept at a temperature a few degrees above that of the open air. But in long periods of continued cold this advantage disappears. Also a properly sited wall protects the plants growing near it from the harmful cold drying winds. But it must be emphasized that the soil at the base of a wall is often drier than that further away; therefore, except during frost, this soil should be kept moist by watering. It should also be kept compacted, not loose, as the air above compacted soil is warmer.

The plants described here are, speaking broadly, hardy in the open in the south and south-west, and also in maritime areas as far north as the west coast of Scotland.

1 LEPTOSPERMUM **scoparium nichollsii.** The leptospermums are shrubs and small trees native to Australia, New Zealand, and Tasmania. None of them are hardy everywhere, but this red variety of the white *L. scoparium* is moderately frost-resistant on a wall. There is a form with larger flowers. The dwarf form of *L. scoparium*, which is hardier, is not a very attractive plant. The white *L. pubescens* is also fairly hardy. Several new species and hybrids have been introduced in recent years, but the only one as hardy as *L. s. nichollsii* is 'Red Damask'. They all flower profusely, mostly in June.

2 ABUTILON **vitifolium album.** This and the lavender-blue type from Chile are very beautiful mallow-like shrubs which, against a wall, are hardy as far north as parts of eastern Scotland. It may be grown in the open in the south, and though it will be cut to the ground in severe winters, provided the plant is not too old, it will 'break' again from the base. Like most members of the mallow family, it grows very rapidly and is short lived, even under the best conditions. A striking but more beautiful species is *A. megapotamicum* from Brazil, but it is suitable only for the mildest places. Its yellow petals are in a tubular shape, enclosed in a conspicuous red calyx.

3 MIMULUS **glutinosus puniceus.** *M. glutinosus*, sometimes known as Diplacus, is a native of California where it grows by the road-side. It is variable in colour from cream to orange-buff and crimson. It is a reasonably hardy shrubby plant and has been much used as a pot plant in conservatories because its attractive flowers continue a long time. *See* also p. 75.

4 MYRTUS **communis. (Common Myrtle).** This has been in cultivation since the 16th century and is fairly hardy against a wall. The white flowers in July are fragrant. In classical times myrtle was associated with the Goddess of Love, and a sprig was at one time an essential part of a bridal bouquet. Though *M. communis* is about the hardiest, there are other myrtles suitable for a protected position. *M. luma* from Chile, which may become a small tree, has beautiful cinnamon bark. *M. lechleriana* is a more recent introduction with white fragrant blossom in May.

ACACIA **dealbata (Mimosa).** This shrub grows very quickly and flowers while young, but is suitable only for very mild climates. It cannot survive a hard frost.

ABELIA **floribunda.** An evergreen shrub with masses of tubular rose-red flowers. Against a sunny sheltered wall it will withstand 15 degrees of frost. *See* also p. 171.

CALLISTEMON **linearis (Bottle Brush).** The beauty of this genus lies in the stamens, scarlet in *C. linearis*, the hardiest species. It will grow as a slender bush about 6 ft. tall.

CORONILLA **glauca.** For long-flowering this glaucous-leaved shrub from southern Europe, with heads of bright yellow pea-shaped flowers, is conspicuous. It is early-flowering and grows 6 ft. or more tall.

DESFONTAINEA **spinosa.** A shrub from Chile and Peru with holly-like leaves and tubular, waxy, scarlet-and-gold flowers. It needs a lime-free soil, and begins to flower at an early age.

EMBOTHRIUM **coccineum longifolium.** Another shrub from Chile which needs a lime-free soil. It has curious-shaped scarlet flowers, with long tubes and long protruding styles, which cluster along the branches. It dislikes sun on its roots, so a smaller shrub should be planted at its base to give shade.

1 LEPTOSPERMUM SCOPARIUM NICHOLLSII   2 ABUTILON VITIFOLIUM ALBUM
3 MIMULUS GLUTINOSUS PUNICEUS   4 MYRTUS COMMUNIS

LABIATE SHRUBS FOR DRY SUNNY PLACES

This large family of herbaceous plants (*see* p. 153), sub-shrubs, and shrubs mainly inhabit dry regions, particularly those bordering the Mediterranean and also Central Asia. They all have a lip to the flower (hence the name), and this lip is intimately concerned with the process of fertilization, being the landing ground for bees or other insects. The impact of the insect sets off a hammer-like mechanism which causes the anthers to deposit pollen on the insect's back. Most labiates have downy leaves and stems and contain essential oils, features which are characteristic of plants from hot and dry areas. It is these oils which makes the herbs mint, sage, and thyme of value in cookery, and lavender, patchouli, and rosemary of value in perfumery. In the garden the labiates require the hottest and driest positions possible, and some need winter protection.

1 LEONOTIS **leonurus** (**Lion's Tail**). A half-hardy plant from South Africa suitable only for mild districts or a sunny position sheltered by a wall. It is easily propagated, and a few rooted cuttings should always be kept in reserve. It flowers in the late autumn, much later than the other plants on this page, and therefore is liable to be damaged by early frosts.

2 LAVANDULA **spica** 'Hidcote Purple' (Lavender). A native of Mediterranean regions, lavender has been cultivated in Britain since the 16th century, mainly because of its fragrance, strongest in the flower heads. Several varieties exist, most, if not all, collected in the wild. The most vigorous is *L. s. gigantea*, sometimes known as the 'Grappenhall' variety, which may grow up to 5 ft. 'Twickle Purple' is a semi-dwarf, late-blooming, bushy form with long spikes of rich lavender blue. The best garden varieties are *L. s. nana*, 'Munstead Violet', purple and early; 'Folgate' and 'Beechwood', both deep blue; and 'Hidcote', the deepest of all. Very dwarf varieties suitable for the rock garden are 'Baby Blue' and 'Baby White', about 6 ins. tall. There are white and lilac-pink varieties of *L. spica*, but these are less attractive.

3 SALVIA **officinalis** (**Common Sage**). This excellent pot-herb is an essential herb garden plant; but there are a number of varieties with coloured leaves which are also attractive in hot, dry places in the flower garden (*see* p. 108). *S. o. aurea* has golden yellow leaves; *icterina*, green and gold; *sturnina*, green and white; *purpurascens*, the commonest and reddish-purple; and *tricolor*, green, white, yellow, and pink. Some of the best, however, are not easy to come by. The brilliant scarlet and crimson shrubby salvias are not hardy enough to grow as perennials, but some, such as *S. splendens*, can be grown as half-hardy annuals (*see* p. 127).

4 PHLOMIS **fruticosa** (**Jerusalem Sage**). A free-flowering shrub 2–4 ft. tall, which cannot be regarded as perfectly hardy in cold areas. The more striking plant, *P. chrysophylla*, with brighter yellow flowers and foliage covered with golden hairs which give it a distinct yellow tinge, is not entirely hardy either.

5 ROSMARINUS **officinalis** (**Rosemary**). The ordinary pale violet form with highly aromatic foliage has been in cultivation for over 400 years. It has been used for making rosemary tea, a remedy for headaches, and for flavouring sauces. It is a variable plant, with many differences in colour and habit. *R. o.* 'Corsican Blue' (which has other names) and also 'Severn Sea' have bright coloured flowers. 'Tuscan Blue' has distinct broad leaves and very bright flowers which it does not produce very freely. 'Miss Jessop's Upright' is a very erect form suitable for a low hedge. There is a prostrate rosemary, *R. prostratus*, but it is not hardy. In cold places it is worth remembering that young plants are hardier than old.

COLQUHOUNIA **coccinea**. A very showy labiate shrub, with scarlet and yellow flowers in late summer; but it needs a wall except in mild places. It comes from the Himalayas, as also does its variety *vestita*, which is perhaps somewhat hardier. The crushed leaves are fragrant.

THYMUS x **citriodorus**. A very small bushy shrub 4–12 ins. high, suitable for the front of the border. It is lemon-scented and has several forms, of which the gold and silver variegated are the most attractive. *See* also p. 89.

RUTA **graveolens** (**Rue**). An evergreen shrub 2–3 ft. tall, with dull yellow flowers. The variety 'Jackman's Blue' has attractive blue foliage and a very bushy growth.

HYSSOPUS **officinalis**. An aromatic, partly ever-green, rounded bush, 1–2 ft. tall, and covered with spikes of bluish-purple flowers. There are white and red varieties. It has been cultivated for a long time.

1 Leonotis leonurus   2 Lavandula spica 'Hidcote Purple'   3 Salvia officinalis
4 Phlomis fruticosa   5 Rosmarinus officinalis

POTENTILLAS AND GEUMS

Both the groups of plants on this page belong to the very varied family, Rosaceae. They are perennial plants of temperate and cold regions, and there are native species of both in Britain. They are easily grown in most situations, including some shade, though Potentillas in particular do better in full sun and dry soil. They can be propagated by seed or division but, since many hybridize readily, varieties can be relied on to come true only by division.

1-4 POTENTILLA (Cinquefoil). The name comes from *potens*=powerful, for the plant was supposed to have medicinal qualities. It is sometimes called the strawberry plant because the leaves and flowers are similar in shape. It has a fruit which looks not unlike a little strawberry.

Many potentillas are prostrate in growth and may, when fully grown, cover a square yard; but most can be made to grow upright if given support. They are very useful for covering gaps in herbaceous borders — for example, planted next to large plants such as oriental poppies which flower early and are then cut down, leaving a gap. Many of the best garden varieties are hybrids of *P. argyrophylla*, *P. atrosanguinea*, and *P. nepalensis*, as well as some others, and the most common colours are orange, scarlet, crimson, and yellow. Some varieties have attractive silver foliage.

As well as those illustrated there are many other single, semi-double, and double varieties. 'Etna' is a tall silver-foliaged plant with dense crimson single flowers. Of the doubles, 'Golden Queen' is a semi-double buttercup-yellow with orange spots; 'Melton' has flame-gold double flowers; and 'Monsieur Rouillard' is a deep blood-red double variety. *P.*

rupestris, a tall single species, is white; and *P. fragiformis* is a dwarf yellow hairy species.

There are also potentillas suitable for the rock garden, such as *P. nitida rubra*, a tiny silver carpeter with large deep pink flowers, and the also tiny, buttercup-yellow *P. verna nana*. For shrubby potentillas, *see* p. 161.

5-6 GEUM (Avens), from *geuo*=to flavour, because the roots of some species have a pleasant taste. Most of the large-flowered garden varieties, both single and double, have been developed from *G. chiloense*, which grows 1–2 ft. tall.

As well as those illustrated, there are the following good varieties: 'Borisii', single orange-scarlet and an attractive edging or ground cover plant; 'Mrs. Bradshaw', semi-double deep scarlet; 'Prince of Orange', double bright orange-yellow; and 'Leonard's Variety', a form of the species *G. rivale* (Water Avens), with nodding flowers, old rose in colour, and about 1 ft. tall.

The species *G. montanum* is a dwarf plant with orange golden-yellow flowers, suitable for rock gardens (*see* p. 34).

1 Potentilla x 'Gibson's Scarlet'
2 Potentilla nepalensis 'Miss Willmott'
3 Potentilla atrosanguinea
4 Potentilla x tonguei
5 Geum 'Fire Opal'
6 Geum chiloense 'Lady Stratheden'

SUN-LOVING PERENNIALS FOR MODERATELY DRY SOIL

The plants illustrated opposite are all easy to grow and are not particular about soil or situation so long as there is a fair amount of sun. Most of them have been well-known in British gardens for many years.

1-2 TRADESCANTIA virginiana (Spiderwort). An American plant named after John Tradescant, gardener to King Charles I. Most garden varieties are derived from *T. virginiana*, a native of the eastern states of the U.S.A. It has various country names, such as 'Moses in the Bullrushes' because of the cluster of flowers amid rush-like leaves, or 'Trinity Flower' because of the three-petalled flowers. The individual flowers last for one day only, but there are always more to follow, and they continue the whole summer. The flowers, with their silky petals and prominent stamens are lovely, but the rather informal plants generally look a little untidy and are perhaps more suited to a woodland garden or shrub border than a herbaceous border. They are tolerant of almost any conditions, and can be easily increased by division in March. They grow from 1½–2 ft. tall.

As well as those illustrated, other good varieties are the white *T. v. alba*: white flushed blue 'Iris Prichard'; white with blue filaments 'Osprey'; pale pink-purple 'Purewell Giant'; deep violet-purple 'Purple Dome'; rose-crimson 'Taplow Crimson'; and carmine-rose *T. v. rubra*.

3 OENOTHERA fruticosa 'Yellow River' (Evening Primrose). Evening Primroses, most of which open only in the evening and some of which scent the air with their fragrance, come from North America. Although tolerant of most soils, they prefer a well-drained sandy loam and they need sunshine. They continue to flower for a long time and grow 1–2 ft. tall. *O. glabra* has attractive bronze foliage and buds as well as bright yellow flowers. *O. perennis* (also called Sundrops) and *O. tetragona riparia* are rather dwarfer. *O. speciosa* has white, slightly fragrant, shaded rose flowers. There are also biennial and annual species (*see* p. 127).

4 VERONICA TEUCRIUM 'Royal Blue' (Speedwell). The veronicas are a very large group which includes plants which flower at most times of the year and range from flowering shrubs (*see* p. 161) to dwarf perennials suitable for rock gardens (*see* pp. 41 and 81). There are several good herbaceous-border species, such as the varieties of *V. teucrium*, *V. spicata*, and *V. incana*, which are reliable and give good colour for a long period, even in the less choice places in the border. Most of them grow about 1½–2 ft. tall, though the light blue *V. exaltata*, and the blue or white forms of *V. virginica* grow a good deal taller. *V. incana*, which is rather dwarf, has silver foliage and deep blue flowers.

5 PLATYCODON grandiflorus mariesii (Chinese Bellflower). This campanula-like plant from China and Japan is named from Greek words *platys*=broad and *kodon*=bell, and is sometimes called the Balloon Flower because the buds are balloon-like before they open. It has tap roots like a parsnip, which can be dug up, stored, and replanted without any ill effects. But the plants are not easy to divide and are best propagated from seed. The variety illustrated grows 9–12 ins. tall, but most other varieties grow up to 2 ft. There are white and pink single forms and also a semi-double blue variety.

SALVIA. Most salvias have woody roots which are not easy to divide, so they are best grown from seed. Some are grown as half-hardy annuals (*see* p. 127); others are shrubs (*see* p. 105); others flower rather later in the season (*see* p. 153). Of summer-flowering perennials *S. haematodes* has light blue flowers, *S. nemorosa* violet-purple, and *S. argentea* white flowers with silver foliage. In some varieties much of the colour comes from the conspicuous bracts which persist for a long time. *S. nemorosa*, for example, has red bracts, and in *S. sclarea turkestanica* they are rose and pale blue. Salvias need a hot, dry situation, and some are best grown as biennials.

1 Tradescantia virginiana 'J. C. Weguelin'   2 Tradescantia virginiana 'Leonora'
3 Oenothera fruticosa 'Yellow River'   4 Veronica teucrium 'Royal Blue'
5 Platycodon grandiflorus mariesii

TALL HERBACEOUS PLANTS FOR LIGHT SHADE

More plants will grow in shade than many people imagine, especially if the soil is not dry. There are many places in the garden in gaps between shrubs or trees which can be made colourful with the right plants, but the soil must be well dug and enriched with humus and manure; otherwise it will dry out and the plants will fail.

1 LACTUCA bourgaei, *lac*=milk — a milky juice flows from the stems when they are cut. The salad lettuce (*L. sativa*) belongs to this genus, though one does not usually see its flower. The decorative species are sometimes called Mulgedium. They are easy to grow, though preferring deep moist soil in semi-shade. The handsome heads of soft lavender flowers and well-cut leaves look particularly effective in wild or woodland gardens. *L. bourgaei* grows up to 6 ft. tall, but *L. alpina* has large lilac flowers on stems only 3 ft. tall.

2 KIRENGESHOMA palmata. A Japanese plant needing a half-shady position in a moist, leaf-mouldy soil. The word *ki* means 'yellow' in Japanese. The waxy, usually more or less nodding flowers are carried on 3-ft. slender purple stems above large glaucous leaves, handsomely veined and toothed. It flowers rather later than the other plants on this page.

3 GENTIANA asclepiadea (Swallow-wort), usually called Willow Gentian because of its narrow willow-like leaves. The type has gentian-blue flowers with paler stripes and purple spots within, and grows on long arching stems. There is also the white form, *alba*, which is illustrated, and a blue and white form, known as *bicolor*. It does best in a shady position, but can be grown in the open if the soil is consistently moist. It grows 1–2 ft. tall, is vigorous and hardy, and will quickly become naturalized in the right environment.

Another quite easy gentian of about the same height is *G. trichotoma* (*G. hopei*) from West China, which has clear blue flowers on branched stems. *G. pneumonanthe* is much smaller, with purplish-blue, green-spotted flowers on 6–12 in. stems. Very much taller is the stately *G. lutea* which has pale yellow-spotted flowers on unbranched stems 4–6 ft. tall. Both these last species do well planted by the waterside.

For other gentians, *see* pp. 35 and 177.

4 ARUNCUS sylvester (Goat's Beard). This used to be called *Spirea aruncus*. It is not so dependent on a moist soil as most of the plants on this page — in fact, it succeeds well in a fairly dry loamy soil in light shade. It grows up to 5 ft. and with its massive creamy-white plumes and attractively-cut foliage, it is suitable for a prominent position and looks well growing by itself so that its handsome shape can be seen.

5 CAMPANULA alliariifolia. This campanula from the Caucasus is sometimes known as *C. cordifolia* because of its heart-shaped leaves. The lower leaves are large and grey-green, toothed, and of a rough texture. It is an ideal plant for informal positions and odd corners in light shade, growing up to 2 ft. tall, and though it increases fairly quickly, it is never a nuisance.

Another June-flowering campanula easy to grow in most situations and tolerant of shade is *C. latiloba*. It grows 2 ft. or more tall and has large pale violet-blue flowers in the upper leaf axils on unbranched stems. It has also a white form. *C. persicifolia*, June–July flowering, is also easily grown. It has large, widely-spaced lavender-blue flowers on slender leafless stems. There are white and also double forms. The variety 'Telham Beauty' has very large silver-blue flowers, but is less vigorous. *See* also p. 157 for later-flowering species.

LYTHRUM salicaria (Purple Loosestrife). There are several garden varieties of this British wild flower. They are easy to grow and showy and, like the species, prefer a damp soil. The erect spikes of flowers grow on 2–4-feet-tall stems. The variety 'Robert' is clear pink; 'Brightness' is rose-pink; and 'Rose Queen' is rose-purple.

1 Lactuca bourgaei   2 Kirengeshoma palmata   3 Gentiana asclepiadea alba
4 Aruncus sylvester   5 Campanula alliariifolia

SUN-LOVING HERBACEOUS PLANTS WITH SPIKES

A well-designed border needs plants of different shapes and heights. The plants described on this page are all tall with slender spikes of flowers which look well rising above mounds of foliage or rounded clumps. These plants are suitable for the back of the border in the sunny parts, whereas those described on p. 110 will grow in the more shady parts.

1-3 VERBASCUM (Mullein). Most verbascums are hardy biennials and should be sown in June or July to flower the following summer. As a matter of fact, they sow themselves freely, and there are usually enough seedlings for one's purpose — though the colours do not necessarily come true. There are a few perennial species and hybrids, most of the garden varieties being descended from the robust *V. x caledonia*. *V. phoeniceum* (Purple Mullein) is a perennial with varieties in many pastel shades, but it can also be grown as a biennial.

Verbascums will grow on any rather dry light soil and thrive on chalk. Many of the biennials grow up to 5 ft. tall or more: for example, the sulphur-yellow very tall *V. olympicum*, the pure white V. 'Miss Willmott', and the large rich yellow V. 'Harkness Hybrid'. The varieties illustrated 'Cotswold Beauty' (2) and 'Cotswold Queen' (3), both with lilac anthers, are 3–4 ft. tall; and the pink-purple perennial *V. phoeniceum* is 2–3 ft. There is a dwarf salmon-buff variety, 'Maud Pugsley', which is about 15 ins.

Some Verbascums have thick woolly leaves. *V. bombyciferum* (V. 'Broussa') has the whole plant covered densely with fine white hairs, and the woolly winter rosette of large leaves is very decorative. The native British mulleins, especially the Great Mullein (*V. thapsus*), have a woolly appearance.

4 SIDALCEA. A member of the mallow family, growing 3–4 ft. high and bearing flowers like a small hollyhock. The modern garden varieties derive from crossing the white *S. candida* and the lilac or pink *S. malvaeflora*, and range from palest pink to deep rose. Sidalcea thrives in any soil, and can be easily propagated by dividing the plants. They flower from early July to late August: the varieties 'Rev. Page Roberts' (flesh pink), 'Rose Queen' (rose-pink), and 'The Duchess' (carmine-rose) are early flowering, and the deep rose 'Monarch' and silver-pink 'Elsie Heugh' do not flower till August.

ALTHAEA rosea (Hollyhock). Although this is a perennial, it is usually best grown as a biennial (*see* p. 130) because of its tendency to suffer from hollyhock rust. It is an excellent town garden plant where it seems to suffer less from disease. There are both single and double forms ranging from white, lemon, and pale pink to salmon, crimson, and deep maroon.

5-6 LYSIMACHIA (Loosestrife). This genus, of which there are native British species, may have been named after a King of Thrace called Lysimachas, who may have first discovered the soothing properties of the plant; or the name may have come from *lysis* = abatement and *mache* = strife — in other words, loosestrife. The lysimachias prefer a fairly moist soil, indeed, the native *L. thyrsiflora* often grows partly in water, and *L. ephemerum* (5) can be grown as a waterside plant.

Lysimachias vary a great deal in appearance. *L. punctata* (6) is like the native yellow Loosestrife (*L. vulgaris*) in appearance and makes dense thickets of upright stems 2 ft. or more tall, flowering in June. *L. clethroides* has white flower spikes in the shape of a crook, which look best grown against a wall or another plant so that they all face the same way. It flowers in July to September. *L. nummularia*, the native Creeping Jenny, is a prostrate plant with bright yellow flowers, which spreads by creeping roots and is useful for growing on moist banks. There is an even better golden-leaved form.

DICTAMNUS albus (fraxinella). This has spikes of white or pale purple (or in the variety *D. albus caucasicus*, rose-pink) flowers. The ash-like leaves have a lemon scent, and the stems exude an inflammable oil which can be ignited on a still summer evening without damaging the plant — hence its name Burning Bush.

POLYGONUM bistorta superbum (Bistort). This is a garden variety of the native wild plant, with stiff spikes of tiny, thickly clustered, rosy-pink flowers and often attractively coloured leaves. It grows best in a moist soil and is 2–3 ft. tall. It tends to spread unless the running roots are cut back each spring. For other polygonums, *see* pp. 149, 164, and 176.

LIATRIS. A hardy, handsome plant of the daisy family from North America, which grows well in any moderately good light soil and lasts well when cut. *L. callilepis* has close spikes of heather-purple flowers about 3 ft. tall from July into September.

1 Verbascum nigrum   2 Verbascum 'Cotswold Beauty'   3 Verbascum 'Cotswold Queen'
4 Sidalcea 'Sussex Beauty'   5 Lysimachia ephemerum   6 Lysimachia punctata

113

THISTLE-LIKE PLANTS

All the plants on this page belong to the Daisy family and do well in any ordinary soil. Some do better in a poor dry soil, and all like sun. They are easy to grow from seed, and many of them are not suitable for a small garden. Except for Echinops and Cynara, there are species of all of them which are native to Britain.

1-2 ECHINOPS (Globe Thistle), *echinos* = hedgehog, *ops* = like. These are natives of Spain eastwards to India. They are usually blue, though there are whitish and silvery-grey species (*E. sphaerocephalus*). They dry well for winter decoration (*see* p. 190), but must be cut just before reaching full bloom; otherwise they fall to pieces when dry. They vary in height from 'Veitch's Blue' (1) which is 2 ft. tall to 'Taplow Blue' or *E. sphaerocephalus* which are 5 ft. or more. *E. ritro* (2), about 3 ft. tall, can be grown well as a biennial, sown in May or June.

3 CIRSIUM rivulare atropurpureum. Most of these thistles are not suitable for the garden, but this 3-ft.-tall crimson species with bold foliage makes a striking variety among other border plants.

4-5 CENTAUREA (Knapweed). There are several British wild Knapweeds and also some showy garden plants suitable for dry soils. The well-known Cornflower (*C. cyanus*) and Sweet Sultan (*C. moschata*) are annuals (*see* p. 87). The perennials have thistle-like leaves, often with silver linings, though some of the more silvery species, such as *C. rutifolia* (*candidissima*), are less hardy. They vary in height from the yellow *C. macrocephala* (3–4 ft.) to *C. montana* (1½ ft.), which has white, pink, crimson, and deep blue varieties. Some Centaureas spread very quickly by seed and can become tiresome weeds in a small garden.

CARLINA acaulis (Carline Thistle). A silvery white flower, 9–12 ins. tall, with shiny thistle-like leaves, which does best on poor, stony soil.

CYNARA cardunculus (Cardoon), *kynos* = dog, for the spines surrounding the flowerhead are likened to a dog's teeth. This is a tall handsome plant from Mediterranean lands, with large silver leaves and purple thistle-like heads. The Globe Artichoke (*C. scolymus*), grown as a vegetable is also very ornamental, and can look handsome in a large garden where there is room.

ONOPORDON acanthium (Scotch or Cotton Thistle). This native thistle, up to 5 ft. tall, has handsome large purple flowers and grows very well on poor soil. As the plant is top heavy and the roots not deep, it needs good staking.

SILYBUM marianum (Milk Thistle). A biennial thistle with rose-purple flowers and conspicuous white veins in the leaves. It has become naturalized in waste places in Britain, particularly on limestone near the sea.

SERRATULA coronata. A large and tall Saw-wort from Russia, with tufted purple thistleheads and deeply-cut leaves with a bronze tinge. There is also a dwarf, late-flowering variety (*see* p. 177).

1 Echinops 'Veitch's Blue'   2 Echinops ritro   3 Cirsium rivulare atropurpureum
4 Centaurea dealbata steenbergii   5 Centaurea macrocephala

BRIGHT SUMMER BULBS, HARDY OR HALF-HARDY

The flowers shown on this page and p. 71 show what beautiful and interesting bulbous plants, apart from lilies, may be grown, not only in the spring, but all through the summer. Many of the plants on this page, however, which come from hot countries, mainly Africa, are not hardy in Britain and must either be lifted in the autumn or given protection through the winter.

1 GLADIOLUS **nanus** 'Peach Blossom'. *G. nanus* is the result of a cross made in England by a Chelsea nurseryman between the species *G. tristis*, (pale yellow) and *G. cardinalis* (bright red), both from South Africa. None of these early-flowering gladioli are hardy in cold places and even in warm ones are best planted in a south border under a wall, if they are to be kept in the open. For cultivation in pots they are excellent, in which case the pots should be plunged in a cold frame until March and then moved into a cool or cold greenhouse. They fail if given much heat. As well as the variety illustrated, one of the original ones, 'The Bride', pure white, is still a favourite. There are several new strains of early flowerers, but these have not yet been well tested. For autumn-flowering gladioli, *see* p. 174.

2 CURTONUS **paniculatus (Antholyza paniculata).** A native of the Transvaal and Natal and quite hardy in Britain. The flowers on 4-ft. stems, together with the long-pleated leaves, add a distinct note to any border.

CROCOSMIA **masonorum.** A plant somewhat similar in growth and recently introduced from South Africa, with large clear-orange blossoms, all facing upwards, on 2-ft. arching stems. It appears to be quite hardy, which has been fully tested in the 1962–3 winter.

3 MONTBRETIA 'Solfaterre'. Montbretias are the results of a cross between *Crocosmia aurea* and *C. (montbretia) pottsii*, and the group is now correctly known as *Crocosmia x crocosmiiflora*. The older and small-flowered varieties, such as the one illustrated, are very hardy and vigorous plants which will grow almost anywhere, and are suitable for planting in rough grass. The newer varieties have stems up to 3 ft. and larger flowers. The first of these was the pale orange 'Star of the East' which, with others of the same group, was bred at Earlham in Norfolk. They are not as hardy as the older ones, needing some protection in cold districts and in hard winters, and are best planted in spring. Good varieties, with flowers about 3 in. across, are: 'Comet', golden-orange with a band of crimson and a yellow centre; 'His Majesty', scarlet shading to gold; 'James Coey', vermilion with orange centre; and 'Lady Wilson', clear-orange and very large.

4 ACIDANTHERA **bicolor murielae.** An Abyssinian tender plant, but worth growing because as well as being beautiful it is very fragrant. The flower stems are 2½–3½ ft. tall and may bear six or more flowers. The corms should be planted in late April and usually flower in September. They must be lifted before severe frost sets in, dried off, and kept in a warm place during the winter. Without winter warmth they will not flower freely the next summer. They make good pot plants.

5 TIGRIDIA **pavonia** 'Giant Rouge'. Tigridias come from the mountains of Mexico and are extremely showy late-summer bulbous plants. They are hardy in the south and west and mild districts generally, where they will increase by self-sown seed. Elsewhere they must be lifted when the foliage becomes yellow, dried, and stored in a frost-free place. Each flower lasts only one day, but a succession of six or more are produced from the same stem.

Tigridias like plenty of moisture while in growth, as in nature they grow in damp situations. There is a wide range of colours from pure white to yellows, scarlet and crimson, and even lilac; some are spotted, some not.

DIERAMA **pulcherrimum (Wand Flower).** This South African plant has a corm-like rootstock. The leaves are like iris leaves, and from the slender stem up to 5 ft. long dangle large bells, white, pink, mauve, or purple. Dierama is fairly hardy, but in cold places needs a border against a wall. When suited, it will produce plenty of self-sown seedlings. These must be transplanted as seedlings, for established plants very much dislike disturbance. There are named varieties, but seedlings will give a wide variety.

GALTONIA **candicans.** A lily-like plant from South Africa named after the 19th-century traveller, Francis Galton. It grows about 3–4 ft. high, and the stems carry fifteen or so fragrant, pure white, drooping flowers. It will grow well in a sunny position in well-drained, light, rich soil, and if the bulbs are buried 6–7 ins. deep, they will survive the winter. They dislike being disturbed.

1 GLADIOLUS NANUS 'PEACH BLOSSOM' 2 CURTONUS PANICULATUS 3 MONTBRETIA 'SOLFATERRE'
4 ACIDANTHERA BICOLOR MURIELAE 5 TIGRIDIA PAVONIA 'GIANT ROUGE'

TALL HERBACEOUS PLANTS FOR COOL, MOIST SOILS

1 DIGITALIS ambigua (Foxglove), digitus=finger, the individual flowers being like the fingers of a glove. Although the native purple foxglove, *D. purpurea*, is best treated as a biennial, there are several good perennial foxgloves also suitable for a shady border, among shrubs, or in a woodland garden. They do best in a leafy soil which does not easily dry out. If the central spike is cut out when the flowers start to fade, the side shoots will develop and produce good flowers. Propagation is by seed, or the plants of the perennials can be divided.

Crosses with *D. purpurea* and other European foxgloves have produced varieties in pure white, primrose, yellow, pink, and crimson, and ranging in height from 3–4 ft. or more to dwarf varieties from 1–2 ft. The hybrid *D. x mertonensis* has handsome old-rose flowers, richly spotted, and dark green foliage. *D. lutea* is honey-coloured and rather short. An unusual strain 'Excelsior' has been developed from an American sport with pure white flowers born horizontally all round the spike. This strain produces bold spikes 5 ft. or more tall in a variety of colours.

2 ASTRANTIA major, *astron*=star. An old-fashioned plant typical of cottage gardens, and, though not spectacular, having individuality and charm of its own. It lasts well when picked and is useful in floral decorations. It has local country names: 'Hattie's Pincushion', or 'The Melancholy Gentleman'. It will grow in any ordinary soil so long as it is sufficiently moist, especially damp woodland, and can be increased by division or seed. It grows up to 2 ft. tall. There is a smaller species, *A. carniolica*, which is up to 1 ft. tall, and has a reddish variety, *rubra*.

3 CIMICIFUGA racemosa (Bugbane, Bugwort), *cimex*=bug, *fugo*=flee, because an insecticide was made from the plant, especially from *C. foetida*. Cimicifugas are hardy graceful plants which, if grown in a moist and shady situation, grow taller than the other plants on this page, up to 6 ft. or more, and flower in July and August. They have handsome foliage. They look particularly attractive in the woodland garden, a good place to grow them for some, though not *C. racemosa*, have a rather unpleasant smell, unattractive in a flower border. They are best increased by division.

C. cordifolia (*americana*) is a creamy-white species on dark stems about 3 ft. tall; and the variety 'White Pearl' has branched stems and pale green leaves. *C. japonica* from Japan, also white, is late-flowering.

ACTAEA spicata (Herb Christopher, Baneberry), *aktaia*=elder, because the leaves resemble those of the elder tree. This moisture and shade-loving plant, a rather rare native of Britain, can be grown in a shady corner of the border or in woodland. The whitish flowers are rather insignificant, somewhat like a spiraea, but the clusters of large berries carried on stiff stems above the leaves are decorative when they turn a shiny purplish-black. They are poisonous — hence the name Baneberry. *A. spicata alba* has white berries, and *rubra* has red berries. They grow from 2–3 ft. tall.

THALICTRUM (Meadow Rue). This belongs to the same family as the last two plants. Some species are very attractive flowering plants (*see* p. 149); others are grown more for their foliage, resembling maiden-hair fern, than for their yellowish feathery flowers which are not very showy. *T. speciosissimum* and *T. flavum* are useful border plants for shady places and make good clumps of attractive foliage. The conspicuous long stamens make the otherwise rather inconspicuous flowers attractive. The former grows very tall — up to 6 ft. *T. minus*, which is shorter, has elegant foliage. The Alpine Meadow Rue (*T. alpinus*) is described on p. 34.

4 DICENTRA formosa 'Bountiful' (Bleeding Heart), *di*=double, *kentron*=spur. Dicentras are old-fashioned cottage-garden plants very useful for moist shady north borders, where not many other plants will succeed. They have several country names, such as 'Lyre Plant', 'Dutchman's Breeches', 'Lady in the Bath'. The fern-like, slightly glaucous foliage, which is crimson when it first appears, is one of its charms. The dwarf varieties grow well under trees and make good ground cover. As the roots are very brittle, they should not be disturbed more than possible, and to increase them, the clumps should be carefully lifted and divided in July. Most dicentras grow about 18 ins. tall and start flowering in May. The species *D. eximea* is rather smaller and has a white form. *D. spectabilis* is the tallest and most handsome, with rosy-crimson flowers, but it is tender to late spring frosts.

1 Digitalis ambigua   2 Astrantia major
3 Cimicifuga racemosa   4 Dicentra formosa

BOLD WATERSIDE OR MOISTURE-LOVING PLANTS

All these plants are large, some of them very large, with rather a coarse growth and showy flowers. In order to reach their full size they all need moisture, and some do better beside a pond. They are best propagated by division in the spring.

1-2 LIGULARIA *ligula*=strap, because of the strap shape of the petals. Most of them come from China, and they are closely related to Senecio, with which they used to be grouped. They have big circular leaves and stout flower-stems set with large, fleshy, daisy-like flowers. The two species illustrated grow about 4 ft. tall; the bronze-centred 'Gregynog Gold' is rather shorter; and the golden-yellow *L. wilsoniana*, and the deep yellow hybrid *L. x hessei* grow up to 5 or 6 ft. Some varieties have dark stems and purplish leaves.

SENECIO (Ragwort). This is an enormous and very varied genus with about 1,300 species, ranging from huge tree-like plants of the tropics to the common ragworts and groundsels of the British countryside. There are also late-flowering garden shrubs (*see* p. 161).

Among the summer-flowering herbaceous species is the white *S. smithii*, a 3-ft. plant from Chile. Rather later-flowering are the 2-ft. carmine-purple *S. pulcher* from Uruguay, and the much taller *S. tanguticus* from China, which has a feathery mass of small yellow flowers with silver bracts.

3-4 LOBELIA, named after Matthew Lobel, physician to James I. This is another very large and varied genus. ranging from the little half-hardy annual *L. erinus* (*see* p. 140) to the giant lobelias from Central Africa. The tall herbaceous lobelias are not completely hardy and need winter protection; in cold districts they should be lifted and wintered in a frame. Most of them are in flower by July and last into October. Their colours range from vermilion, scarlet, violet, purple, blue, and white, and some varieties have rich crimson or beetroot-coloured foliage.

Two very good species, the 3-ft. vermilion *L. fulgens* (3) with coloured foliage and the 4–5-ft. *L. cardinalis* with green foliage cross freely with the blue *L. syphilitica*, producing varieties such as the rich purple 4-ft. 'Purple Emperor' and the rather shorter vermilion-red 'Queen Victoria' with bronzy-purple foliage. *L. syphilitica* is blue and about 2 ft., and has a white form.

5 BUPHTHALMUM speciosum. A large, daisy-like, aromatic plant from South Europe, about 4 ft. tall, which looks its best in a large border or in bold groups in a woodland garden. There is also a much shorter September-flowering American species, *B. salicifolium* (*see* p. 147).

HERACLEUM villosum (Cartwheel Flower). This enormous cow parsnip, also known as *H. giganteum*, is a magnificent plant for a wild garden where there is room for a really imposing plant. It grows 8–10 ft. tall, has leaves a yard wide, and immense heads with thousands of little white flowers. The stout cylindrical stems are copper-coloured. It sows itself freely, and so it is better to cut off the seed heads before the seeds fall.

RANUNCULUS lingua grandiflora (Greater Spearwort). This is a garden variety of the rather rare British *R. lingua* of marshes and fens. It has the same spear-like leaves, and very large yellow buttercup flowers on stems 2–3 ft. long.

1 Ligularia veitchiana   2 Ligularia clivorum   3 Lobelia fulgens
4 Lobelia vedrariensis   5 Buphthalmum speciosum

SUMMER PERENNIAL DAISIES, PINK AND BLUE

1 CATANANCHE **caerulea (Cupid's Dart).** A plant introduced from South Europe as early as 1596, but never very common. The long, wiry flower-stems rise about 2½ ft. from thick clumps of grassy foliage, and the buds are encased in overlapping silvery bracts, which give the effect of a patch of silver in the border. Catananches flower over a long period from July onwards, and are excellent for cutting and also for drying for winter decoration (*see* p. 190). They do best in a dry border, and survive the winter better if some of the flower stalks are removed after the end of August. They are best increased by seed.

VARIETIES: *C. c. major*, extra large, lavender blue; *major alba*, white; *bicolor*, blue and white.

2 ECHINACEA **purpurea**, sometimes known as the purple cone flower (*echinos* = hedgehog), is classed as *Rudbeckia purpurea* (*see* p. 147). It was introduced to Britain from America in 1799, and it and its varieties help to give much-needed colour to a border in August. Their sturdy stems, about 2½ ft. tall, and the enormous daisy flowers ranging in colour from rose-red to smoky purple, with conspicuous dark or orange centres, are excellent for cutting. The wide-spaced petals are usually rather narrow, although the newest variety, E. 'Robert Bloom', has broader petals.

VARIETIES: 'Abendsonne', rose-red; 'Earliest of all', deep pinky-purple; 'Robert Bloom', carmine-purple with orange centre; 'The King', smoky purple with dark centre and 4 ft.

3 PYRETHRUM **(Chrysanthemum coccineum).** This has been grown in Britain for a very long time, but the typical cottage-garden plant of the 19th century had small flowers and harsh colours compared with the magnificent pyrethrums of today. These flowers, both single and double, grow on long, sturdy stalks and include many lovely colours. Their main flowering time is May and June, but most varieties have a second flowering in late August and September. They do best in a fairly light soil, and should be planted in the spring and divided at least every third year, also in the spring. They grow about 2 ft. tall.

VARIETIES: (*Single*) 'Snow White'; 'Brenda', large rose; 'Evenglow', light salmon; 'James Kelway', crimson-scarlet; 'Marjorie Robinson', rose-pink; 'Sam Robinson', large deep pink; 'Salmon Beauty'; 'Scarlet Glow'.
(*Double*) 'Andromeda', deep rose; 'J. N. Twerdy', deep crimson-red; 'Panorama', pale pink; 'Princess Mary' and 'Progress', rose-pink; 'Queen Mary', peach-pink; 'Victoria', large full white; 'White Queen Mary'.

CHRYSANTHEMUM **uliginosum** An old plant which used to be called a pyrethrum, and is now coming back to favour. It has large white, green-centred daisies on stiff 4–6-ft. stems, and although its name implies a love of moisture, it grows well in any position. It flowers later than pyrethrums — in August to November.

4 ERIGERON **(Fleabane).** Erigerons have been grown in Britain since 1628 and comprise a very large family ranging from the tiny *E. mucronatus* from Australia, with its clouds of pink and white daisies all through the season, to *E. glaucus*, the fleshy rock aster of seaside cliffs and walls. Erigerons make good mid-border plants, and some of the old cottage-garden varieties, such as *E. speciosus* 'Quakeress' and the little pink *E. philadelphicus*, are well worth growing.

Modern erigerons have larger flowers in much stronger colours and a more robust habit of growth. They start flowering in June and may still be producing odd blooms in September. They can be increased by division in October or March, and also by cuttings.

VARIETIES: 'Unity', pink, 2 ft.; 'Charity', light lavender-pink, 2 ft.; 'Dimity', copper buds and pink flowers, 1 ft.; 'Vanity', late pink, 2½ ft.; 'Foerster's Liebling', deep violet-pink semi-double, 1½ ft.; 'Darkest of all', deep violet with golden eye, 1½ ft.; 'Dignity', violet, 2 ft.; *macranthus* (*Mesa-grande*), deep blue, 2 ft.; 'Mrs. F. H. Beale', blue, 1 ft.; 'Wupperthal', violet-mauve, 2½ ft.

CHRYSANTHEMUM **maximum.** The old Shasta Daisy of Victorian borders, but modern varieties, especially double ones, are more interesting and not so tall. They last well in water when picked. Most of them flower in July.

VARIETIES: 'Esther Read', double white, 2 ft.; 'Horace Read', double white with quilled petals, 2 ft.; 'Phyllis Smith', single with narrow fringed petals, 3 ft.; 'Wirral Supreme', large white solid double flowers, 4 ft.

5 ASTER **amellus.** The asters derived from *A. amellus* are much shorter than ordinary michaelmas daisies (*see* p. 179). The large flowers, often 3 ins. across, are borne in broad, branched heads on sturdy stems, with dark, rather rough foliage. A well-grown clump gives the effect of a rounded bush, 2–2½ ft. high, which seldom needs staking. The flowers will last a week in water if cut while still young.

Amellus asters do not increase quickly. They must be planted in spring and divided also in spring, when the woody crowns can be lifted, and each flowering stem with its complement of fine roots pulled from the plant. Cuttings of side shoots can also be taken in autumn.

VARIETIES: *July-flowering:* 'Junifreud', lavender-blue, rather short.
August-flowering: A. x *frikartii* 'Wonder of Stafa', clear blue; 'Lac de Geneve', soft blue.
September-flowering: 'Bessie Chapman', violet-blue; 'King George', dark violet-blue with orange eye; 'Brilliant', deep rose-pink, 2 ft.; 'Mrs. Ralph Woods', rosy-pink; 'Sonia', medium pink.

1 Catananche caerulea major   2 Echinacea purpurea 'The King'   3 Pyrethrum 'E. M. Robinson'
4 Erigeron 'Unity'   5 Aster x frikartii 'Wonder of Stafa'

GREENHOUSE SHRUBBY PLANTS FOR BEDDING

None of the plants on this page are hardy, but all can be grown in a cool greenhouse and bedded out in early summer, usually to follow spring-flowering plants such as wallflowers, polyanthus, and bulbs. Such bedding out is also often done with half-hardy annuals, but the perennial shrubby plants are more reliable for continuous colour, especially in bad weather. Bedding out, however, is a good deal of work and depends on considerable greenhouse space. This popular form of Victorian gardening is now largely confined to beds immediately near the house or to public gardens and parks.

1 HELIOTROPIUM peruvianum (Cherry Pie), *helios* = sun, *tropos* = turning. A greenhouse shrub very popular in Victorian days and first introduced in 1757. Most of the varieties grown are derived from *H. peruvianum*, which in Peru can grow into a tall shrub. For bedding, compact plants are grown from cuttings taken in the autumn; but taller plants, 1½–2 ft. tall, raised from seed are used in some bedding schemes to combine with shorter plants. They do not need much heat but cannot stand frost. There are a number of varieties in deep purple, violet, blue, lilac, and white. These come true from cuttings but not from seed.

2 PELARGONIUM, *pelargos* = stork, because the 'beak' of the fruit resembles that of a stork. The plants commonly, though incorrectly, known as geraniums, have been among the most popular bedding plants because they give non-stop colour throughout the season. They are invaluable window-box plants for town houses.

There are several groups of pelargoniums, of which the most popular are the zonal pelargoniums (geraniums), so called because the roundish lobed leaves have more or less apparent dark horseshoe markings. The very many garden varieties are hybrids mainly developed from *P. zonale* and *P. inquinans*, which have pink, red, carmine, or white flowers. The modern varieties include doubles as well as singles and purple, orange, salmon-pink and other shades, as well as the well-established and popular vermilions, such as 'Paul Crampel' and 'Gustav Emich'. There are a number with variegated leaves, often with yellow or pale green background and black, red, gold, or dark green zones.

Ivy-leaved pelargoniums (derived from *P. peltatum*), with single or double flowers, are not so suitable for bedding, except for very elaborate schemes, but can be used for growing over walls or hanging over the edge of tubs.

Regal or show pelargoniums, such as the one illustrated, have larger and fewer flowers, toothed leaves, and a rather shorter flowering period. The petals, as with the pink 'Carisbrooke', are sometimes fringed. They are very showy but are often subject to attack from aphis and white fly.

Scented-leaved pelargoniums, many of which have been cultivated for a long time, are grown for foliage rather than flowers. The leaves vary in shade and are scented lemon, almond, rose, peppermint, or nutmeg.

3 BEGONIA, named after Michel Begon, a 17th-century French Governor of Canada. There are a great many both tuberous- and fibrous-rooted varieties which are excellent for bedding and give a rich show in splendid colours of both single and double flowers for a long season. Their foliage also is very decorative. Both kinds can be grown from seed, but, in fact, the tuberous-rooted kinds are generally bought as tubers, lifted and dried off in the autumn, and kept through the winter in a frost-proof place.

The tuberous-rooted begonias are the larger and more showy. They prefer a fairly cool moist situation and a peaty loamy soil. In the spring they are started into growth in boxes of moist peat in a moderately warm greenhouse, and are planted out in June. The fibrous-rooted begonias make compact bushy plants about a foot high with smaller flowers, generally in shades of white, pink, and red. They are useful bedding plants as they will stand up to bad weather.

4 COLEUS blumei. Coleus are foliage plants only, the flowers being unimportant. They are usually grown from seed as half-hardy annuals, but they can also be grown from cuttings. There is a wide variety of foliage colours, a good strain of mixed seed such as 'Prize', 'Monarch', or 'Giant' producing many interesting plants from which cuttings can be taken. The plants can be kept compact and well shaped by pinching off the points of the shoots at an early stage.

DAHLIA, dwarf bedding. These dwarf hybrids are usually grown from seed sown in late March and planted out in rich soil in full sun in June. The single-flowered or 'Coltness' group grow 12–18 ins. high and come true from seed in whites, yellows, and various shades of pink, scarlet, and crimson. Small decorative double or semi-double dahlias grow rather taller and make bushy plants which need no staking. It is important to remove the flower heads as they fade in order to prolong the flowering season. For other dahlias, see p. 167.

CHRYSANTHEMUM frutescens (Marguerite or Paris Daisy). A very reliable shrubby daisy from the Canary Islands with white ray petals and yellow disks, which flowers continuously through the summer. This plant and 'geraniums', lobelias, and calceolarias were the popular Victorian bedding plants.

1 HELIOTROPIUM PERUVIANUM   2 PELARGONIUM 'SHOW' VARIETY
3 BEGONIA, TUBEROUS-ROOTED, 'SUSAN HOLT'   4 COLEUS BLUMEI

TALLER HALF-HARDY ANNUALS. 1

All the plants on this page can be grown as half-hardy annuals, that is, sown in February or March under glass and planted out when danger of frost is over, usually in May. In this way they have a long enough season of growth and avoid late frosts. The China Asters, Stocks, Salvias, and Antirrhinums are very popular bedding out plants.

1 CLEOME spinosa (Spider Plant). A plant from the southern states of North America which grows 3-4 ft. tall. It is covered with spines, and the leaves when bruised have an unpleasant smell. The light purple flowers have long spidery stamens. There is a pink variety 'Pink Queen', and a white one. The plants remain in flower for a very long time. They need a warm, well-cultivated soil which should never get too dry.

2 CALLISTEPHUS chinensis (China Aster). The original plant which came from China and Japan had single purple flowers, and grew about 2 ft. tall. There is now a great variety of types, single, double, incurved, anemone-flowered, ray-petalled, etc. — flowering from 6 ins. to 3 ft. tall, with button-like to large shaggy flower heads. There is almost every shade of colour, and they flower from June to October. They grow best in a rich, well-cultivated loam, and will tolerate some shade.

3 OENOTHERA trichocalyx (Evening Primrose). Oenotheras come from the temperate regions of North and South America. The common one, O. biennis, is a hardy biennial which will sow itself and does well in light shade. The best forms have primrose-yellow flowers and bright red flower stems and calyces, and grow to a foot high. O. odorata, which is like a less stout O. biennis but very fragrant, can be grown either as a biennial or a hardy annual.
The species illustrated, O. trichocalyx, comes from California and, although a biennial, is better grown as a half-hardy annual. The grey-leaved, branching, plant is 12–18 ins. tall, and the pure white fragrant flowers stay open during the day. Another species, O. acaulis, which can be grown as a half-hardy annual, is a trailing plant suitable for rock gardens, and has white flowers shading to rose, or yellow in the variety aurea. For perennial oenothera, see p. 109.

4 DIANTHUS barbatus 'Summer Beauty' (Annual Sweet William). These bushy plants, 15–18 ins. tall, flower in July and August and have the full range of Sweet William colours. See page 79.

5 SALVIA splendens (Scarlet Sage). A tender perennial from Brazil, grown in Britain as a half-hardy annual. If planted out in early June, it will flower from July into the autumn. Dwarf varieties such as 'Blaze of Fire' and the illustrated 'Dwarf Salmon' are early flowering and grow to 12 ins. tall. The varieties 'Fireball' and 'Harbinger' are rather taller and flower rather later. Another half-hardy perennial best treated as a half-hardy annual is S. farinacea, which is 2–3 ft. tall and has long spikes of lavender-blue flowers with white hairy calyces and shiny bright leaves. 'Blue Bedder' is a deeper blue form. See also pages 105, 108, and 153.

GILIA rubra. This plant is best treated as a half-hardy biennial, sown under glass in September. It grows 3–4 ft. tall, and the stems, clad with finely-cut foliage, carry spikes of brilliant scarlet flowers from July to October. There are also less tall hardy-annual species, such as the lavender-blue G. capitata, and G. tricolor in shades of white, lavender, and pink, with gold or purple centres. G. x hybrida is a dwarf variety, 3–6 ins. tall, in a wide range of colours.

ANTIRRHINUM majus (Snapdragon). The garden varieties have been developed from a branching perennial plant of Mediterranean countries, usually crimson magenta, but occasionally white. There are varieties in most colours except blues, and the plants range in size from 3 ft. or more to about a foot. Although fairly hardy, they are best grown as half-hardy annuals, but will sometimes persist, and will naturalize in old walls and such places. They need well-cultivated, well-drained soil, but without fresh manure.

MATTHIOLA incana (Ten-week Stocks). Strains of these (Brompton Stocks) can be grown as hardy biennials to flower in May and June (see p. 33). Other strains, such as 'Giant Perfection', can be sown under glass in March and flower about 10 weeks later. They need an open situation, rich soil with some lime, good drainage, and enough moisture in the summer. There is now a strain, 'Hansen's 100% Double', which produces all double flowers.

1 Cleome spinosa   2 Callistephus chinensis 'Giant Ray'   3 Oenothera trichocalyx
4 Dianthus barbatus 'Summer Beauty'   5 Salvia splendens 'Dwarf Salmon'

TALLER HALF-HARDY ANNUALS. 2

For general notes on these half-hardy annuals see p. 126.

1-2 AMARANTHUS. These plants, which have been grown in English gardens since Tudor times, have several common names, such as 'Prince's Feather' (*A. hypochondriacus*) and 'Joseph's Coat' (*A. melanchŏlicus tricolor*), a species with very ornamental foliage. The scientific name means 'not withering', for the flowers hold their colour for a long time. Some species, the well-known 'Love Lies Bleeding' (*A. caudatus*), for example, can be treated as hardy annuals, but most do better if sown under glass and planted out in a sunny place in late May. They flower better in not too rich a soil but with sufficient moisture. They grow well in pots.

A. caudatus grows 2–3 ft. tall and has long, drooping, red panicles of flowers. The one illustrated, *A. c. viridis* (2), is a green form. *A. salicifolius* (1) has rather more upright flower spikes. The varieties of *A. melancholicus* with their rich crimson, yellow, and bronze-green foliage are rather more dwarf.

CELSIA cretica. This plant is, in fact, fairly hardy, and can be grown as a hardy biennial (*see* p. 33) in favourable positions and will flower in June. If grown as a half-hardy annual and sown in March, it throws up tall spikes of large, sweetly-scented, golden-yellow flowers, spotted brown, in July and August. It is closely related to and much resembles verbascum (*see* p. 113).

3 SALPIGLOSSIS sinuata. A good mixture from any reliable seedsman produces a remarkable range of rich colours in these sticky, hairy plants from Chile — members of the potato and tobacco family (*Solanaceae*). The plants grow 2–3 ft. tall, and the large flowers may be ivory and gold, golden-yellow, rich crimson or violet, blue and gold, or many other combinations of colour. They do much better in a warm situation protected from the wind and in a rich soil. They enjoy heat but should not be allowed to get dry while making their early growth.

4 NICOTIANA alata (Tobacco Plant). In tropical America, where this plant comes from, it grows as a perennial, but it will not stand frost. There is also a very sweet-scented, white-flowered species from Australia, *N. suaveolens*, which does well as a pot plant. The common Tobacco, *N. tabacum*, has red flowers. *N. alata* has greenish-white flowers, and there are hybrids in pink, red, and crimson. Most nicotianas remain closed during the day but open in the evening when their scent fills the air; but the variety 'Sensation Mixed' is open during the day also. They need rich, well-cultivated soil, but will thrive in partial shade, so long as it is not too dry.

DATURA (Angel's Trumpets). Most daturas, members of the potato and tobacco family, are rather tender shrubs or small trees, but *D. metel* and varieties of it can be grown as half-hardy annuals, about 2–4 ft. tall. The large trumpet-shaped flowers are yellow or white tinged with purple and are sweet-scented. They need warm positions and do best in the south.

IMPATIENS (Balsam). The name refers to the violent discharge of the seeds from the pod, when ripe. The most attractive Balsams, *I. balsamina* and *I. holstii*, are tender annuals suitable for greenhouses or warm situations in the south. These grow about 18 ins. tall and have large red or scarlet flowers. *I. roylei*, which is a rather coarse plant 5–6 ft. tall, is a hardy annual and has conspicuous purple or white flowers.

1 Amaranthus salicifolius   2 Amaranthus caudatus viridis   3 Salpiglossis sinuata
4 Nicotiana alata

TALLER HARDY ANNUALS

All the plants on this page need open sunny positions and well-drained soil. They are easy to grow, though members of the Malvaceae (Mallow family) sometimes get hollyhock rust which attacks their leaves. Nigella and the tall double godetias can be grown as biennials and survive all but severe winters, making large plants which flower in May. Hollyhocks, if not attacked by rust, will survive as perennials. Gypsophila, malope, and lavatera should be sown in late April.

1 GYPSOPHILA **elegans.** Most gypsophilas are perennial (*see* p. 148). This slender annual grows 12–18 ins. tall and has white, pink, rose, and crimson varieties. Gypsophilas like a dry soil and do well if old brick rubbish is mixed with the soil.

2 MALOPE **trifida.** *Malope* is an old Greek name for a kind of annual mallow, a close relative to lavatera. It is a Mediterranean native, and there are white, purple, pink, and deep crimson varieties. Malope is easily grown but prefers a sandy soil. It grows about a foot tall.

LAVATERA **trimestris.** This annual mallow from the Mediterranean region makes a robust spreading plant, 2–3 ft. tall or taller. It can make a good flowering hedge and will continue to produce large mallow-like flowers in white and shades of rose all through the summer.

ALTHAEA **rosea (Hollyhock).** A very well-known English cottage-garden flower of the Mallow family, which is best grown from seed as an annual or biennial. It thrives very well in town gardens, and there are both single and double varieties in a wide range of colours.

3 NIGELLA **damascena (Love-in-a-Mist).** The name comes from *niger* =black, because of the colour of the seeds. If grown as an annual it grows a foot or more high, but as a biennial it makes a strong, branching plant 1½–2 ft. tall. There are deep blue and white varieties, and the seed pods as well as the flowers are decorative.

N. hispanica (Fennel Flower) has grey foliage and its deep violet-blue flowers have blood-red stamens.

4 GODETIA. These annuals from the western states of U.S.A. are named after C. H. Godet, a 19th-century Swiss botanist. There are two main groups, the taller ones which derive from *G. amoena* and grow 2 ft. or more tall, and the semi-dwarf ones which derive from *G. grandiflora* and grow about a foot tall. As well, there is the distinct 'Lavender Gem' variety, probably derived from *G. viminea*, which has a more slender growth and lavender and white flowers with deep purple stamens.

There are both single and double or azalea-flowered godetias and a wide range of colours — mostly whites, pinks, and crimsons but also salmon, scarlet, orange, and mauve-blue. They should be sown as early in spring as the season allows so as to give as long a growing time as possible. They have a long season of flowering and are very useful for bedding and also for window-boxes.

CLARKIA. A Californian annual of the same family as godetia and grown in the same way. It is named after Captain William Clark who explored the Rocky Mountains and beyond in 1806. Like godetia, there are single and double forms in a wide range of colours. Those derived from *C. elegans* grow about 2 ft. or more tall, while *C. pulchella* produces shorter and more branched plants. Clarkias can be sown in the autumn and survive if the winter is not too severe, in which case they make taller, stouter plants.

1 GYPSOPHILA ELEGANS   2 MALOPE TRIFIDA   3 NIGELLA DAMASCENA
4 GODETIA 'SUTTON'S INTERMEDIATE BRILLIANT'

BRIGHT SMALL HARDY ANNUALS

These and the plants shown on p. 135 can all be grown from seed sown in the spring in the open ground where they are to flower. When large enough to handle, they should be thinned out enough to allow room for each plant to grow to its full size. Many of these bright hardy annuals came originally from California. They will grow in any ordinary garden soil.

1 SILENE oculata (Viscaria). Originally bright purple, this gay hardy annual can now be obtained in a mixture of colours, including white, shades of pink, red and carmine, pale blue and rich delphinium blue. Either mixed colours or separate colours true from seed can be bought. Viscarias are very suitable for an informal garden, usually growing 12–15 ins. tall. Dwarf-growing varieties only 6 ins. high are also available. If sown in pots in September and kept in a cool house through the winter, they will flower in April and May as house plants. Other Silenes are shown on pp. 135 and 177.

2 MENTZELIA lindleyi (Bartonia aurea), a very showy Californian hardy annual, descriptively called 'Blazing Star'. The plant grows 1½–2 ft. tall, and the golden-yellow flowers are 2 ins. across. They do not open in dull weather, but glow in the sunshine and will open in water if gathered. They are slightly fragrant.

3 LINUM grandiflorum rubrum (Scarlet Flax). Linums are mostly European or North African plants which have been grown since prehistoric times for their fibres (linen) and for the oil in their seeds (linseed). Common Flax (L. usitatissimum), which is the species developed commercially, has attractive pale blue flowers and is well worth growing, especially for the wild garden. L. grandiflorum, one of the most showy of hardy annuals is a slender plant, 12–15 ins. high. It looks best massed in groups in a mixed border. The petals have a silky sheen on them which is very attractive when the flowers rustle in a slight breeze. There is also a white form. Linums will grow in any well-drained soil but prefer sand and leaf-mould. There are also perennial linums and dwarf shrubs suitable for the rock garden (see p. 42).

4 CONVOLVULUS tricolor (minor). The garden dwarf convolvulus is a showy hardy annual from Southern Europe. The bushy plants grow 12–15 ins., and when in full sun make a brilliant show in flower. Pale blue, dark blue, rose, and pink varieties can be obtained. For the climbing convolvulus see p. 163.

5 NEMOPHILA menziesii insignis is a slender spreading plant growing to a height of 6–8 ins. It is useful for edging, and for patches in the front of a border or in a rock garden, and it will tolerate light shade and enjoys a moist cool situation. There are various forms of Nemophila menziesii, including pure white, deep purple, and spotted. It is very hardy and can not only be sown in the spring for summer flowering but also in favourable situations in autumn for spring flowering.

6 PHACELIA campanularia. This Californian plant, which grows 8–9 ins. high and has attractive greyish foliage, is suitable for edging and for patches in the rock garden. Its bright colours attract bees. It should be sown in March or April in a sunny position, and also in a protected place in September for spring flowering.

P. viscida, also gentian-blue but with rose shading, grows slightly taller than P. campanularia and has fresh green foliage. P. tanacetifolia is taller still and has curled flower-heads of soft lavender blue; and P. brachyloba, the tallest, has white flowers with yellow eyes.

PLATYSTEMON californicus (Cream-cups of California), a grey-leaved hardy annual with small poppy-like cream-coloured flowers born on 9–10 in. stalks. It is very hardy and frequently sows itself in the garden; so it is very suitable for autumn-sowing. Like most annual poppies (see p. 83), it prefers a sandy loam soil.

LIMNANTHES douglasii. This low-growing Californian hardy annual has shiny green foliage and open yellow flowers edged with white, which are beloved of bees. It is a good edging plant, growing about 6 ins. high. It is hardy and may be sown in the open in September to flower in April–June, as well as in the spring for summer flowering.

1 SILENE OCULATA   2 MENTZELIA LINDLEYI   3 LINUM GRANDIFLORUM RUBRUM
4 CONVOLVULUS TRICOLOR   5 NEMOPHILA MENZIESII   6 PHACELIA CAMPANULARIA

PALE, SMALL, HARDY ANNUALS

These, like the plants shown on p. 133, are easily grown from seed in any ordinary soil, though acid soils need dressings of lime. An important factor is the preparation of the seed-bed, which should be worked well at a time when the soil is not wet and sticky. The seeds are sown thinly and evenly, and then lightly covered with fine soil. Many of the plants given here, such as linaria, alyssum, malcomia, and silene, are hardy enough to be sown in the autumn and so to flower in early summer. There are a great many hardy annuals, and these pages can make only a selection.

1 ASPERULA (Woodruff). There are both perennial and annual asperulas which are related to the wild Woodruff (*A. odorata*) and Squinancy Wort (*A. cynanchica*), both of which are white. *A. orientalis* grows about 12 ins. tall and comes from Asia Minor. It does well in moist shady places — for example, in a woodland garden. It is very fragrant.

2 LINARIA (Toadflax). The dwarf *L. maroccana* illustrated here comes from Morocco and grows 9–12 ins. tall. The delicate snapdragon-like flowers come in a wide range of colouring, including purples and crimsons, and look best if grown in patches in the border or rock garden. *L. alpina* can be grown either as a perennial or annual. It is a spreading plant only 2–6 ins. high, and the violet-blue flowers have an orange patch on the lips. There are white and flesh-pink varieties. *L. reticulata*, another tiny annual, has deep purple flowers with copper-coloured or yellow lips.

COLLINSIA bicolor. Another snapdragon-like annual from California, growing 12–15 ins. tall and bearing lilac and white flowers on long slender spikes. Collinsia will tolerate light shade and is suitable for a woodland garden.

3 ALYSSUM maritimum (Sweet Alyssum). Most alyssums are perennials (*see* p. 41), but this species, correctly called *Lobularia maritima*, is a spreading, branching annual, growing about 6–9 ins. tall. The dwarf, carpet-making form, 'minima', is useful for growing between stones on a path or terrace. Sweet Alyssums, of which there are also rose-pink forms, are very sweet-scented and attract bees.

IBERIS (Candytuft). The plant is named after Iberia, an old name for Spain, where it is a native. It looks not unlike Sweet Alyssum and grows 6–12 ins. tall in a wide variety of colours. *I. umbellata* 'Rich Purple' and 'Dwarf Carmine' are good varieties, and *I. amara* 'Improved White Spiral' has fine large flowers.

4 MALCOMIA maritima (Virginian Stock). Although belonging to the same family as No. 3, the Cruciferae, malcomias are very different from the true stocks (*see* pp. 33, 127). Mixtures include a variety of colours which blend well together, the plants growing 6–9 ins. tall. They can be grown in cracks in paving stones and will tolerate shady places.

IONOPSIDIUM acaule (Violet Cress). This is another Crucifer suitable for crevices in shady places. The tiny tufted plant, only 2–3 ins. high, is covered with small violet-blue flowers. It often seeds itself about.

SPECULARIA speculum (Venus's Looking-glass). A campanula-like, violet-blue flower on slender branching stems, growing 9–12 ins. tall. There is a white and also a double form.

5 ECHIUM plantagineum. A dwarf, compact, annual borage, growing up to 12 ins. tall with sweet-scented flowers attractive to bees. It has been much improved in recent years and will succeed both in cold, wet seasons and also in dry.

6 SILENE (Catchfly). A large genus of annuals and perennials of which several are British wild flowers, including the dwarf reddish purple Moss Campion (*S. acaulis*). *S. pendula,* illustrated here, is very hardy and if sown in the autumn will flower in May and June. If sown in the spring, it will flower into September. There is a wide range of colours in both double and single flowers. *S. armeria* with rose-pink flowers is rather taller and often naturalizes itself in old walls. (*See* also pp. 133 and 177.)

EUPHORBIA (Spurge). This very large group consists mostly of shrubs and perennial herbs (*see* p. 13), but there are a few annuals. *E. heterophylla* (Mexican Fire Plant) grows about 2 ft. tall and has small orange-red flowers surrounded by bracts blotched with red and white. The dark-green foliage is sometimes variegated. *E. marginata* (Snow on the Mountains) has flowers with large white bracts and much white in the leaves. It flowers in September and lasts well.

RESEDA odorata (Mignonette). A plant grown mainly for its fragrance, though some of the newer, larger flowered varieties such as 'Golden Goliath' and 'Crimson Giant' are more showy. Reseda grows well in a rich compost with feeds of liquid manure.

MATRICARIA A hardy daisy-like plant, more attractive in its double forms. *M. eximia* (*Chrysanthemum parthenium*) has double varieties, 'Golden Ball' and 'Silver Ball', which make compact plants 10–12 ins. high and suitable for edgings. *M. maritima* 'Bridal Robe' is rather taller and has pure white double flowers.

1 ASPERULA ORIENTALIS   2 LINARIA MAROCCANA   3 ALYSSUM MARITIMUM
4 MALCOMIA MARITIMA   5 ECHIUM PLANTAGINEUM   6 SILENE PENDULA

ANNUAL DAISIES — MOSTLY FROM AMERICA

All the species described on this page have originated in North America, except for the Calendula, which is a native of southern Europe. Many come from Mexico or California, and some can be grown either as half-hardies, sown in gentle heat in March or April and planted out in May or June, or as hardies, sown in the open in May. Rudbeckia and calendula, if sown in June or July, can be treated as biennials (*see* p. 33). There are perennial species of many of these American daisies (*see* p. 147).

1 ZINNIA. The original species, *Z. elegans* illustrated here, was introduced to Britain from Mexico over 150 years ago. A wide range of colouring and different forms have now been developed, both single and double. Giant dahlia-flowered or giant mammoth zinnias grow 2–3 ft. tall with double flowers up to 5 ins. across. The miniature pompon or Lilliput zinnias grow 9–12 ins. tall with compact double flowers. *Z. haageana* (*angustifolia*) is a dwarf bushy species with single or semi-double flowers which will withstand bad weather and are useful for bedding.

Zinnias are best treated as half-hardies and they need rich soil and hot sunshine. The flowers last for a long time.

2-3 COSMOS (from a Greek word meaning 'beautiful). These are half-hardy plants from Mexico. The most usual species, *C. bipinnatus* (2), is a very slender well-branched plant about 3 ft. or more tall, with long wiry stems carrying large flowers in shades of white, pink, crimson, and purple. *C. diversifolius atrosanguineus* (Black Cosmos) grows only about 18 ins., and carries velvety-red flowers rather like single dahlias. *C. sulphureus* 'Orange Ruffles' (3) is a very slender plant with rather smaller flowers.

COREOPSIS (Tick-Seed). Both the scientific and popular names refer to the shape of the seed — *koris* =bug, *opsis* =like. The hardy annual coreopsis varies in colour from yellow to crimson-brown. *C. tinctoria atrosanguinea* is a fine form with rich dark-red flowers and grows 2–3 ft. tall. *C. drummondii* has a more spreading growth and clear yellow flowers with a crimson ring round the disk. *C. maritima* (often called *Leptosyne maritima*) has very large golden-yellow flowers and can be grown as a half-hardy annual or rather tender perennial. It makes a vigorous branching plant about 2 ft. tall.

BAERIA coronaria. A low-growing hardy annual from California. Its masses of golden-yellow flowers and finely-cut foliage make an attractive edging.

LAYIA elegans. This is a useful, showy, hardy annual for sunny places, which grows about 1 ft. tall and has yellow flowers tipped with white. There is a white variety.

4 RUDBECKIA hirta hybrida (Black-eyed Susan). These showy annual rudbeckias range in colours from lemon-yellow to bronze and crimson with dark centres. They are vigorous plants growing 2–3 ft. tall, with flowers often 3–4 ins. across. *R. bicolor* is not so tall. The variety 'Autumn Glow' has golden-yellow petals with rich, dark maroon disks, while 'Sutton's Crimson and Gold' has large flowers variously marked with chestnut and crimson.

HELIANTHUS annuus (Sunflower). The common Sunflower came to Britain from America over 300 years ago. In good soil it will grow 8 or more feet tall, each stem carrying a huge, usually yellow-red flower a foot or more across. Hybrids have been produced, of which a very good one is Sutton's 'Autumn Beauty', ranging in colour from pale primrose to chestnut-brown. These plants, which branch freely and grow 4–5 ft. tall, are very showy and not so coarse.

TITHONIA (Mexican Sunflower). These Central American daisies are half-hardy. *T. rotundifolia*, the best of them, grows about 5 ft. tall and carries striking rich orange-red dahlia-like flowers, 2–3 ins. across.

5 CALENDULA officinalis (Pot Marigold). The word *calendae* means 'first day of the month' and indicates that these marigolds flower nearly all the year round in sheltered places. *Officinalis* means that the plant was used medicinally by herbalists. Marigolds were used for flavouring soups or stews, hence the old English name 'Pot'.

The original marigolds have single orange flowers. Hardy varieties now grown, such as 'Orange King', 'Primrose Queen', 'Apricot Queen', are double, and there are taller, more shaggy varieties such as 'Sunshine' or 'Radio'. A good, single, long-stemmed variety with long orange petals and a dark chocolate centre is 'Nova'. Calendulas can be sown in the autumn and will survive all but severe winters and flower in March or April. They will grow in the poorest of soils. The variety illustrated is a new form, 'Crested Mixed'.

1 ZINNIA ELEGANS   2 COSMOS BIPINNATUS   3 COSMOS SULPHUREUS 'ORANGE RUFFLES'
4 RUDBECKIA HIRTA HYBRIDA   5 CALENDULA OFFICINALIS

ANNUAL SOUTH AFRICAN DAISIES

This colourful group of garden plants will grow and flower well in Britain if treated as half-hardy annuals. Most of them should be sown in March or April under glass and planted out in sunny positions in light soils in May. Many of them tend to close up except when the sun is shining. As with many of the daisy family, they hybridize freely, and a number of varieties of different colours have been produced.

1 GAZANIA. Gazanias, which hybridize very freely, have been much improved in recent years and will continue to flower the whole summer from June to the first autumn frosts. Two mixtures of colour are now available — red and bronze shades and pink and cream shades. They are very easily raised from seed if sown in early March in a cool greenhouse or a little later in a cold frame. They will stand more cold than many African daisies, and so can be hardened off and planted out early in May. They should be planted 12 ins. apart as the plants tend to spread. The flower stems rise 6–10 ins. above the attractive dark green foliage. A good strain of hybrids has flowers as much as 3 ins. across. Gazanias are not fastidious as to soil but must be planted in the sun; otherwise the flowers will not open. Although usually grown as annuals, gazanias are perennials and may be propagated by cuttings taken in autumn and wintered in a cold frame.

2-3 ARCTOTIS (**African Daisy**). The name means 'bear's ear', to which the pappus scales bear a resemblance. There are many hybrid varieties, such as Sutton's Special Hybrids (2) with a wide range of colours, including white, pink bronze, rich red, crimson, cream, yellow, orange, and wine shade, and *A. grandis* hybrids (3) with colours mostly pastel shades of white, ivory, buff, and salmon. The plants grow vigorously and have attractive grey foliage. They provide excellent cut flowers for day-time decoration, though they tend to close at night. They do well on a good loam in an open sunny situation, and treated as half-hardy annuals, will continue to flower until cut down by frost in autumn.

A new group of hybrids raised by Messrs. Sutton between Venidium and Arctotis has been recently developed. They are like the arctotis special hybrids but are more vigorous, bushier, and rather more hardy, though not fully hardy. The flower stems grow as much as 2 ft. tall.

VENIDIUM. This is an African daisy very much like arctotis, but without the pappus and of a rather coarser growth. *V. fastuosum* grows 2–3 ft. tall and has very large, showy, rich orange flowers with purplish-black disks and blotches at the base of the petals. The leaves are grey and hairy.

4 DIMORPHOTHECA (**Namaqualand Daisy or Star of the Veldt**). The name comes from Greek words *dis* =two, *morphe* =shape, *theca* =fruit, because the flower produces two forms of seeds — flattened fruit from the disk florets and rod-like corrugated fruits from the ray florets, each producing an identical plant. The usual dimorphotheca grown in gardens is *D. aurantiaca* with bright orange flowers, and hybrids of white, yellow, and apricot. These are not very hardy and are best sown under glass and planted in well-drained soil in May. The flower illustrated, *D. pluvialis ringens*, is rather more hardy and grows rather taller — about 12 ins. This can be sown in April in open ground in light soil in the south. All dimorphothecas need sunny situations.

5 URSINIA. These orange or yellow South African daisies vary from *U. pygmaea* 'Brilliance', growing only 6 ins. high, to the taller *U. anethoides*, the most commonly grown, which may reach 2 ft. and flowers very freely. There is now a mixture under the name of U. Hybrids, which includes a wide range of orange and lemon tones.

FELICIA. Most of these African daisies are shrubby perennials. *F. amelloides*, the 'Blue Daisy', makes a pretty pot plant and can be used for bedding out (*see* p. 125). *F. bergeriana*, the 'Kingfisher Daisy', however, is a dwarf half-hardy annual, about 4–5 ins. tall, and its mass of small azure-blue flowers make a good show in a sunny spot in the rock garden or at the front of a border.

ASTER. The South African asters are mostly blue and are all half-hardy. *A. pappei* has many small blue flowers on stems some 6 ins. long. *A. rotundifolius* is of a low shrubby growth and has rather larger flowers.

1 Gazania hybrid   2 Arctotis 'Sutton's Special Hybrids'   3 Arctotis grandis hybrids
4 Dimorphotheca pluvialis ringens   5 Ursinia pygmaea 'Brilliance'

SMALL HALF-HARDY ANNUALS. 1

Half-hardy annuals are plants which, to ensure their full development in a normal British summer, should be sown in a cool greenhouse in February or March, pricked out into boxes, and after a few days of hardening off, planted out from mid-May onwards, when risk of frost is over. The small half-hardy annuals of this page and the next are among the most brilliantly coloured of garden flowers and normally remain in flower for a long time. They need sunny positions and a well-drained soil, with plenty of moisture in the early stages.

1 VERBENA **hybrida.** Although these South American plants are perennials, in Britain they are best treated as half-hardy annuals. They make compact bushy plants 12–15 ins. tall and have a wide range of colours, 'Giant Blue', 'Lawrence Johnston' (cherry-red), and 'Firefly' (scarlet) being attractive varieties. They normally come true from seed. Most are very sweet-scented.

V. bonariensis can be treated as a hardy perennial. It grows 3–4 ft. tall with blue or purple flowers, and is effective massed in a semi-wild garden. *V. rigida*, also a perennial, is much smaller and has small spikes of violet-purple flowers.

2 BRACHYCOME **iberidifolia (Swan River Daisy).** An Australian annual, rather like a miniature cineraria, in shades of blue, pink, and purple, and also white. It grows 9–12 ins. tall.

COTULA **barbata (Pin-cushion Plant).** A little tufted plant from South Africa with a great many pale-yellow, cushion-like, daisy heads on long, fine stalks. It is a good edging or rock-garden plant.

3-4 DIANTHUS **chinensis (Annual Pinks).** There is a great variety of forms and colours developed from the original wild *D. chinensis* in China and particularly in Japan. The most widely grown group, *Heddewigii*, were raised from seed imported from Japan by Carl Heddewig to St. Petersburg (Leningrad) in the 19th century. 'Brilliant Fringed Mixed' is a good variety of single pinks ranging from white to crimson and scarlet. The double forms, including 'Black

Prince', have also many colours with various markings. (*See* also p. 79.)

(*See* also p. 79.)

PORTULACA **grandiflora (Sun Plant).** The yellow, pink, scarlet, or purple cup-shaped flowers of this little plant from Brazil open in direct sunshine and close in shadow. It is excellent for carpeting a hot sunny bank. It is hardier than the other plants on this page and prefers a rather poor dry soil.

5 AGERATUM (*a* =not, *geras* =old). The name refers to the fact that the flowers hold their colour for a long time. The garden varieties are derived from *A. conyzoides* and *A. houstonianum* and vary from 6 to 18 ins. in height and in colour from pale lavender to deep mauve.

ANAGALLIS **linifolia (Pimpernel).** This grows as a perennial in its native Mediterranean countries, but in Britain does best as a half-hardy annual. It is a free-flowering showy little plant, about 6 ins. high, and there are rose, crimson, lilac, and blue varieties. Like all pimpernels, the flowers tend to close in bad weather.

LOBELIA **erinus.** Although really a perennial, the dwarf blue lobelia is better grown as a half-hardy annual in Britain. It needs rich soil which does not dry out and benefits from weekly doses of a general fertilizer. There are varieties in white, pink, and different shades of blue.

1 VERBENA HYBRIDA 'GIANT BLUE'   2 BRACHYCOME IBERIDIFOLIA
3 DIANTHUS CHINENSIS 'BRILLIANT FRINGED' 4 DIANTHUS CHINENSIS 'BLACK PRINCE'
5 AGERATUM 'BLUE MINK'

SMALL HALF-HARDY ANNUALS. 2

For general notes on half-hardy annuals see p. 140. The plants illustrated here are useful for window boxes or for patches in the front of a herbaceous border. They all like a well-drained soil and full sunshine, and should not be planted out until risk of frost is over.

1 PHLOX **drummondii.** The annual phlox is named after Thomas Drummond who first brought seeds to Britain from Texas 1835. There are now two types: 'grandiflora', about 18 ins. tall, and 'nana compacta', about 9–12 ins. tall and very compact. There are a great many colour variations : self-coloured, bicoloured, and tricoloured. For example, there are forms with rose tubes and purple lobes, or purple without and white within, or crimson with a white base and yellow centre. In a well-cultivated loam, plenty of sun, and enough moisture, especially when first planted out, they will continue to flower the whole summer.

2 NEMESIA. These South African flowers of the snapdragon family, introduced to Britain over 60 years ago by Messrs. Sutton of Reading, are quite hardy. *N. strumosa*, the most satisfactory to grow, can be sown in the open, but they are better treated as half-hardies. They prefer a light soil with plenty of humus, and grow about 18 ins. tall. Seeds of individual colours can be obtained, but good mixtures produce a fine range of colours.

ALONSOA **warscewiczii.** A South American snapdragon-like perennial, best treated in Britain as a half-hardy annual. It is a bushy plant with bright green leaves and scarlet flowers which withstand bad weather particularly well.

3 PETUNIA. Originally South American plants, there are now three main types: large-flowered, either single or double, which are best suited to greenhouse cultivation; the bedding varieties, mostly single and some more compact and dwarf than others; the balcony varieties which are single and have a vigorous trailing habit of growth, very suitable for window boxes and hanging baskets.

Petunias range in colour from white to pink, crimson, violet, and blue, and come true from seed. They will not stand frost, but in a light loam will continue to flower all through the summer. If they grow straggly, they can be cut back and will produce flowering shoots.

NIEREMBERGIA **caerulea.** A petunia-like, South American, fairly hardy plant, growing about 9 ins. tall and producing an abundance of deep violet-blue

flowers with yellow throats. They are very suitable for sunny patches in the rock garden. The plants may be kept through the winter in a cool house or well-protected frame and will flower again from May onwards.

4 TAGETES **(French and African Marigolds).** In spite of their names both French marigolds (*T. patula*) and African marigolds (*T. erecta*) come from Mexico and were introduced to Britain over 300 years ago. Both have been greatly improved and flower freely and continuously throughout the summer. French marigolds are the more dwarf — bushy plants 12–15 ins. tall. There are also 'petite', cushion-like varieties very useful for edgings. They range from lemon to orange and mahogany red, both single and double. The African marigolds now mostly grown are the Carnation-flowered, such as 'Guinea Gold' and 'Primrose', and Chrysanthemum-flowered with shaggy heads. They are about 2½ ft. tall.

5 MESEMBRYANTHEMUM. This is a very large genus of succulent plants, mostly from South Africa and many suitable only for greenhouse culture. *M. criniflorum* grows well as a half-hardy annual, making low, spreading plants 4–6 ins. high and covered with daisy-like flowers in a wide range of pastel shades. It is useful for edgings or for sunny patches in the rock garden.

ARNEBIA **cornuta.** A flower of the Forget-me-not family, growing 15–18 ins. tall, with hairy foliage and deep yellow flowers, each marked with five brownish-black spots.

A. echioides (Prophet Flower) is a hardy perennial of a shorter, more spreading growth, which flowers in May and grows well in the gritty soil of a rock garden or dry wall.

CALANDRINIA **umbellata (Rock Purslane).** A South American bushy plant about 6 ins. high, with dark green leaves and vivid crimson-magenta flowers. It grows well in light sandy soil, and in a protected place will survive through a mild winter. *C. grandiflora* is taller, with rose-coloured flowers.

1 PHLOX DRUMMONDII 'VIVID SCARLET'   2 NEMESIA STRUMOSA
3 PETUNIA 'RED SATIN'   4 TAGETES PATULA 'LITTLE MARIETTA'
5 MESEMBRYANTHEMUM CRINIFLORUM

HYDRANGEAS

Most people are familiar with the large-leaved balloon or 'mop-headed' hydrangeas, which are garden varieties of the wild Japanese *Hydrangea macrophylla*, and flourish particularly in south and west coast seaside resorts.

There are many wild species of hydrangea in the Far East, all of which bear two types of flower: an outer ring of more or less showy ones, which are sterile and therefore bear no seeds, and an inner mass of small, less showy ones which are fertile. In many of the garden varieties of Japanese hydrangeas all the flowers are showy and sterile and these are classed botanically under *H. macrophylla hortensia*. They are reproduced by cuttings.

1 **Hydrangea villosa** is a wild species from China, so called because the shoots, leaf, and flower stalks are densely hairy. If left to itself it makes a straggling bush up to 9 ft. high, but it can be pruned in Spring more or less to any height desired, and the flowers appear in August on the new growths. It is a plant for half or full shade in any ordinary soil. Another similar species, but with more handsome foliage, is *H. aspera macrophylla*.

2 **Hydrangea paniculata grandiflora** is a garden form from Japan in which all or nearly all the flowers are of the large showy sterile type. As they mature they fade to pink.

The plant is hardy and can be made to grow to any size desired by spring pruning. If it is cut right back and not too many shoots allowed to grow, it will make very large heads; but, in fact, these are less beautiful than the smaller ones which result from moderate pruning. It will grow in any reasonable soil in any position and flowers in August and on into September. The flowers, if cut just before the colour begins to dull, are excellent for drying for winter decoration (*see* p. 190).

3 **Hydrangea macrophylla** 'Blue Wave'. This cultivated variety of the wild hydrangea, has retained the characteristics of its flower head — the outer sterile and inner fertile flowers. These varieties are now called 'Lace Caps'. They vary in colour through various shades of pink and crimson to white, and in acid soils the red shades will become some shade of blue. The plant illustrated is so named because it becomes blue in acid soils, but this one has obviously been grown in a limy soil. Pink hydrangeas may be persuaded to blue if watered in the winter with a solution of aluminium sulphate, and the advice of a nurseryman had best be sought about the strength of the solution. As the autumn advances, the flowers turn a fine maroon-purple and can then be picked and dried. When they turn brown they can be cut off, but not with long stalks as this would remove growth buds needed for next season.

Many of the 'Lace Caps' and 'Mop Heads' are not hardy in very cold districts, but 'Blue Wave' is hardy anywhere except in extremely cold areas. The plants have large leaves which are surprisingly wind resistant. All *H. macrophylla* are best planted in spring in half shade in any good soil.

Good varieties of 'mop heads' are: 'Ami Pasquier', dwarf, rich crimson; 'Mme Emile Mouillere', large white turning to rose; 'Parsival', deep crimson; 'Générale Vicomtesse de Vibraye', rich pink which blues well and is hardy.

Hydrangea serrata is a species from Japan and Korea which is smaller in all its parts and hardier even than *H. macrophylla*. It has lace-cap flowers on a smaller scale with white, pink, or blue sterile flowers changing in colour as they age.

Good varieties are: 'Grayswood'; 'lilacina'; and 'rosalba', the latter being especially hardy.

1 HYDRANGEA VILLOSA   2 HYDRANGEA PANICULATA GRANDIFLORA

3 HYDRANGEA MACROPHYLLA 'BLUE WAVE'

SUMMER PERENNIAL DAISIES, MOSTLY AMERICAN

1 BUPHTHALMUM. Many of the garden as well as wild daisies are called 'Ox-eye' because of the resemblance of the centre of the flower to the eye of an ox. This plant gets its name from two Greek words, *bous* (ox) and *opthalmos* (eye). The variety illustrated, *B. salicifolium*, is so called because of its narrow willow-like leaves. It is a native of Austria, and flowers earlier than the other buphthalmums, bearing its solitary flowers in June or July. It will grow on almost any soil and spreads rapidly by means of underground runners.

SPECIES: *Buphthalmum salicifolium*, 2 ft.; *B. speciosum*, 4 ft., a variety suitable for moist soils near pools (*see* p. 121).

2 HELENIUM. *Helenion* is an ancient Greek name for 'a plant'. Heleniums thrive in a sunny position in any ordinary soil and bloom for many weeks in the late summer. The flowers last well in water. They are propagated by division in autumn or spring, or can be grown from seed.

VARIETIES: *Helenium autumnale* 'Bishop', warm orange-yellow, 3 ft.; *rubrum*, bronzy-crimson, 4 ft.; 'Bruno', mahogany-red, 3 ft.; 'Butterpat', yellow, 3 ft.; 'Chipperfield Orange', yellow streaked crimson, 4 ft.; 'Crimson Beauty', browny-red, 2 ft.; 'Gold Fox', tawny-orange, 3 ft.; 'Moerheim Beauty', bronze-red, 3 ft.; 'Wyndley', coppery orange, 2 ft.

3 COREOPSIS (**Tick-Seed**). The name comes from Greek words meaning 'like a bug', referring to the shape of the seeds. The genus includes both annuals and perennials. They do best in sun in a medium, well-drained soil. As some varieties do not always survive a hard winter, it is wise to keep a reserve in a frame. They are propagated either by seed or by summer cuttings. *C. verticillata* has thread-like leaves in whorls up the stems. For the annual coreopsis *see* p. 136.

SPECIES AND VARIETIES: *Coreopsis verticillata grandiflora*, large flowers of golden yellow, 2 ft.; 'Mayfield Giant', deep yellow, 2½ ft.; 'Sunburst', yellow, double, 2½ ft.; *grandiflora* 'Badengold', deep yellow, 3 ft.

4 HELIOPSIS, from the Greek *helios* (sun) and *opsis* (like), is sometimes called the orange sunflower. It has a bushy, compact habit of growth, with neat, bright green foliage. It is very hardy and will do quite well in poor, dry soil. The flowers are about 3 ins. across and last well, both indoors and out.

SPECIES AND VARIETIES: *Heliopsis scabra incomparabilis*, semi double, orange-yellow, 3 ft.; *gigantea*, large golden flowers, 4 ft.; 'Goldgreenheart', double with green centre, 3 ft.; 'Light of Loddon', yellow, 3 ft.; 'Summer Sun', orange-yellow, 3 ft.

5 RUDBECKIA. These plants get their name from Olaf Rudbeck, a Swedish Professor of Botany. They are sometimes called 'cone flowers' because of the prominent cone-like centres of the single varieties. Although usually grown in sun, they will succeed in a partially shaded border. *R. bicolor* and *R. hirta* are annuals (*see* p. 137).

SPECIES AND VARIETIES: *Rudbeckia laciniata*, large yellow, greenish disk; 'Golden Glow', double rich yellow, tall; *speciosa*, orange, black-purple disk, 2½ ft.; 'Goldsturm', improved variety; 'Goldquelle', double yellow, 3 ft.; 'Herbstsonne', bright yellow, green disk, tall.

6 GAILLARDIA, named after Monsieur Gaillard, a French botanist. They are sometimes called 'blanket flower' because the margins of the petals are like the edging of blanket. Various garden varieties have been developed from the one perennial species, *G. aristata*. They do not breed true from seed, so they are best propagated from summer cuttings or by dividing the plant in spring. There are also annual varieties. They do best in light, well-drained soil in full sun.

SPECIES AND VARIETIES: *Gaillardia* 'Wirral Flame', browny-red, 3 ft.; 'Croftway Yellow', 2½ ft.; *grandiflora*, scarlet-edged yellow, 1½ ft.; 'Mandarin', orange-red, 2½ ft.; *pulchella*, annual, yellow and crimson, 1½ ft.

INULA. These yellow daisies differ from most other species on this page in that they are not American but natives of Europe, Asia, or Africa. *I. crithmoides* and *I. helenium* are British wild plants. The garden species have fringed flowers and soft, hairy leaves and stems. The coarser varieties such as *I. macrocephala* are suited to a woodland garden. They flower from July to October and make good cut flowers.

SPECIES: *Inula magnifica*, yellow, 6 ft.; 'Golden Beauty', yellow, 2 ft.; *hookeri*, rayed yellow, 2 ft.; *orientalis*, orange, 2 ft.

1 BUPHTHALMUM SALICIFOLIUM
2 HELENIUM AUTUMNALE 'BISHOP'
3 COREOPSIS VERTICILLATA GRANDIFLORA
4 HELIOPSIS SCABRA INCOMPARABILIS
5 RUDBECKIA SPECIOSA
6 GAILLARDIA ARISTATA 'WIRRAL FLAME'

147

PERENNIAL FEATHERY FLOWERS

1 HEUCHERELLA **tiarelloides** 'Bridget Bloom' is a cross between a tiarella and a heuchera. The flowers get their colour from the heuchera, while the structure of the plant and the attractive marking of the leaves come from the tiarella. The flower spikes will grow 18 to 20 ins. tall in good soil and light shade, and continue to flower through the summer if conditions are right. Heucherella does not set seed, but the plants can be divided in spring or autumn. A white variety, *alba*, has also been introduced.

2 HEUCHERA (**Alum Root**). These members of the saxifrage family are named after a German Professor, J. E. Heucher, and are excellent plants for the front of the border, being evergreen and flowering over a long period. They should be planted deeply, with only the top of the crown showing, and divided regularly, as the plants tend to get woody. Most of the modern varieties are developed from *H. sanguinea* or *H. brizoides*. They vary in colour from light pink to coral-rose or crimson-scarlet, and the variety 'Orphee' is white. They grow about 2 ft. tall.

New varieties, which flower more freely than the older kinds, include: 'Oakington Jewel', coral-rose; 'Lady Romney', pearl-pink; 'Red Spangles', crimson-scarlet, 1½ ft.; 'Rhapsody', glowing pink; 'Sparkler', bright scarlet.

3 POLYGONUM (**Knot Weed**). Some of the plants in this large family are too rampant for any position but the woodland garden, others are particularly attractive growing near water. Almost all of them tend to spread. The flowers are small and grow in sprays or in tight spikes; the plants vary in size from little rock plants 6–9 ins. tall to stout plants up to 6 ft. or more; and they all flower in late summer and autumn.

SPECIES: *Polygonum campanulatum*, 2–3 ft., not very hardy; *cuspidatum*, white with red-brown stems, 6–9 ft., too vigorous except for wild garden; *cuspidatum variegatum*, pale pink with strikingly variegated cream and pink leaves, 4–6 ft.; *amplexicaule atrosanguineum*, deep rosy-red, 3–3½ ft.; *bistorta superbum*, light rosy-pink, 2–3 ft.; *affine* 'Darjeeling Red', deep pink, mat-forming, 9–12 ins.; *vacciniifolium*, bright rose, late-flowering shrubby rock plant (*see* p. 176).

4-5 THALICTRUM (**Meadow Rue**). Their attractive foliage as well as their small, fluffy flowers make thalictrums valuable border plants. They all like good, rich soil and do best in light shade, although they can be grown in a sunny position if the soil is moist. With the exception of *T. adiantifolium majus*, the hardy maidenhair plant grown for its foliage rather than flowers, which has running roots, they make clumps which can be divided in spring. They can be grown from seed, though this is not reliable with the double varieties.

SPECIES: *Thalictrum dipterocarpum*, 3–5 ft.; *dipterocarpum album*, white, 3–4 ft.; *dipterocarpum plenum* 'Hewitt's Double' (4), 4–5 ft.; *delavayi* (5), 2–4 ft. slender; *speciosissimum* (*glaucum*), pale yellow, good foliage, 3–5 ft.; *aquilegifolium*, mauve and cream, *album*, white, *purpureum*, rosy purple — all early flowering, 2–4 ft.; *alpinum*, dwarf early-flowering (*see* p. 34).

GYPSOPHILA (from *gypsos* =gypsum, a chalk-like mineral, and *phileo* =to love). The American name 'Baby's Breath' well describes the clouds of tiny white flowers. It is an invaluable cut flower as a background for other flowers, and can be dried for use in winter decoration (*see* p. 190). Gypsophilas take up very little room when not in flower, though they need deep root space for their roots are large. If they are planted at the edge of a supporting wall, the vast mound of feathery flower stems that they make can push out over the wall without their taking up too much valuable planting space. They like a dryish soil, and if possible lime rubble should be dug into the soil at planting time. The best perennial varieties have been developed from *G. paniculata*, a single white species.

VARIETIES: *Gypsophila* 'Bristol Fairy', double white, 3 ft.; 'Flamingo', double pink, 3 ft.; 'Perfecta', large-flowered double white, 3 ft.; 'Rosy Veil', double pink, 1½ ft., the best perennial for small gardens. For annual species *see* p. 131.

STATICE (**limonium**) **latifolium** (Sea Lavender). This perennial Sea Lavender makes clouds of tiny lavender flowers on stiff, very branching stems, which dry well and keep their colour if cut just before they reach their peak (*see* p. 191). The large leathery leaves turn a warm brown in autumn.

VARIETIES: *Statice latifolium*, lavender, 2–3 ft.; 'Blue Cloud', large flowered, 2 ft.; 'Collyers Pink', 3 ft.; 'Violetta', deep violet blue, 2 ft.

1 Heucherella tiarelloides 'Bridget Bloom'   2 Heuchera sanguinea 'Oakington Jewel'
3 Polygonum campanulatum   4 Thalictrum dipterocarpum 'Hewitt's Double'
                    5 Thalictrum delavayi

PERENNIAL CLUSTER-HEAD COMPOSITES

These are all long-lived, sun-loving perennials, willingly thriving in any garden soil or sand. They often plant themselves in the soft mortar on the tops of old walls, and thence escape to the countryside.

Most of these flowers can easily be dried for winter decoration (*see* p. 190). Their woody stems and hard, papery flower-heads preserve well if cut just before they are fully open and hung, heads downward, to dry. The same qualities keep them looking respectable in rough weather when softer plants are wrecked. So they are excellent for growing in exposed places.

1 SOLIDAGO (**Golden Rod**) from solidare — to make whole, because of its reputed medicinal properties. Golden Rods used to be straggling, invasive plants, but the modern varieties, mostly developed from the tall *S. canadensis* or the dwarf *S. virgaurea*, are neat and compact and do not stray. They increase slowly and are propagated by dividing the plants in spring or autumn. Some of the newer varieties start blooming as early as July, and there are subtle differences in the shape of the flower sprays, the size of the flowers, and the colour of the foliage. They tend to grow rank with less good colour if they are grown in too rich soil.
 VARIETIES: *Solidago* 'Lena' golden-yellow, 2½ ft.; 'Golden Dwarf', yellow, 1 ft., early flowering; 'Lemore', lemon yellow, 1½ ft.; 'Golden Gates', yellow in large, feathery plumes, 2 ft., early flowering; 'Goldenmosa', golden-yellow mimosa-like flowers, 2½ ft.; 'Mimosa', golden-yellow, well-branched, 3½–4 ft.; 'Golden Wings', yellow, 5 ft.

SOLIDASTER **luteus** is a cross between a dwarf white-flowered aster, *A. ptarmicoides*, and a golden rod. It has the appearance of a rather small-flowered, bright yellow michaelmas daisy. It is a rather flimsy plant about 2–2½ ft. tall, and in most gardens is not as successful as a modern solidago.

2-3 ACHILLEA (**Yarrow**) is named after the Greek hero Achilles, who is said to have used the plant medicinally. Achilleas grow in any ordinary soil, but prefer a well-drained sunny position, and they will flower from June or July until the autumn frosts. They have attractive ferny foliage, and the flowers are excellent for winter decoration.
 SPECIES AND VARIETIES: *Achillea filipendulina* 'Coronation Gold' (3), flat golden heads, 2½–3 ft.; 'Schwefelblute' (Flowers of Sulphur) (2), pale

sulphur yellow, grey leaves, 2½ ft.; 'Gold Plate', flat golden heads, 4–5 ft.; *A. millefolium* 'Cerise Queen', cerise, 3 ft.; 'Fire King', deep red, 2 ft.; *A. ptarmica* 'The Pearl', small double white flowers, 2½ ft.; *A. siberica* 'Perry's White', 2–3 ft. The two last tend to spread.

ARTEMISIA **lactiflora**. This is a good plant to grow in a mass in the wild garden. It grows on erect stems 4 or 5 ft. tall, bearing panicles of milk-white flowers. The plant is covered with silky hairs which gives the foliage an attractive greyish appearance, often very effective in the herbaceous border.
 VARIETIES: Artemisia *lactiflora*, 4–5 ft.; *ludaviciana*, very downy, 2–3 ft.; *frigida*, shrubby, yellow flowers, 1–1½ ft.; *mutellina*, rock garden shrub, pale yellow, 2–6 ins. The two last are grown for foliage only, the flowers being uninteresting.

TANACETUM **vulgare** (**Tansy**). Though usually grown as a herb, Tansy is quite decorative in the right place, its finely-cut, fresh green foliage and small, bright yellow button flowers looking well in woodland planting. It spreads too much to be suitable in the flower border. It is very aromatic and was at one time used to flavour Easter puddings. There is a form with more curled leaves known as Crested Tansy.

4-5 ANAPHALIS (**Pearly Everlasting Flower**). These white, ivory-centred flowers with silver evergreen leaves are excellent for drying. The taller varieties, such as *A. margaritacea*, have small leaves and long underground stems; while the dwarf forms such as *A. triplinervis*, have larger leaves and make more compact clumps, though still inclined to run.

1 SOLIDAGO 'LENA'   2 ACHILLEA 'SCHWEFELBLUTE'   3 ACHILLEA 'CORONATION GOLD'
4 ANAPHALIS MARGARITACEA   5 ANAPHALIS TRIPLINERVIS

LABIATE SUMMER HERBACEOUS PLANTS

1 DRACOCEPHALUM. The name means 'dragon-headed' because of the shape of the flowers. It is free-growing, with fleshy roots which tend to spread, and does best in an open but not dry position. The plants are easily divided in spring or autumn. Some varieties have the same strong, rather unpleasant smell and general appearance as the nepetas.

SPECIES: *Dracocephalum prattii*, lavender-blue, 3–4 ft., early flowering; *forrestii*, deep purple, 1–1½ ft.; *hemsleyanum*, violet blue, 1–1½ ft.; *grandiflorum*, blue, large-flowered rock plant, 6–9 ins.

2 MONARDA (**Bergamot**) is named after N. Monardez, a 16th-century Spanish botanist. The garden hybrids are forms of *M. didyma*, an American plant often called 'Oswego Tea' or 'Bee Balm'. The leaves, which are so aromatic that they scent the air nearby, are used in pot-pourri and used sometimes to be added to tea to give a scented flavour. Monardas flower in July, and some varieties, such as 'Croftway Pink' and 'Cambridge Scarlet', last on into August or September. They are surface rooting and spread quickly by matted stems. They look better when grown in masses rather than in small clumps in a border, and they need a moist soil. They are best propagated by division in autumn or spring, even the smallest piece soon making a good plant; and if a clump has been badly damaged by frost, it can be recovered by replanting the uninjured bits. They grow about 2½ ft. tall.

VARIETIES: *Monarda didyma* 'Croftway Pink'; 'Cambridge Scarlet'; 'Magnifica', deep rosy-purple; 'Blue Stocking', violet purple; 'Pillar Box', bright red, rather tall; 'Priory Glow', salmon; 'Snow Maiden', white.

3 PEROVSKIA **atriplicifolia,** named after a Russian botanist Perovski, is sometimes called Russian Sage. It is a shrubby aromatic plant, with small finely-cut silver leaves and long, branched flowering spikes which can be cut back each spring. It will grow in any well-drained garden soil, its flowers lasting well into September, and it can be increased by cuttings or suckers.

STACHYS (*stachus* = spike). These low-growing plants, sometimes listed as betonicas, grow in any ordinary soil about 1–2 ft. tall and spread freely. *S. lanata*, a woolly-leaved cottage-garden plant known as 'lamb's ears', 'lamb's tongue', or 'sow's ears', is a good silver-leaved plant for edging, for ground cover, or for a wall, and dries well for winter decoration (*see* p. 190).

SPECIES: *Stachys lanata*, pink; *lavandulifolia*, rose-purple, dwarf; *macrantha superba*, purple-violet; *macrantha rosea*, pink.

AGASTACHE. The name means 'very much spiked', for these plants, closely allied to monardas, have attractive spikes of small flowers which show up well in the border. The best, *A. mexicana*, needs winter protection.

SPECIES: *Agastache anisata*, blue, 3 ft., scented of anise; *mexicana*, bright rose, 2½ ft.

4 NEPETA (**Catmint**), is a favourite plant for edging a border or planting in paving or on top of a wall. It prefers light, sandy soil and spreads quickly from a small rooted piece. It will flower from May to September. New growth is encouraged if the spent flowering stems are cut from underneath several times during the season, and in the autumn the plant should be cut to 3–4 ins. from the ground, which allows enough protection for the winter.

VARIETIES: *Nepeta x faassenii* (*mussinii*); 'Blue Beauty' (Souvenir d'Andre Chaudron) light blue; 'Six Hills Giant', lavender-mauve, tall.

MELITTIS **melissophyllum (Bastard Balm).** Its name comes from *melitta* =a bee, because of its attractiveness to bees. It has stiff, stout stems and rough green leaves, and the typical labiate flowers are white with bands of wine purple. It prefers semi-shade, and grows well on the edge of a wood. It is best propagated from seed. It flowers earlier than the other species on this page.

MENTHA. Some of the mints are decorative enough for the flower border but they increase so rapidly by underground stems that they may easily over-run more valuable plants. They prefer moist situations and start flowering in June.

SPECIES: *Mentha x gentilis aurea*, golden, variegated foliage, mauve flowers; *rotundifolia variegata* (apple mint) silver variegations, white flowers; *requienii*, peppermint-scented, carpeting rock plant (*see* p. 89).

5 SALVIA. This very large group of annual (*see* p. 127). biennial, or perennial herbs and shrubs (*see* p. 105) derives its name from the Latin *salveo*, to heal, because some species were supposed to have medical properties. Most but not all are hardy and like a rich soil, and nearly all have a long season of flowering — from June or July to September or October. Here we are concerned only with the herbaceous salvias.

SPECIES: *Salvia glutinosa*, pale yellow, sticky stems, 3 ft.; *azurea grandiflora*, light blue, 3½ ft.; *haematodes*, light blue, 2 ft.; *involucrata bethellii*, bright rosy-crimson, 3–4 ft., tender; *officinalis*, see p. 105; *horminum* and *splendens*, see p. 127; *sclarea* (Clary), lavender and white, 5 ft.; *sclarea turkestanica*, rose and pale blue, 4 ft.; *x superba*, purple, 3 ft.; *uliginosa*, azure blue, 4 ft. or more, rather tender in cold areas.

1 Dracocephalum pratti   2 Monarda didyma 'Croftway Pink'   3 Perovskia atriplicifolia
4 Nepeta x faassenii   5 Salvia glutinosa

PERENNIAL SEA HOLLIES AND SCABIOUS

1-4 ERYNGIUM (Sea Holly). There are two distinct sections in this large group: The European species which are mostly blue-flowered and include our native sea holly, *E. maritimum*, and the South American species with greenish-grey or whitish flowers, some of which are not hardy in cold districts. They all need sunny positions in the garden, and do best in a light sandy soil. The wild sea holly can sometimes be established in a garden if given conditions which resemble its native seashore, for example, in gravel at the edge of a path.

The European species do not like to be disturbed when once established and are best increased by seed. The South American eryngiums, which have an attractive habit of growth with striking spiny leaves and flower spikes up to 14 ft., can be divided in spring or autumn and can also be grown from seed.

All the eryngiums dry well (*see* p. 190) so long as they are cut before seeds have begun to set; otherwise they will 'moult'. The delicate filigree and the steely blue colouring of the European species are particularly beautiful when dried. The biennial species, *E. giganteum*, becomes quite white and desiccated after it has flowered, and is often called 'Miss Willmott's Ghost', after that great gardener Miss Ellen Willmott.

EUROPEAN SPECIES: *Eryngium alpinum* (2), 2 ft., July-September; *giganteum* (biennial) (3), 3 ft., August; 'Jewel' (4), 3 ft., July; *amethystinum*, light blue, 1½ ft., July-September; 'Blue Dwarf', blue, 2 ft., July; *planum*, small blue flowers, 2 ft., July; *x oliverianum*, amethyst, 3 ft. or more, July-August; *tripartitum*, small dark-blue flowers, 4 ft., July-August; 'Violetta', intense violet-blue, 2½ ft., August-September.

SOUTH AMERICAN SPECIES: *E. bromeliifolium* (1), pale green, 2–3 ft., June-July, not very hardy; *agavifolium*, green, 3 ft. or more, September; *pandanifolium*, purple-brown, 10–14 ft., October-November, tender.

5 SCABIOSA caucasica (from *scabies* = the itch, a disease which this plant is said to cure). A country name is the 'pincushion flower'. It is one of the most popular garden plants because it blooms for at least 4 months from July to October, needs no staking, and is an excellent flower for cutting, lasting a long time in water and blending well with other flowers. *S. caucasica* is pale blue but is now superseded by its varieties.

There are also annual species (*see* p. 87), and dwarf rock garden species (*see* p. 89).

Scabious must be planted in spring, and increased by division, also in the spring; or cuttings can be taken in September. It will grow anywhere, even in light shade, and in ordinary fairly light soil. It does not do well in heavy clay soil.

VARIETIES: *Scabiosa caucasica* 'Clive Greaves', mauve, 2 ft.; 'Emily', white, 3 ft.; 'Coronation', blue-mauve, 2½ ft.; 'Imperial Purple', deep violet-blue, 3 ft.; 'Miss Willmott', creamy-white, 2 ft.; 'Moonstone', light blue, 2 ft.

CEPHALARIA. This closely resembles a scabious but grows a great deal taller. It has rather small flowers for its size, but they are produced in great profusion and continue for 3 months. The thin pale-coloured flowers of this plant need a good background to show them up, and can otherwise look rather flimsy. Cephalaria can be naturalized in a wild garden.

SPECIES: *Cephalaria tatarica*, pale yellow, 5–6 ft., June-August; *syriaca* (annual), pale blue.

6 STOKESIA is named after Dr. Stokes, an English botanist, and was introduced to Britain from North America in 1766. It is sometimes called 'Stokes' aster', for it is rather like a China aster (*see* p. 127). It has good evergreen foliage and varieties vary in colour from white to blue and purple. It is useful in giving colour in August in the front of the border, and does best in a warm, sunny position. It is best propagated by taking rooted cuttings in spring and inserting them in sharp sand in a cold frame.

VARIETIES: *Stokesia laevis* 'Blue Moon', deep hyacinth blue, 2 ft.; 'Blue Star', large star-shaped blue flowers, 1 ft.

1 ERYNGIUM BROMELIIFOLIUM   2 ERYNGIUM ALPINUM   3 ERYNGIUM GIGANTEUM
4 ERYNGIUM 'JEWEL'   5 SCABIOSA CAUCASICA 'CLIVE GREAVES'   6 STOKESIA LAEVIS

SUMMER BORDER PLANTS FOR RICH SOILS

1 ACANTHUS, from the Greek *akanthos* = prickle, and sometimes called 'Bear's breeches'. This was first introduced to England from South Europe in 1548. In classical times the acanthus leaf served as the motif for ornamental carving, particularly for Corinthian capitals. Its handsome leaves are evergreen and make wonderful garden furnishing; but acanthus is better planted in isolation rather than in a border because its deeply delving roots wander and are difficult to eradicate. Its majestic flower spikes dry beautifully (*see* p. 190), but they must be cut before the seeds are formed for otherwise the seeds shoot from the calyces when the spikes are brought into a warm room. It is best propagated by dividing the plant in the autumn.

SPECIES: *Acanthus spinosus*, 4 ft., purple, July-September; *spinosus spinosissimus*, rose, 3 ft. July; *mollis latifolius*, rosy-purple and white, 4 ft., July-August.

2 ACONITUM, from the Greek *akon* = dart, because the juice of the plant was used to poison arrow-heads. Monkshood or Wolf's-bane are common names. Though it will grow in full sun, aconitum does best in light shade — at the back of a border, for example, or under trees. A shrub border makes a good background, so long as the plants are not allowed to dry out. Aconitum can be propagated by dividing the tuberous roots in spring or autumn. Winter aconite is a different genus (*see* Eranthis, p. 7).

SPECIES: *Aconitum wilsonii*, 'Barker's var.', 5 ft., August-October; *variegatum bicolor*, blue and white, 3 ft., July; *neomontanum*, violet-blue and hairy, 3 ft., June-August; *lycoctonum*, creamy yellow, 4 ft., July; *napellus roseum*, rose, 3 ft., July.

3 CAMPANULA (**Bellflower**), from the Italian *campana* = a bell. This very large family includes also annuals and biennials (*see* p. 32) and many small meadow or rock plants (*see* pp. 81 and 90). Here we are concerned with the larger herbaceous border plants. Some, such as *C. latiloba* (*see* p. 111), will grow where little else succeeds, and some, such as *C. rapunculoides*, can be a tiresome weed and are best confined to a wild garden. The tall *C. pyramidalis*, the 'chimney bellflower', which is best treated as a biennial, can be used in an orthodox position in a flower bed, in the greenhouse as a pot plant, or even where it sows itself in a wall. The great majority of campanulas grow equally well in sun or shade, though most like good soil and a watering or mulching in dry weather. Many of them increase by small white running roots, which makes propagation easy.

SPECIES AND VARIETIES: *Campanula lactiflora* 'Loddon Anna', 3–4 ft. or more; 'Prichard's Var.', deep blue. *C. latifolia* 'Brantwood', violet-purple, 2½–3 ft.; *C. macrantha alba*, white, 4 ft. *C. latiloba alba*, white, 3–4 ft.; 'Percy Piper', deep blue, 3 ft. *C. pyramidalis*, bright blue, 4–5 ft.; *alba*, white, 4–5 ft. *C. persicifolia* 'Beechwood', pale blue; 'Snowdrift', white; 'Gardenia', double white; 'Wirral Bell', double blue — all 2½ ft., June-July. *C. alliariifolia*, creamy-white, 2 ft., June. *C. glomerata*, rich violet-blue, 1½ ft., June.

4 PHLOX, from the Greek word for 'flame'. The herbaceous perennial phloxes are derivatives of the American *Phlox paniculata* and they flower from July to October. They do best in a cool moist position, with plenty of manure and humus, and should be mulched in dry weather for, being shallow rooted, they suffer from drought. They prefer semi-shade and, in fact, the brilliant cerise and flame shades tend to bleach in full sun. The dwarf rock-garden species, *P. subulata*, however, needs a sunny position (*see* p. 41). Most species grow about 3 ft. tall. For the annual phlox, *see* p. 143.

Eelworm is the principal pest of phloxes, and immediately the plants show twisted brittle leaves, swollen stems, and poor and stunted growth, they should be dug out and burnt. The roots of phlox tend to become very woody unless the plants are divided fairly frequently. They can also be increased from cuttings of non-flowering shoots taken early in the year.

VARIETIES: *Phlox paniculata* 'Eventide'; 'Bleu de Pervanche', periwinkle blue; 'The King', violet-purple; 'San Antonio', deep purplish-red, 2½ ft.; 'Brigadier', salmon-scarlet; 'Leo Schlageter', glowing vermilion, 2 ft.; 'Charles Curtis', cherry-red, 2 ft.; 'Evangeline', rose-pink; 'Mia Ruys', pure white, 1½ ft.; 'Rembrandt', white, 3 ft.

1 ACANTHUS SPINOSUS 2 ACONITUM WILSONII 'BARKER'S VAR.'
3 CAMPANULA LACTIFLORA 'LODDON ANNA' 4 PHLOX PANICULATA 'EVENTIDE'

TALLER LATE SUMMER SHRUBS

Although spring and early summer is the main season for flowering shrubs (*see* pp. 23 – 27 and 59 – 61), there are many shrubs which flower in late summer and even in the autumn. The majority of these shrubs need full sun and do well in a poor soil. The 'brooms', in particular, need a poor soil to do their best.

1 CEANOTHUS **azureus** 'Gloire de Versailles'. Most species of ceanothus come from western North America, mainly California, and are not very hardy, particularly the evergreen spring-flowering species such as *C. papillosus*, *C. rigidus*, and *C. veitchianus*. However, by crossing the Mexican *C. azureus* with the hardy species *C. americanus*, both deciduous, a hardy late-flowering race has been produced. In the open 'Gloire de Versailles' reaches about 4–5 ft., and on walls it will go up to 10 ft. It is best planted in the spring and given a little protection in the first winter in exposed places.

> OTHER VARIETIES: 'Henri Desfosse', indigo blue; 'Marie Simon', pink; 'Perle Rose', rosy red; 'Topaze', dark blue; 'Indigo', very dark blue but rather tender; 'Autumnal Blue' and 'Burkwoodii', evergreen late-flowering hybrids of uncertain hardiness.

2 HOHERIA. The hoherias or 'ribbon woods', so called from the way the bark peels off, are natives of New Zealand with a Maori name. They are tall shrubs or small trees with bunches of white cherry-like flowers. They are none of them really hardy and are plants for the south and west rather than colder areas, though the deciduous *H. glabrata* or *H. lyallii*, with their profusion of honey-scented, cup-shaped white flowers, are more likely to survive the winter. These flower rather earlier than *H. sexstylosa*. Hoherias grow very rapidly and are easy to cultivate.

3 ESCALLONIA. Named after a Spanish traveller, Senor Escallón, these are shrubs or small trees from South America, mostly Chile. The majority of the species are not hardy, but many of the evergreen and free-flowering garden hybrids now usually grown are hardier. *E. x. iveyi*, the hybrid illustrated, is not one of the hardy ones and is best grown only in the south and west. The older hybrids *E. x. edinensis* (rose pink), *E. x. exoniensis* (white) and *x. langleyense* (rosy) are likely to succeed in any reasonable climate, and so are the newer ones with better flowers such as 'Apple Blossom' with large pink and white flowers and any of the Donard varieties such as 'Donard Brilliance' (crimson) and 'Slieve Donard' (pink). All these grow from 4–6 ft. tall and are very wind resistant. They make excellent hedges as they will stand clipping. If cut down by frost they will grow again. *See also* p. 58.

4 RHUS (**Sumach**). This is a large genus of mainly hardy trees and shrubs, many of which are poisonous — for example, Poison Ivy (*R. radicans*), Poison Oak (*R. toxicodendron*). Some species produce dyes from the leaves (*R. coriaria*) or from the wood (*R. cotinus*); the sap of *R. verniciflua* yields Japanese lacquer; and the crushed berries of *R. succedanea* yield wax.

The Venetian Sumach, *R. cotinus* 'Notcutt's variety' (Royal Purple), has large, feathery, silky plumes bearing a few flowers and turning smoky grey in the autumn — hence its name 'Smoke Tree'. The purple leaves of this variety turn scarlet in the autumn. It grows as a bushy shrub, 6–10 ft. tall. *R. cotinoides*, which may grow much taller, has even more brilliant autumn colouring.

BUDDLEIA. A genus of shrubs and small trees, named after a 17th-century botanist Adam Buddle. The best late summer species is *B. davidii*, which has long mauve spikes of flowers very attractive to the August butterflies. Many brighter coloured varieties have recently been introduced — for example, 'Royal Red' (claret), 'Empire Blue' (dark purple-blue), and 'White Profusion'. Buddleias can be pruned in the spring to keep them a good shape and stop them growing too big.

GENISTA **aethnensis** (**Mt. Etna Broom**). This flowers later than most genistas, and is illustrated on p. 61. It produces masses of golden-yellow pea-shaped flowers on feathery branches in July. It can grow up to 15 ft., but if pruned carefully after flowering can be kept as a smaller shrub.

SPARTIUM **junceum** (**Spanish Broom**). Another shrub of the pea family which has large bright-yellow flowers on erect spikes. It may start flowering in June but lasts on into September. If not pruned back after flowering, it becomes leggy and gawky.

TAMARIX. Although tamarisks do grow in inland places, they are essentially seaside shrubs. Though most of them if left alone would grow into small trees, the August-flowered ones can be kept smaller and in shape by spring pruning. They have feathery foliage and plumes of small pink or white flowers. Two species, *T. parviflora* and *T. tetrandra*, flower in April or May, but most flower in late summer. *T. pentandra*, especially its variety *rubra*, has rosy-red flowers in August and September. *T. hispida*, also an autumn flowerer, has bright pink flowers on a compact shrub 3–4 ft. high.

1 Ceanothus azureus 'Gloire de Versailles'   2 Hoheria sexstylosa   3 Escallonia x iveyi
4 Rhus cotinus 'Royal Purple'

LOW-GROWING LATE SUMMER SHRUBS

In most gardens there are places beneath standard trees or towards the front of shrub borders where low-growing plants are needed to fill in empty spaces. The more or less permanent small shrubs are the plants best suited for such places, for the digging necessary for growing herbaceous or annual plants would disturb the roots of the bigger trees or shrubs. The plants shown on the opposite page will do well in such situations, especially if occasional top-dressings of fertilizers are given. Most of these shrubs continue to give colour for a long period and some have very decorative foliage.

1-2 VERONICA. The evergreen shrubby veronicas, sometimes called hebes, are very different from the herbaceous Speedwells (*see* p. 109). They mostly come from New Zealand and include also small trees and dwarfs suitable for the rock garden. The ones with narrow leaves are usually the most hardy; those with larger leaves and flower-heads are hardy only in the south and maritime districts. The flower spikes, usually 2–4 ins. long, may be white, pink, lilac, mauve, or purple. They can be pruned to the size required when frosts are over, as they all flower on the new growths. They are propagated very easily from cuttings of young wood from June to August.

HARDY SPECIES AND VARIETIES: *Veronica brachysiphon* (1), bushy shape, up to 6 ft. unless pruned; 'White Gem' is a more dwarf variety; 'Warley Pink' (2), hybrid of unknown parentage, 3 ft.; *anomala*, 3–4 ft., pale pink, early flowering; 'Eversley Seedling', rosy-lilac; *pimelioides glauco-caerulea*, 1 ft., deep purple, grey foliage, and black stems.

TENDER SPECIES AND VARIETIES: *Veronica speciosa* hybrids, ranging from white to crimson and purple; 'Autumn Glory', violet; *salicifolia* Spender's Variety, white; 'Mrs. Winder', blue-purple with purple foliage.

3 HYPERICUM (St. John's Wort). The hardy, shrubby hypericums are easy to grow and add a touch of gold to the garden from July to October. *H. x. moserianum*, the one illustrated, is a hybrid between the common 'Rose of Sharon' *H. calycinum*, which is too much of a weed for the border but will grow under trees, and *H. patulum*, a species from the Himalayas, China, and Japan. Its large flowers, 2½ ins. across, are produced over a long period. Its only fault is that in hard winters it may be cut back to the ground and take some time to recover. *H. patulum* 'Hidcote' is a neat, very free-flowering dwarf bush which can be cut back freely. *H. reptans* is a mat-forming species suitable for growing over a mound. It produces large, golden-tinged crimson flowers in the autumn. *See* also p. 65.

4 SENECIO. The name comes from *senex* =old man, and refers to the white or grey hair-like pappus of the seeds, familiar in weeds such as groundsel and ragwort. In New Zealand many senecios are shrubs or trees up to 20 ft. tall. Their beauty lies mainly in their thick leaves with felted white or buff undersurfaces, which enable them to withstand strong salt-laden winds. The garden shrubs which have come from New Zealand are mostly about 2–5 ft. tall and not very hardy. *S. monroi*, the species illustrated, and its near relative *S. compactus* are suitable only for mild districts, but *S. laxifolius* is rather more hardy.

OLEARIA, another group of daisy-like plants, often with felted leaves, from New Zealand or Tasmania. *O. gunniana* has pure white flowers with yellow centres, and there are also some blue-flowered forms. *O. semidentata* has large, solitary, pale purple flowers with dark purple centres. Both these species are hardy only in mild districts. The hardiest species is *O. haastii*, a bushy shrub some 5 ft. tall, with white and yellow flowers. All have leathery, white-felted leaves and are good sea-side shrubs.

5 CERATOSTIGMA willmottianum. This hardy shrub of the plumbago family, a native of China, continues flowering from July until the frosts come. Close planting is essential for effect, as usually only two or three flowers are open in a head at the same time. Except in mild areas or mild winters, it is cut to the ground each year, but comes again in the spring, growing to about 2–3 ft. Sometimes self-sown seedlings appear, and if these are potted up and kept in a frame for a year or two, they can then be planted out.

The perennial herb *C. plumbaginoides* is also hardy and grows 1–1½ ft. tall. The flowers are a brilliant purple-blue.

6 POTENTILLA fruticosa 'Primrose'. In this large group of mainly herbaceous plants (*see* p. 107) are some hardy and long-flowering shrubs, ranging in colour from white through yellow to orange. Some of the best garden varieties have been bred from far eastern species, some of which have not only beautiful flowers but attractive silvery foliage. Most vary in height from 2–4 ft., and one or two, such as *P. glabra mandshurica* (white) and *P. fruticosa micrandra* (yellow) are prostrate or dwarf enough for the rock garden.

SPECIES AND VARIETIES: *Potentilla glabra veitchii*, pure white; *fruticosa ochroleuca*, pale cream; 'Katherine Dykes', canary-yellow; *f. arbuscula*, sulphur yellow, low-growing; *f. beesii*, gold with silver foliage; *f. farreri*, bright yellow; f. 'Tangerine', orange.

1 VERONICA BRACHYSIPHON   2 VERONICA 'WARLEY PINK'   3 HYPERICUM X. MOSERIANUM

4 SENECIO MONROI   5 CERATOSTIGMA WILLMOTTIANUM   6 POTENTILLA FRUTICOSA 'PRIMROSE'

ANNUAL AND HERBACEOUS CLIMBERS

1 CONVOLVULUS **althaeoides (Riviera Bindweed).** A mediterranean perennial plant with slender silver leaves and deep pink flowers, like up-turned limpet shells. It has running roots which will spread, and so it is sometimes planted in a container, such as a drain pipe, to confine its roots. If it is grown among shrubs or herbaceous plants it will twine round them, but it does them no damage. Its trailing stems will grow about 4 ft. long.

For the annual convolvulus *see* p. 133.

2 LATHYRUS **latifolius.** Everlasting peas come from Eastern Europe and are easily-grown, long-lived perennials, reaching 6–8 ft. and making their own way over trellis or fence, without training. They are often used, especially in cottage gardens, to cover porches and old tree stumps, and will also grow horizontally as ground cover under trees. Small pieces dibbled into sandy soil soon make roots.

L. latifolius has large rose-pink flowers, but there are modern varieties in other colours. The one illustrated is *latifolius albus* 'White Pearl'; and there is a deep pink variety called 'Pink Beauty'.

Lathyrus odoratus, the well-known 'Sweet Pea', is an annual climber developed from an insignificant but sweet-scented wild flower in Sicily. It is now produced in almost every colour except yellow. It can be grown as a hardy annual to flower late in the year, but the best results come from sowing in October under glass, wintering the seedlings in a cold frame, and planting out in March.

OTHER SPECIES OF CLIMBERS: *Lathyrus magellanicus* 'Lord Anson's Pea', bluish-purple, vigorous and long-lasting; *L. rotundifolius*, red; *L. violaceus*, violet-blue, half hardy.

COBAEA **scandens.** This native of Mexico, sometimes known as 'Cups and Saucers' or 'Cathedral Bells', is named after Father Cobo, a Spanish missionary and naturalist. The flowers, borne on long stems, are pale green when they open and become violet or dark purple after a day or two; they are followed by very decorative large green fruits. Cobaea is best treated as a half-hardy annual, the flat seeds germinating best if sown on edge. In mild districts it will survive the winter, especially if protected. There is also a white-flowering variety.

3-4 TROPAEOLUM. This is a group of mainly annual climbers, including the common nasturtium (*T. majus*) which originated in South America. The annual species grow very quickly and are useful for covering walls or fences, especially as they will grow even on a north wall. Once established, they generally reappear year after year from seeds shed on the ground in the year before.

T. peregrinum (3), or Canary Creeper, comes from Peru. It can be sown under glass in March or in the open in late May or June, and will flower all summer. It enjoys a rather richer soil than other nasturtiums.

T. majus (4), also from Peru, will grow anywhere in any soil and sows itself freely. It is effective trailing from a window box or falling down a bank. There are now a large variety of colours from primrose to crimson and mahogany (but not blue), and there are single and double types as well as dwarfs and those with variegated leaves.

T. speciosum, 'Flame Flower' or 'Scotch Creeper', is a fleshy rooted perennial tropaeolum from Chile which is hardy but prefers northern rather than southern districts. It takes a little time to settle down, but once established it will produce its scarlet flowers from June to October. It needs good, well-drained soil and some shade. If planted on the north side of a hedge, it will work its way up to the sun.

ECCREMOCARPUS **scaber (Chilean Glory Flower).** A semi-woody perennial which climbs by tendrils to 10–15 ft. It has delicate fern-like leaves and sprays of red or orange tubular flowers, which are produced on the young shoots. It likes to clamber through a shrub or another climber, and flowers until late autumn. It is not hardy in cold districts and does best on a south or south-west wall, with winter protection for the roots. If sown in heat in March or April it will flower in the same season, like a half-hardy annual.

5 IPOMOEA **rubro-caerulea (Pharbitis tricolor),** 'Morning Glory'. The name ipomoea means 'like bindweed' for it belongs to the convolvulus family. Its flowers, which last for one day only, are at their best in the morning. Once the plants start to flower they produce blossoms in quick succession. As it has few leaves, this climber looks best if grown through another climber or a shrub. Most ipomoeas are greenhouse or stove plants, and this one does best if treated as a half-hardy annual and planted in a warm position. The variety *praecox* is the most hardy.

OTHER SPECIES: *Ipomoea purpurea elatior*, dark purple; *Hybrida* 'Darling', wine-red with white throat; 'Pearly Gates', pure white; 'Scarlet O'Hara', scarlet.

HUMULUS **lupulus (Hop).** This is a hardy, decorative climbing perennial which will quickly cover sunny walls or fences and tree stumps. It has panicles of greenish-yellow flowers. The plant should be well-watered and mulched in dry weather, and cut down in October. An annual hop, *H. japonicus variegatus* has decorative variegated leaves. Hops grow well in town gardens.

1 Convolvulus althaeoides   2 Lathyrus latifolius albus   3 Tropaeolum peregrinum
4 Tropaeolum majus   5 Ipomoea rubro-caerulea

LATE SUMMER CLIMBERS

1 CLEMATIS. Certain varieties of clematis flower from July onwards and are vigorous climbers. Some grow better up a wall; some look best when allowed to grow over other shrubs or small trees or over a shed. The species described here originated in north and east Asia. They prefer a rich and well-drained soil.

SPECIES: *Clematis orientalis*, a slender plant with very vigorous growth, can be grown on an east, west, or south wall. If it has grown too much it can be cut back drastically in February. The finely-cut leaves are smooth, and the flowers have petals almost as thick as orange peel. After flowering, silky seed heads hang on for many weeks. *C. rehderiana* has greeny-cream, bell-shaped flowers, cowslip-scented and produced in panicles throughout the late summer. Both this and *C. tangutica* are useful for growing over uninteresting shrubs or small trees. *C. tangutica* covers itself with golden lanterns in late summer and is still flowering when the first blooms have turned to silky seed heads, which hang on until winter. *See also* p. 63.

2 SOLANUM jasminoides (Potato Vine). This graceful twining plant from Brazil has clusters of soft pale-blue flowers, produced in great abundance from mid-summer until checked by frost. It is easily propagated by cuttings, but is not very hardy, and does best on sheltered south or south-west walls. Any excess growth can be trimmed in February. There is a commonly seen white variety, *S. jasminoides album*. *S. crispum*, the Chilean Potato Tree, is a rampant climber or can be grown as a shrub, though it is only really hardy on a sunny wall. It produces bluish-mauve flowers, with conspicuous yellow centres, nearly the whole year round. It is evergreen except in very hard winters.

3 JASMINUM officinale produces its deliciously scented flowers until November. It will grow anywhere, even on a north wall, but it needs careful training to prevent its growing in a tangle and usually should be trimmed back after flowering. It can be increased by layers or cutting.

SPECIES: *Jasminum officinale affine*, larger flowers, shaded pink on the outside. *J. stephanense*, a cross between *J. beesianum*, the 'red' jasmine, and *J. officinale*, pale pink flowers and attractive glossy black fruits; a vigorous climber.
For the winter-flowering jasmine *see* p. 3.

4 PASSIFLORA caerulea (Passion Flower). A native of South Brazil which can be grown on a sheltered south wall as far north as the Midlands, but elsewhere is best treated as a cool greenhouse climber. Its flowers are scented, and the egg-shaped fruits turn orange in the autumn. The plant is evergreen in mild localities. There is a variety, *P. caerulea* 'Constance Elliott', which has pure white flowers.

CAMPSIS radicans (Trumpet Creeper). A vigorous climber from North America, which has been grown in England for 300 years. It clings by aerial roots and needs plenty of room to develop. Though hardy, it does best on a warm south wall. It takes a year or two to produce its tubular, rust-red flowers. The hybrid variety *C. tagliabuana* 'Mme Galen' has very fine salmon-red flowers and is nearly as hardy as *C. radicans*.

POLYGONUM baldschuanicum (Russian Vine). This is, in fact, a native of Bokhara, and is a rampant twining plant which will quickly smother any unsightly object in one season. It will grow in shade but does best in full sun, and is covered with clusters of small, pink-flushed, white flowers throughout the summer.

LONICERA. Most honeysuckles flower in May and June (*see* p. 63), but some start flowering in June and flower through July and August. Many of these are tender plants, such as *L. sempervirens*, the trumpet honeysuckle, and can be grown out-of-doors only in sheltered places in the south. Some, however, are hardy, and often have very decorative fruits. They climb up to 20–30 ft.

HARDY SPECIES: *Lonicera japonica* has very fragrant cream flowers tinged with pink and appearing in the leaf axils of growing shoots. It is semi-evergreen and can be cut back after flowering. *L. japonica flexuosa* has yellow flowers tinged with purple. *L. japonica halliana* is pure white tinged with yellow. *L. periclymenum belgica* (early) and *serotina* (late) are garden forms of the wild honeysuckle, with purplish-red and yellow flowers.

TRACHELOSPERMUM. These climbers, introduced from China in 1844, are most suitable for cold greenhouses, but will grow in sheltered southern districts. *T. jasminoides* has clusters of very fragrant pure white jasmine-like flowers on slender stems. In France it is sometimes used to cover a house as we would use ivy. *T. crocostomum* is hardier and has fragrant yellowish flowers.

1 Clematis orientalis   2 Solanum jasminoides   3 Jasminum officinale
4 Passiflora caerulea

DAHLIAS

Dahlias, named after Dr. Dahl, a Swedish pupil of Linnaeus, are natives of Mexico. They range from the tree-like *D. imperialis* with large single lilac flowers to the small scarlet-flowered *D. coccinea*. They were introduced to Spain in 1789 and were first grown in England in 1798. They will grow in any soil so long as it is not too dry, and give a great deal of colour from early August to the first frosts. The small bedding varieties grown from seed can be treated as half-hardy annuals, and bedded out about June (*see* p. 125). The larger kinds are increased by cuttings or by division of the clumps of tubers. When the first frosts blacken the foliage, the tubers are lifted and, the soil removed, stored in a dry, frostproof place. In March they are brought into the light and sprinkled with water to make them sprout. They are planted out when severe frosts are over — usually in April. They like a well-manured soil and a feed of bone meal when planted, and also a mulch of manure or compost and some watering in the hot weather. They are improved by disbudding, and the dead heads must be removed. Tall dahlias need to be well staked. A vast number of dahlias have been developed, the varieties mentioned here being only an arbitrary selection of the main types. They are now classified into eleven main sections by the Royal Horticultural Society and the National Dahlia Society.

SINGLE-FLOWERED DAHLIAS. These have a single ring of florets round a central disk, and most are dwarf bedding types.

VARIETIES: 'Coltness Gem', bright red; 'Northern Gold', golden yellow with dark foliage; 'Shirley Yellow', light yellow; 'Princess Marie-José', lilac pink.

1 COLLARETTE DAHLIAS resemble single-flowered dahlias, except that there is a ring (or collar) of shorter ray florets round the centre.

VARIETIES: 'Aureoline', orange-yellow; 'Lady Friend', pale pink; 'Swallow', white; 'Admiral', crimson with white collar; 'Gerring's Elite', red with yellow collar.

2 DECORATIVE DAHLIAS. These are fully double, the rings of florets hiding the central disk except with fully-blown flowers. They range in size from the large-flowered exhibition types, 10 ins. or more in diameter, to the miniature types which are 3–4 ins.

VARIETIES: (*a*) Large: 'Croyden Masterpiece', orange-bronze; 'Lavender Perfection'; 'Liberator', red; 'Axford Triumph', deep apricot; 'Frieda Gaylord', pink.

(*b*) Medium (6–8 ins.): 'Ballego's Glory', velvety-red edged gold; 'Ormerod', orange-scarlet and yellow; 'Yellow Show'; 'Jersey Beauty', salmon-pink; 'Peace', white.

(*c*) Small (4–6 ins.): 'Gerrie Hoek', pink; 'Edinburgh', purple with white tip; 'Chinese Lantern', orange.

(*d*) Miniature (2–4 ins.): 'Arabian Night', dark red; 'Doris Duke', pink; 'Newby', salmon-apricot.

3 ANEMONE-FLOWERED DAHLIAS. The flowers, which are cushion-shaped, have outer rings of broad florets and inner rings of tubular florets. There are still only a few varieties of this type.

VARIETIES: 'Comet', dark crimson; 'Honey', apricot-pink; 'Bridesmaid', white.

PAEONY-FLOWERED DAHLIAS are like single dahlias but with two or three rows of broad ray florets round a central disk. Few varieties are now grown, far the most popular being 'Bishop of Llandaff', a bright red dahlia with dark purplish foliage.

4 POMPON DAHLIAS. The flowers are made up of short tubular florets, sometimes forming almost a complete ball. They vary in size from the large-flowered types with a diameter of 3–4 ins. to the small-flowered pompons which may be an inch or less.

VARIETIES: (*a*) Large: 'Nellie Birch', deep crimson; 'Mary Patterson', yellow; 'Jean Lister', white.

(*b*) Medium: 'Golf Ball', orange; 'Leo', rich red.

(*c*) Small: 'Rosea', lavender-mauve; 'Rosalinda', pink; 'Wiluna', deep rosy-lilac; 'Py', yellow.

CACTUS DAHLIAS. Star-shaped, double flowers with narrow, pointed florets, usually hiding the central disk. They are subdivided like Decorative Dahlias, with the same dimensions.

VARIETIES: (*a*) Large-flowered: 'Good Catch', yellow; 'Pride of Holland', pink; 'Smokey', very dark crimson; 'Gunyah Glory', deep purple.

(*b*) Medium-flowered: 'Polar Beauty', white; 'Firerays', reddish flame; 'Eclipse', wine-red.

(*c*) Small-flowered; 'Pirouette', pale lemon; 'Andries Orange'; 'Cheerio', wine-purple tipped with silver; 'Doris Day', deep red.

OTHER DAHLIAS. Several types do not fit into any of the above sections. 'Show' (self-coloured) and 'Fancy' (bicoloured), similar to large pompons, are little grown because of their weak stems. The best orchid-flowering dahlia is the double, light-orange-bronze 'Giraffe', good for floral decoration. Star dahlias, small flowers with two or three rows of pointed florets round central disks, are, apart from 'White Star', seldom grown.

1 Collarette Dahlia   2 Decorative Dahlia   3 Anemone-flowered Dahlia
4 Pompon Dahlia

PENSTEMONS AND FUCHSIAS

Fuchsias, penstemons, and the close relatives of penstemons, phygelius and chelone, are a group of shrubs or woody herbs which are mostly natives of South or North America. Only some of them are completely hardy. Although they can be grown from seed, they are best propagated from cuttings. Those of fuchsias are taken in spring and rooted in a greenhouse; those of penstemons are taken in late summer and wintered in a cold frame for planting out in May. Treated like this, penstemons and fuchsias are good plants for bedding (*see* p. 125). They need a well-drained soil preferably with peat or leaf mould and some sharp sand. Hardy species and hybrids will survive the winter out-of-doors. It is wise not to cut down the previous season's growth of penstemons until the following spring when danger of frost is over. Fuchsias are usually cut down before the winter and covered with 6 – 8 inches of ashes or leaves.

1 PENSTEMON. The name means five (*pente*) stamens (*stemon*). They are natives of North America, and there are many species and garden hybrids ranging from herbaceous plants growing 3–4 ft. tall to rock plants such as the prostrate May-flowering *P. newberryi* (*see* p. 67). There is a large range of colours, the hybrids mainly being descended from the reddish-purple to white *P. cobaea* and the scarlet *P. hartwegii*.

SPECIES: *P. heterophyllus*, blue suffused rose, 1 ft. or more, spreading habit; *P. campanulatus*, small flowers, nearly hardy, early-flowering; *P. c.* 'Evelyn', 9 ins., soft pink; *P. c.* 'Garnet', 2 ft., ruby-red; *P. c. purpureus*, purple; *P. grandiflorus*, lavender-purple, large flowered, 2–3 ft.

Hybrids: 'Alice Hindley', 2–3 ft., pale lavender; 'Castle Forbes', 2 ft., crimson with white throat; 'Hewell's pink bedder', 1½ ft., salmon, with white throat; 'Newbury Gem', 1½ ft., scarlet; 'Stapleford Gem', 2½ ft., pale iridescent blue.

CHELONE (**Turtle Head**). A hardy perennial closely related to penstemon — indeed the light coral-red *C. barbata* is often listed as *P. barbatus* and is easy to mistake for a penstemon. Apart from this species, the erect flower spikes with flowers closely bunched at the end look very different from most penstemons. There are white (*C. glabra*), violet-purple (*C. nemorosa*), and deep rose (*C. obliqua*) species, and they range from about 1½–3½ ft.

2 PHYGELIUS **capensis (Cape Figwort)**. This South African shrub is named from two Greek words *phuge* = flight and *helios* = sun, because in Africa it prefers to grow in light shade. In England it does best in a sunny site. In a herbaceous border it rarely exceeds 3 ft., but grown against a south wall it will grow to 8–10 ft. It has dark evergreen foliage and flowers from July to autumn. A very severe winter may cut it to the ground, but its running roots are seldom killed.

There is a bright scarlet improved variety, *P. c. coccineus*, which starts flowering as early as May.

3-4 FUCHSIA. Fuchsias are named after Leonard Fuchs, a 16th-century German botanist. The majority of the hardy fuchsias now grown are varieties of or hybrids from *F. magellanica*, and there are a large number of less hardy varieties which flower from July till the frosts. Some are suitable for growing to hang over a wall; some are dwarf and suitable for a rock garden; some have ornamental foliage.

VARIETIES: Fuchsia *m.* 'Margaret' (3), 2 ft.; 'M. Brown' (4); 'Mrs. Wood', flesh pink and white, 3 ft.; 'Mrs. Popple', 2 ft., red and violet; 'Mme Cornelisson', 2 ft., deep carmine tube and sepals, semi-double white petals; *m.* 'Musgrave's' variety, 4 ft., scarlet and violet; *m.* 'riccartonii', 4 ft. or more, bright crimson and purple, makes a good sea-side hedge and is very hardy; 'Tom Thumb', 1 ft., carmine and purple, and almost as hardy.

1 Penstemon heterophyllus   2 Phygelius capensis   3 Fuchsia magellanica 'Margaret'
4 Fuchsia 'M. Brown'

LATE SUMMER AND AUTUMN SHRUBS

1 CLEMATIS **heracleifolia 'Cote d'Azur'.** Most people think of clematis as climbing plants (*see* pp. 63, 164, 165), and the semi-shrubby dwarf plants are not frequently grown. The type *C. heracleifolia*, which comes from China, has pale blue flowers and grows about 3 ft. tall; 'Cote d'Azur', illustrated here, is deeper in colour; and the variety *C. heracleifolia davidiana* is an indigo blue. This latter, which is fragrant, does not have flowers which curl back like those of a hyacinth and is a little taller than the others. These are useful plants for the front of a shrub border and are excellent on limy soils.

2 HIBISCUS **syriacus 'Coeleste'.** Most Tree Hollyhocks are natives of hotter climates, where they may grow to tree height. Those that are hardy enough to grow in Britain are tall shrubs which tend to look rather gaunt in the spring because the leaves appear late. *H. syriacus*, in spite of its name, is a native not of Syria but of India and China. In Britain it needs all the sun possible and a well-drained though not necessarily rich soil. It tends often to fail in very wet districts or in wet autumns. There are single and double varieties, the singles being on the whole the more beautiful.

OTHER VARIETIES: *H. syriacus* 'Hamabo', blush-pink with central crimson blotch; 'Snowdrift', pure white; 'Woodbridge', rose pink with maroon blotch; 'Jeanne d'Arc', double pure white with pink reverse.

3 ABELIA **grandiflora.** Most abelias are not very hardy, although excellent shrubs for the south and west and coastal areas. The hybrid *A. grandiflora* is one of the hardiest, its coloured sepals persisting well into the autumn and its bright green leaves being semi-evergreen. It usually grows about 4 ft. tall and flowers from July to October. It is hardy in all but very severe winters.

OTHER SPECIES: *A. triflora*, native of the Himalayas and hardy; the clusters of small pink-tinged white flowers which appear in June are very fragrant; the plant grows up to 10 ft. high. *A. schumannii*, suitable for warm places; a long flowering season of rosy-pink blooms.

4 EUCRYPHIA x **intermedia.** These lovely small trees from Chile and Australasia are mostly rather tender and suitable only for protected places in the south. They all need a moist soil with plenty of humus, leaf-mould, or peat, and most dislike lime. The flowers of all the species are very similar. *E. x. intermedia*, a cross between *E. glutinosa* and *E. lucida*, is fairly hardy and will tolerate a little lime if given plenty of humus.

OTHER SPECIES: *E. glutinosa*, the hardiest eucryphia but will not tolerate lime; grows about 15 ft. tall; the leaves colour late in the autumn. *E. cordifolia*, tender except in the south but will tolerate lime. *E.* 'Nymansay', a hybrid rather more hardy than *E. cordifolia* and a lime tolerator.

5 CARYOPTERIS x **clandonensis.** The caryopteris are natives of East Asia, their name meaning 'nut' (*karyon*) 'winged' (*pteron*), referring to the fruit. This hybrid between *C. mastacanthus* and *C. mongholica* is a charming dwarf shrub (3–5 ft.) for full sun in a dry position, and like many hybrids it is hardier than its parents. The plant is aromatic with a grey underside to the leaves. It should be pruned back well every spring to keep it a good shape. The 'Ferndown' variety is a deep violet blue, and 'Heavenly Blue' is a new American form not yet fully tested.

LESPEDEZA **sieboldii**, a shrub of the pea family from China and Japan, which produces long panicles or rosy-purple flowers in August and September. The plant often dies down to ground level in winter, but sends up fresh semi-woody stems to a height of 4 ft. or more. It is easily cultivated in light loamy soil in full sun.

INDIGOFERA **gerardiana.** This is another shrub of the pea family which comes from the Himalayas and produces rosy-purple flowers from June to September. It is cultivated like Lespedeza and also may die down to the ground in the winter.

1 Clematis heracleifolia 'Cote d' Azur'   2 Hibiscus syriacus 'Coeleste'
3 Abelia grandiflora   4 Eucryphia x intermedia
       5 Caryopteris x clandonensis 'Heavenly Blue'

171

LATE SUMMER LILY-LIKE PLANTS

There are many plants, which are loosely called lilies of some kind or other, although they do not necessarily belong to the lily family. Also, not all members of the lily family have bulbs like the true lilies. In this plate, schizostylis belongs to the iris family, kniphofia and liriope to the lily family, and alstroemeria to the amaryllis or daffodil family. The first three do not possess true bulbs, and the last has a curious fleshy tuberous root. They are all showy, late-summer, border plants, the schizostylis flowering rather late, and some of the kniphofias, such as *K. praecox*, flowering as early as June. Most do better in a good loam soil with plenty of humus, and all except the alstroemerias need sunny positions. Alstroemerias will tolerate semi-shade.

1-2 SCHIZOSTYLIS (Kaffir lily) is a South African flower which, in its native country, grows in damp places near rivers. In English gardens it is not treated as a bog plant, but it should not be lifted and dried off as bulbous plants often are. Though generally hardy, it is best planted in the spring and in a sheltered but not too dry position. The plants should be watered in a drought.

S. coccinea (1), 'Crimson Flag', is the original species from which other varieties have developed. It grows about 2 feet tall, and in a warm sunny position flowers freely. There is a larger flowered but scarcer major form.

S. c. 'Mrs. Hegarty' (2), first appeared in an Irish garden and was named after the wife of the owner. It is just as easily grown. The paler pink 'Viscountess Byng', found in South Africa by that lady, is not worth growing in cold gardens because it flowers so late, often November. Other colours have been reported in the wild, but so far have not appeared in cultivation.

3-4 KNIPHOFIA (Red-hot Poker), named after an 18th-century German professor J. H. Kniphof. These are African plants, the hardy ones coming from South Africa. The bare stems rise from tufts of sword-like leaves to a height of anything from about 18 inches to 6 or 9 feet. The first kniphofia to be introduced as a garden plant was the late-flowering scarlet *K. uvaria*, from which many hybrids have been introduced. As all kniphofias cross very readily, many attractive seedlings have been raised which are usually stronger than their parents and range in colour from ivory-white, through various shades of yellow, to orange and red. In cold areas they are better with some winter protection and should be planted 6–8 ins. deep and disturbed as little as possible.

DWARF SPECIES: *Kniphofia galpinii* (3), from the highlands of Transvaal, 2 ft.; *K. x.* 'Brimstone' (4); *macowanii*, orange-red, 12–18 ins.; *nelsoni*, orange-scarlet, slender, late flowering, 18–24 ins.; *rufa*, yellow and orange, 12–18 ins.

TALLER SPECIES: Varieties mainly developed from *uvaria*, 3½ ft. or more; 'Buttercup', yellow; 'Maid of Orleans', ivory, not very hardy; 'Royal Standard', scarlet and gold.

5 ALSTROEMERIA aurantiaca (Peruvian Lily). All the alstroemerias, named after the 18th-century Baron Alstroemer, come from South America but most of them from Chile rather than Peru. The tuber-like roots are very easily broken from the crown, and if so, will not grow. So it is best to buy the plant in a pot and to handle it with the greatest care when planting it. It should be planted in spring, 6–8 ins. deep. Alstroemerias sometimes do not appear above ground for a year after being planted, but normally they will reappear and once established will never fail.

A. aurantiaca, once established, will grow under deciduous trees and may even spread too much. In a border it may be better to grow one of the following varieties: 'Dover Orange', deep orange; 'Orange King', orange-red; *aurea robusta*, golden yellow; *lutea*, bright yellow; or the *A. ligtu* hybrids in pink, apricot, salmon, or cream.

6 LIRIOPE graminifolia (or *L. muscari*) is a seldom grown but useful dwarf evergreen for autumn flower. It makes tufts of narrow deep green leaves and coloured flowering stems about 6 ins. tall or taller in good soils. It comes from Japan and China.

1 SCHIZOSTYLIS COCCINEA   2 SCHIZOSTYLIS C. 'MRS. HEGARTY'   3 KNIPHOFIA GALPINII

4 KNIPHOFIA X 'BRIMSTONE'   5 ALSTROEMERIA AURANTIACA   6 LIRIOPE GRAMINIFOLIA

SOUTH AFRICAN LATE SUMMER BULBS

1 AGAPANTHUS. These plants of the Lily family are native to South Africa. They have a creeping rootstock with thick fleshy roots, and the flowers, some shade of blue or sometimes white, are borne to the number of about thirty in a round head on a stem which may be 2 ft. high. *A. africanus*, the one illustrated and sometimes listed as *A. umbellatus*, has evergreen leaves, and is hardy only in the south and gardens near the sea. Elsewhere it needs protection in the winter, for if the leaves are destroyed by frost, next season's flowering will be affected. It is best planted under a south wall or fence and the crowns protected with dry moss-peat, straw, or bracken in the late autumn, and covered with a cloche or framelight. It is known that the narrower the leaves the hardier the plant; therefore the narrow-leaved and smaller-flowered *A. campanulatus*, which is deciduous, is a better choice for cold gardens. Both the blue and the white forms grow about 18 ins. tall and are very charming. Other varieties hardier than *A. africanus* are the 'Headbourne' Hybrids which vary in colour from pale china blue to deep violet.

All the agapanthus like a good garden soil, not too dry. They should be planted, and also big clumps divided, in the spring. The less hardy ones make excellent pot plants. The pots must be large and can be placed in the open during the summer and removed to a frost-free place in the winter. Such pot plants require plenty of water and a feed with fertiliser every fortnight when in the open.

2 AMARYLLIS belladonna. Another plant coming from South Africa and usually called the Belladonna Lily, although it belongs to the daffodil, not the lily, family. The large trumpet-shaped flowers are some shade of rose-pink and have a delightfully fruity scent. It is really a plant for the south and south-west, and in other districts must be given the hottest, driest, best-drained position available, at the foot of a south wall, with some winter protection, as for agapanthus. Amaryllis must be planted in July, with the tops of the bulbs 4–5 ins. below the surface. The flowers, on 18–24 inch stems, appear before the leaves, which usually come with the August rains, grow through the winter, and die down in May or June. Amaryllis is erratic in flowering, some forms appearing to flower better than others for no obvious reason. There is no infallible recipe for making them flower, though they dislike being disturbed.

3 CRINUM. This is a very large family of which the majority are greenhouse or even stove plants. Some,

but not all, come from South Africa. They have large bulbs with strange, foot-long necks, and the leaves are long and numerous. *C. powellii* is a semi-hardy hybrid which produces rose-pink or white flowers on 3-foot stems in August and September. The flowers do not all open at once, so it remains in beauty for some time. The plant needs plenty of room and to be left undisturbed to grow into a clump. A clump is very difficult to divide, so it is best to keep it going by good feeding and divide only as a last resort. It is rather more hardy than amaryllis, but in colder areas, say in the Midlands, it needs a protected place, and further north it must have winter protection, as for agapanthus. It looks very miserable after the winter but soon recovers when the weather warms up. The bulbs should be planted in late spring in rich well-drained soil and deep enough to bury the base of the neck. When the flowers shoots appear, if the weather is dry, the plant should have several good soakings of water.

There is a lovely pale-pink variety *C. p. haarlemense* and a darker one *C. p. krelagei*.

4 NERINE bowdenii. Most nerines are greenhouse plants, but *N. bowdenii* is hardy — the hardiest of the South African bulbs illustrated here. It will grow in the open in most districts, only needing protection in the colder parts. It is a most valuable bulb for autumn blossom and flowers regularly. The heads of six or seven rose-pink flowers appear on foot-high stems in September or later, usually just as the leaves are dying away.

N. bowdenii needs well-drained but not necessarily rich soil, and will grow well in open spaces among shrubs. The bulbs should be planted with the nose just below the surface. When they get too crowded they can be divided in the spring, just as the new leaves are appearing.

There are paler and darker varieties, a particularly strong-growing large-flowered form being *N. b. gigantea* or 'Fenwick's Variety'.

GLADIOLUS (*gladius* = sword, from the shape of the leaves). This large group of plants of the Iris family come from Southern Europe and Africa. They prefer a light sandy soil and a sunny position and need careful staking. Most species should be lifted towards the end of October and the corms dried and kept in a frost-free place.

So many hybrids have now been raised, that there are gladioli of most colours, flowering from May to October and varying in size from 3–4 ft. tall to dwarf varieties only 6–8 ins. (*See* also p. 117.)

1 AGAPANTHUS AFRICANUS   2 AMARYLLIS BELLADONNA   3 CRINUM POWELLII
4 NERINE BOWDENII

175

LATE ROCK PLANTS

The majority of rock plants flower in the spring and early summer, in their native haunts coming up as the spring sun melts the snow (*see*, for example, pp. 21, 41, 43). But it is not always realized how many good rock plants there are for giving colour in the late summer and autumn. Some of the best gentians and cyclamen, for example, are autumn-flowering.

1 SERRATULA shawii. *Serrula* means 'a little saw' and refers to the serrated leaves of this thistle-like plant. The wild species (*S. tinctoria*) is commonly called Saw-wort. *S. shawii* is a useful plant for a large rock garden or the front of a herbaceous border, for it grows vigorously almost anywhere and is long-lived. Its stiff stems are about 12 ins. tall.

S. tinctoria montana is a very similar plant but only 2–3 ins. tall, and is therefore useful for the trough or miniature garden.

2 GENTIANA farreri. Both spring (p. 35) and summer-flowering (p. 111) gentians are some of the best-known of mountain flowers. *G. farreri* was discovered by R. Farrer in north-west China in 1914, and it, and the hybrids from it, are now well-established late-summer and autumn rock plants. It will grow quite easily in a sunny but not too dry position in a lime-free soil, or in a limy soil if plenty of leaf-mould or peat is added. It can be propagated from cuttings of the young shoots in April.

G. sino-ornata, also from China, has deeper and more purple-blue flowers and shorter flower trumpets. *G. x. macaulayi*, a hybrid between the two and intermediate in colour, is late-flowering and has plenty of hybrid vigour. This hybrid, particularly 'Newberry's' variety, will stand some lime if given plenty of peat.

3 SEDUM cauticola. The word 'Sedum' comes from the Latin for 'sit' because of the way the low, arching, leafy, almost succulent stems of sedums rest on rockery stones. It is a large group, with many native species, the stonecrops. (See also p. 91.)

S. cauticola, if planted in an open sunny position, will flower for the whole of September and October. The young shoots root easily in the spring. This species is closely related to *S. sieboldii* which, especially in its variegated form, is more often cultivated. *S. stahlii*, a Mexican species and not very hardy, has slender stems 4–8 ins. long bearing yellow flowers. *S. spectabile* from China has stout, erect stems 12–18 ins. high and is an excellent late-flowering border, rather than rock, plant (*see* p. 178).

4 SILENE schafta. There are a great many garden Catchflies, some of the best of which are annuals (*see* pp. 133, 135). Most of them flower earlier than the flowers on this page, but *S. schafta*, although it may start flowering as early as June, in a sunny position will continue into October. The new improved form 'Abbotswood' has larger and deeper rosy-magenta flowers. *S. acaulis exscapa*, Moss Campion, is a very attractive rock cushion plant flowering in early summer.

5 CYCLAMEN neapolitanum. These Mediterranean plants are named from the Greek word *kyklos*, meaning 'circular', because the flower stalks of some species twist spirally after flowering. This autumn-flowering species is very hardy and will grow in almost any situation, especially under trees and shrubs. There is also a white form. This and the spring-flowering cyclamen (*see* p. 7) set seed very easily, and produce flowering corms in about 2–3 years, if seed is sown as soon as ripe.

ERICA. There are ericas in flower most of the year round. The late summer and autumn flowering *E. ciliaris*, Dorset Heath, and *E. cinerea*, Bell-heather, are both lime-haters, though some of the spring varieties (p. 3) tolerate lime.

POLYGONUM vacciniifolium, a mat-forming rock polygonum from the Himalayas. It makes a carpet of evergreen leaves from which appear short spikes bearing many bright pink flowers. It grows very well over a bank or wall in full sun. (*See* also p. 149).

PAROCHETUS communis (Shamrock Pea). This bright blue pea-shaped rock plant was introduced from the Himalayas in 1820. It will grow in any moist well-drained soil, preferably partially shaded. If it is happy, it will spread rapidly, but it may not survive a severe winter. It has bright green clover-like leaves.

ZAUSCHNERIA californica, a fuchsia-like flower sometimes called Humming Bird's Trumpet. The scarlet flowers grow on loose spikes from spreading branches. It is not very hardy and will survive the winter only in a sheltered sunny place in the south. Elsewhere it can be preserved by taking cuttings in September and growing them in sandy soil in a cool house. It prefers rather poor soil.

1 Serratula shawii 2 Gentiana farreri 3 Sedum cauticola
4 Silene schafta 5 Cyclamen neapolitanum

LATE FLOWERING PERENNIALS

1-3 ASTER (Michaelmas daisy). These are easily grown plants which have been greatly improved in recent years. The first aster to be called Michaelmas daisy was *A. tradescantii*, which was brought to England from America in 1633 by John Tradescant, son of Charles I's Dutch gardener. Its sprays of tiny white flowers with yellow centres appear late and are sometimes spoilt by frost.

The garden hybrids grown today come from American species, far the biggest group being *A. novi-belgii* (1) the New York aster, of which new varieties are being added every year. *A. novae-angliae*, the New England aster, grows tall and shaggy with stiff stems. It is showy in the garden but not so good for cutting, and some varieties shut up at night. *A. ericoides* (2), sometimes called the white heather aster, has tiny flowers on long wiry stems and increases rather slowly from a woody rootstock. *A. cordifolius*, so named because of its heart-shaped leaves, has graceful sprays of small star-like flowers, usually lavender or white and sometimes with crimson centres. *A. macrophyllus* (3) has large, hairy, heart-shaped leaves, sturdy stems, and open sprays narrow-petalled flowers. It is a very suitable aster for a woodland garden and once established is difficult to eradicate.

Michaelmas daisies increase very quickly and need to be divided often, the strong outside shoots being used and the centre discarded. To get show specimens all but two or three stems on each plant should be removed in early growth. The plants can be prevented from growing too tall, and so difficult to stake, if they are cut back to 1–1½ ft. in July.

Some asters are subject to mildew, particularly in a very dry season, and this can be prevented by spraying the plants with karathene in the last week of June and again in early August.

VARIETIES: (1) *Aster novi-belgii* 'Elizabeth Bright', pink, 3 ft.; 'Gayborder Supreme', large rose-pink, semi-double, 5 ft.; 'Prosperity', heather-pink, double, 4 ft.; 'Miss Muffet', deep rose, 2½ ft.; 'Arctic', white, double, 5 ft.; 'Blandie', creamy-white, semi-double, 3 ft.; 'Ada Ballard', lavender-blue, very large, 3 ft.; 'Blue Gown', clear light blue, 4½ ft. (late); 'Harrison's Blue', blue-violet, semi-double, 4 ft.; 'Royal Velvet', violet, 2 ft.; 'Beechwood Rival', deep red, 3½ ft.; 'Gayborder Royal', crimson-purple, semi-double, 2½ ft.; 'Winston Churchill', claret-red, 2½ ft. DWARF: 'Lady Henry Maddocks', soft pink, 9 ins.; 'Margaret Rose', bright rose-pink, semi-double, 9 ins. (late); 'Snowsprite', white, semi-double, 9 ins.; 'Audrey', lilac-mauve, 1 ft. (late). (2) *A. ericoides* 'Delight', white, 2 ft.; 'Chastity', white, 2½ ft. (late); 'Ringdove', rosy-mauve, 3½ ft. (late); 'Blue Star', pale blue, 2½ ft. (late). (3) *A. macrophyllus*, lavender-blue, 1½–2 ft. (early). *A. novae-angliae*, 'Barr's Pink, bright mauve-pink, large semi-double, 5 ft.; 'Harrington's Pink', soft salmon-pink, 4 ft.; 'Crimson Beauty', rose-red, 4½ ft. (late); 'September Ruby', deep rose-red, 3 ft.; 'Treasure', lilac, 3 ft. *A. cordifolius* 'Silver Spray', white, 4 ft. (late), 'Sweet Lavender', lilac, 3 ft.

4 ANEMONE japonica (hupehensis). These tall autumn-flowering anemones, introduced originally from China and Japan, are adaptable plants which will grow anywhere, even in a cold, north-facing border or in walls. They are excellent plants for lightening a shrub border and last very well in water when cut. They resent disturbance and take a little time to settle down after planting. They can be increased by dividing the roots in October or March or by root cuttings. They will flower from August to October according to whether they are grown in sun or shade, and most of them grow from 2–3 ft. tall or taller.

VARIETIES: *A. vitifolia robustissima*, 3 ft.; *A. hupehensis* 'Louise Uhink', white, semi-double, 3 ft.; 'Honorine Jobert', white, single, 3½ ft.; 'September Charm', clear pink, 1½ ft.; 'Queen Charlotte', pink, large semi-double, 3 ft.; 'Mont Rosa', rose-pink, double, 2 ft.; 'Lorelei', rose-pink, single, 3 ft.; 'Bressingham Glow', ruby-red, semi-double, 1½ ft.

SEDUM. The tall autumn-flowering herbaceous stonecrops are useful late border plants, flower for many weeks, and are attractive to butterflies. They need no staking and their foliage is attractive all through the year. They do best in full sun, and can be divided in autumn or spring. They grow about 12–18 ins. tall and flower from August to October.

SPECIES: *Sedum spectabile*, bright pink; *s.* 'Autumn Joy' rose-salmon, tinted bronze; *s.* 'Brilliant', deep rose; *maximum atropurpureum*, copper-red leaves and stems and pale pink flowers; *telephium* 'Munstead Dark Red'. (*See* also pp. 91, 177.)

1 ASTER NOVI-BELGII 'ELIZABETH BRIGHT'   2 ASTER ERICOIDES 'DELIGHT'
3 ASTER MACROPHYLLUS   4 ANEMONE VITIFOLIA ROBUSTISSIMA

BORDER CHRYSANTHEMUMS

Chrysanthemums (*Chrysos*=golden, *anthos*=flower) have been bred over centuries from native plants by Chinese and Japanese gardeners. In China their cultivation dates back to about 500 B.C. They were not introduced successfully to Europe until the end of the 18th century. By the 1860's the National Chrysanthemum Society was holding exhibitions of both Chinese and Japanese types.

Chrysanthemums are a very large group containing many well-known garden flowers. The genus includes pyrethrums (*C. coccineum*) and shasta daisies (*C. maximum*), *see* p. 123; marguerites (*C. frutescens*), *see* p. 125; and annual chrysanthemums (*C. carinatum*), *see* p. 87. There are also British wild flowers — corn marigold, ox-eye daisy, and feverfew — of the chrysanthemum genus. There is a great variety of greenhouse chrysanthemums. It is not always easy to distinguish between some greenhouse and outdoor varieties, for many early-flowering greenhouse chrysanthemums will survive a not too severe winter out-of-doors, especially if given some protection, while most outdoor varieties are safer wintered in a cold frame in cold districts.

We are concerned here only with border chrysanthemums, and the illustrations opposite are all varieties of the new races, such as Korean Chrysanthemums, which are reasonably hardy herbaceous plants.

TYPES. There are about four different types of early-flowering chrysanthemums which can be grown out-of-doors: (1) Incurving, the florets turning inwards to form a loose ball; (2) Reflexed, the inner florets turn inwards but the outer turn outwards; (3) Pompon, small-flowered double; (4) Single, including races such as Charm and the original Koreans. The newly-developed herbaceous types, introduced from the U.S.A., have been achieved by crossing the early-flowering, single, branching varieties with other varieties and so achieving a wide range of chrysanthemums which can be grown as herbaceous plants.

Border chrysanthemums range from dwarf or cushion types, 12–18 ins. tall and making compact clumps, to plants up to 3½ ft. Of the varieties illustrated, 'Ember Day' and 'Wedding Sunshine' are 3 ft. tall; 'Cardinal', and 'Eugene Wanderer' are 2½ ft.; 'Brilliant' and 'Dusky' are 2 ft.; and 'Denise' is 1½ ft.

CULTIVATION. Chrysanthemums can be treated as autumn bedding plants, cuttings being taken from last year's plants and kept through the winter in a greenhouse or cold frame. They are planted out in the spring and are often disbudded carefully to produce fine flowers. The more hardy Korean and other varieties are treated as herbaceous plants; they stay out-of-doors all the year and consequently flower earlier.

Border chrysanthemums must also be started from rooted cuttings, planted out about mid-April. They prefer a sunny or semi-sunny position and well cultivated soil, into which rotted manure has been dug. In heavy soil plenty of compost should be used and the cuttings should be planted in peat and sand. They need protecting at first from the sparrows who will strip the leaves if they can. If the cuttings have not already been stopped (the central shoots pinched out), this should be done some 10 days after planting, and once again not later than the first week in July. They benefit from a watering with a chrysanthemum fertilizer at intervals.

Except in warm districts, it is safer to cover the plants with at least 2 ins. of ashes or a layer of bracken or peat early in December, and for further protection not to cut down the tops till the spring. The new shoots must be guarded against slugs. Every other year it is better to lift the plants in the spring and divide them, just as michaelmas daisies are divided (*see* p. 179). Cuttings can also be taken, as already stated, in the autumn.

BORDER CHRYSANTHEMUMS

1 'EMBER DAY'   2 'WEDDING SUNSHINE'   3 'CARDINAL'
4 'EUGENE WANDERER'   5 'BRILLIANT'   6 'DENISE'
7 'DUSKY'

AUTUMN BULBS

The majority of bulbs and corms are spring or early summer flowerers, but there are a few very beautiful autumn-flowering bulbs, the most important being the colchicums. In their native countries these burst into flower with the coming of the first autumn rains after the hot summer. All these plants have also spring or early summer flowering species (*see* p. 11).

1-3 C O L C H I C U M . These members of the lily family mostly come from the Mediterranean and Near East (Colchis is a Greek name for a region east of the Black Sea). *C. autumnale* (Meadow Saffron), however, is a British wild flower. The leaves, which are very large, appear in late winter or spring and die down in June. As the flowers come up on long tubes before the leaves, they are best planted among low shrubs which will give them some protection from wind and rain. The flowers can be easily distinguished from those of crocuses by the six showy stamens — crocuses have only three. When the clumps grow big, they should be divided in June, and the corms replanted in early August with the tops about 2 ins. below the surface.

    C. cilicium (1) and the deeper coloured variety *C. cilicium purpureum* are very free-flowering and not so tall nor the leaves so large as most colchicums. There are several varieties of *C. speciosum, atrorubens* (2) being the darkest and *album* (3) being a beautiful white. They flower in September and October, while the variety *bornmulleri*, with a greenish-white tube and white throat, flowers earlier — in late August. There are also many hybrids, some globular, some starry in shape. 'Princess Astrid' and 'Autumn Queen' are rosy-violet varieties which come early, and 'Violet Queen' is a late variety. *C. agrippinum*, with its smaller leaves, is suitable for the rock garden.

4-5 C R O C U S , autumn. Though most crocuses are spring-flowering (*see* p. 11), there are several which flower in the autumn. Those illustrated flower after the leaves have died down, but others flower with their leaves. They are mostly relatively small, both foliage and flowers, and need sunny positions to encourage them to open. They do better on light soil. Apart from a few white forms, they are always some shade of blue, violet, or purple, often beautifully marked, and sometimes with a finely divided orange or scarlet stigma.

C. nudiflorus (4) is a native in parts of south-west Europe and is found naturalized in some places in Britain. It is variable in colour and has a white form. It spreads by underground runners which form new corms at the end. *C. speciosus* (5) spreads freely by seeds and cormlets and has many varieties, the bluest, 'Oxonian', being unfortunately the least vigorous. *C. clusii* is a dwarf species from Portugal. *C. kotschyanus* (*C. zonatus*) is an early species, rosy-lilac with orange spots at the base of the flower. *C. pulchellus* with an orange throat flowers in October, and *C. salzmanni* is a strong plant flowering into November.

6 S T E R N B E R G I A lutea angustifolia. This form of the species *S. lutea* is the best garden variety, for it continues to produce many flowers from September into November. It flowers with its leaves and is very weatherproof. The bulbs should be planted 4–6 ins. below the surface and should be left undisturbed.

Z E P H Y R A N T H E S candida. Like Sternbergia, this belongs to the daffodil family. Most are rather tender spring or summer flowerers, but *Z. candida* is hardy and produces white, crocus-like flowers on 6 in. stems among rush-like leaves. It should have some protection in hard winters.

L E U C O J U M autumnale (Autumn Snowflake). Leucojum, another of the daffodil family, is best known as a spring flower (*see* p. 7). This autumn species has little white, pink-tinted bells on 3 in. stalks. It needs to be planted in groups of a dozen or so in a choice spot in rather sandy soil in order that it may make a show.

1 COLCHICUM CILICIUM
2 COLCHICUM SPECIOSUM ATRORUBENS
3 COLCHICUM SPECIOSUM ALBUM
4 CROCUS NUDIFLORUS
5 CROCUS SPECIOSUS
6 STERNBERGIA LUTEA ANGUSTIFOLIA

ROSE FAMILY SHRUBS: AUTUMN BERRIES AND LEAVES. 1

As the autumn advances, many gardens depend for colour on the foliage and coloured fruits of trees and shrubs. A large number of these belong to the Rose family, to which belong apples, pears, cherries, almonds, and many others. Some find a place in the flower garden only because of their autumn display; others, such as most of the apple genus (malus) have lovely spring blossom as well. Some, including the many prunus species, blossom but make no autumn show. Many would grow much too large for small gardens unless they were firmly cut back. There are many improved varieties and hybrids of the wild species suitable for gardens.

1 MALUS (Latin for 'apple'). The decorative crab apples vary from large trees 30–40 ft. high to shrubs of 5–8 ft., though most of them are tall. Many are derived from the native wild crab (M. *pumila*), from the Siberian crab (M. *prunifolia*), or from Chinese or Japanese species. They almost all have showy spring flowers in white, pink, and wine-red, and the apple-shaped fruits vary in size from that of a small cherry to 1 in. or more in diameter. In colour they may be yellow, orange, scarlet, or purplish-red. Some, for example the Siberian crab and 'John Downie', a variety of the wild crab, have large, brilliant yellow and scarlet edible berries which make excellent jelly. Some have coppery-coloured or purplish young foliage (M. x. *lemoinei* and M. x. *aldenhamensis*); the leaves of others turn orange and red in the autumn (M. *coronaria* 'Charlottae').

M. x. 'Golden Hornet' (1) is a newer variety, a seedling of a Japanese hybrid of the Siberian crab. It has white flowers, and the fruits hang late in the year.

PYRUS (Latin for 'pear'). Many species which used to be listed under 'Pyrus' are now included in the Malus or Sorbus lists: for example, Pyrus *malus floribunda* is now M. *floribunda*. Pears are not much grown for their decorative value, but the abundance of pure white flowers and snowy white down on the young leaves give P. *nivalis* and P. *salicifolia* a spring beauty, but no particular autumn interest.

2-5 SORBUS (Mountain Ash or Rowan). A big genus stretching across the northern hemisphere, of which our native S. *aucuparia*, with its bunches of orange berries, is well-known. Many new species have been introduced from the Far East and are grown not for their flowers but for the berries and vivid autumn foliage. In time they form big trees, but the species described here can be kept to a reasonable size for many years and bear fruit when relatively small. Birds usually destroy the orange berries, but in some areas they do not take the white, pink, or yellow ones so readily.

S. *cashmeriana* (2), a recent introduction, has the largest berries of any known sorbus, graceful foliage, and pinkish flowers. If only one can be grown, this is probably the best sorbus to choose.

S. *Rock* 23657 (foliolosa) (3). This sorbus was first exhibited under the name S. *foliolosa*, but this has now been withdrawn, and it has no official name except the collector's number. The famous American collector Dr. Rock found it in China. Its pale butter-yellow berries are freely produced from an early age, and it has rich autumn foliage colour.

S. *hupehensis* (4-5), has the same tree-like growth as has No. 3 and may reach 40 ft. But it has smaller flowers and fruits. The greyish foliage has good autumn colouring, and the fruits, pinkish at first, turn white as they get ripe. There is a smaller growing variety, S. *hupehensis aperta*, with pearly fruits, which is better for small gardens. From time to time a new hybrid sorbus appears. The variety, No. 5, illustrated here and called 'Red Tip', is an example. It apparently originated in Holland and is claimed to have a pyramidal habit of growth which makes it suitable for a restricted space.

Other smaller varieties of sorbus, with elegant fern-like foliage and suitable for smaller gardens, are S. *koehneana* with small white berries on red stalks, S. *poterifolia* with pink flowers and deep pink fruits, and S. *vilmoriniana* with dull rose fruits changing to pink-tinged white.

6 COTONEASTER. This is a large genus of hardy, deciduous or evergreen shrubs or small trees. Almost all the species and varieties have red, orange, or purplish-black berries; there are a very few new varieties with yellow berries. The hybrid or seedling variety, C. *exburyensis*, which is illustrated, has yellow-green berries which turn bright yellow when ripe; C. *rothschildiana* has rather deeper yellow fruit.

Some cotoneasters are evergreen prostrate dwarfs, growing only 1–2 ft. high and useful for rock gardens or covering slopes. C. *microphylla* or C. *buxifolia* are good species. Others are rather small and spreading, such as C. *conspicua*, or larger up to about 10 ft., such as C. *bullata macrophylla*, C. *hebephylla*, and C. *franchetti sterniana*. C. *serotina* is a very good late-flowering species which, unless the birds eat them, will carry its berries through to the spring. The hybrids of C. *frigida* make small trees laden with red berries.

Cotoneasters prefer a limy soil, but will grow in any soil, even a very poor one.

1 Malus x 'Golden Hornet'   2 Sorbus cashmeriana   3 Sorbus Rock 23657

4 Sorbus hupehensis   5 Sorbus x 'Red Tip'   6 Cotoneaster exburyensis

ROSE FAMILY SHRUBS: AUTUMN BERRIES AND LEAVES. 2

The plants described on this page, as on p. 184, all belong to the Rosacaea or rose family, but these species, apart from pyracantha, are all true Roses, and are important for their summer flowers (*see* pp. 93 – 101) as well as their autumn berries.

1-2 PYRACANTHA (*pyr* =fire, *acanthos* =thorn). These are large, evergreen, more or less thorny shrubs or small trees, all of which, except P. *coccinea*, the very popular European 'Fire Thorn', come originally from China. They have white flowers and red, orange, or yellow fruits which are very attractive to birds. They grow vigorously, as much as 12–18 ins. in a year, and will do well on a north wall. They will stand a great deal of clipping back and so can be used to cover a wall or to make a thick hedge.

P. *atalantioides aurea* (1). P. *atalantioides* is the tallest grower and has the largest leaves. The berries are normally reddish, but in this variety they are golden.

P. *rogersiana* (2), being a smaller-growing species, is more suited to small gardens. It has smaller leaves and a more slender and less vigorous growth. It produces enormous crops of berries, normally orange, but very variable. The variety *aurantiaca* has berries tinged with red, and *flava* has golden-yellow berries.

3-6 ROSA. Species of this large genus are to be found throughout the northern hemisphere, though the majority of garden species come from China or Japan. Some of them spread very fast by suckers and can be a nuisance, except in a wild garden. Many are grown more for their flowers than their autumn berries.

R. *soulieana* (3), a Chinese species which has yellowish-white flowers and will form a dense prickly bush up to 10 ft. high. It is better grown in a wild corner or wild garden.

R. *moyesii* (4), also from China, is valuable not only for its splendid fruits but also for its striking blood-red flowers (*see* p. 93). It is a strong grower, but can be kept to a reasonable size by cutting out the old rods at intervals. There are many seedling varieties and hybrids. 'Geranium' has lighter flowers; 'Sealing Wax' has masses of scarlet fruits, but less good flowers; *highdownensis* also has masses of fruits.

R. *rugosa* (5), from North China, Japan, and Korea, makes a vigorous low bush, with handsome foliage and fragrant red or white flowers. It is long flowering and will grow in any soil and position. The variety 'Frau Dagmar Hastrup' bears the largest fruits, has clear rose flowers, and the leaves turn a clear yellow in autumn. *See* also p. 93.

R. *reversa* (6), a hybrid of the alpine R. *pendulina* and the Burnet or Scots Briar R. *spinosissima*. The fruits of the former are large and bright red and those of the latter small and black. The cross has produced fruit of a colour between the two.

CRATAEGUS (**Hawthorn**). *Kratos* =strength and refers to the hardness of the wood. The majority of these small deciduous trees come from North America but some come from Europe into Turkey and also North Africa, and two, C. *monogyna* and C. *oxyacantha*, are natives of Britain. Their flowers are white, but some garden varieties have pink or red flowers, both single and double. They thrive in almost any soil, and they should be grown more than they are for their coloured autumn berries.

Good species are C. x. *carrierei* which has fine blossom and large scarlet fruit; C. *durobrivensis*, the largest flowered species with long-hanging crimson fruit; C. *orientalis*, which is slow growing but has attractive grey leaves and pale orange fruit. C. *submollis* produces clusters of large orange-red berries when the tree is quite young, but they tend to fall rather early.

1 Pyracantha atalantioides aurea   2 Pyracantha rogersiana aurantiaca
3 Rosa soulieana   4 Rosa moyesii
5 Rosa rugosa   6 Rosa reversa

SHRUBS: AUTUMN BERRIES AND LEAVES. 3

The majority of autumn fruits and berries tend to be some shade of yellow, orange, or red; a smaller number are pink, and fewer still are blue or pure white. In a well-furnished garden the inclusion of some of the less common colours adds interest and variety. Pages 185 and 187 are confined to those shrubs belonging to the large Rose family; this page has specimens from a selection of other families.

1 SYMPHORICARPUS 'Mother of Pearl'. This belongs to the same genus as the well-known Snowberry (S. *rivularis*), a native of North America which has become naturalized in Britain. An improved variety, with much larger berries and less liable to spread through suckering, S. *albus laevigatus*, has pure white fruits half-an-inch across and produced in such masses that they weigh down the 6 ft. stems. Also the birds do not eat them as they do the common Snowberry. A new variety is 'White Hedge', upright in growth with upright clusters of pea-sized white fruit. Several pink to red hybrids, of which the oldest is 'Chenaultii', have been developed from the red-fruited S. *orbiculatus*, which itself bears few and small berries. 'Mother of Pearl' (1), 'Magic Berry' (cyclamen pink), and 'Erect' (red) are recent great improvements. The flowers of Symphoricarpus are not very attractive.

2 CLERODENDRON fargesii. Most clerodendrons are stove or greenhouse plants; even the hardy ones need protected positions. They are shrubs or small trees which flower late, August-September, and continue their beauty with a show of berries. The flat heads of off-white, sweet-scented flowers are about 6 ins. across. The leaves have an unpleasant scent when crushed. C. *fargesii*, from China, fruits freely when established, but takes some time to become so. The calyx, the outermost part of the flower, starts green and becomes pink with age. C. *trichotomum* from Japan is slightly less hardy and has calyces which are always reddish and rather darker fruits.

CALLICARPA (*kallos* =beauty, *karpos* =fruit). This is another shrub of the same family as clerodendron, of which only some species are hardy. They have uninteresting flowers, but produce clusters of very attractive bright violet berries in the late autumn. As they do better if they can cross fertilize, more than one specimen should be planted — perhaps C. *giraldiana* (6 ft.) at the back, with C. *dichotoma* (4 ft.) in front. Both of these are hardy.

3 CORNUS alba siberica. C. *alba*, the dog-wood, is too rampant for the ordinary garden, but C. *alba siberica* is much less so and is grown mainly for the beauty of the bright-red young shoots which show up effectively in the autumn and, if cut, will retain their bright colour all the winter. The old wood becomes duller, and therefore it is usual to cut back or 'pollard' the plant, like a willow, each spring. The leaves turn red in the autumn, and the pale blue fruit shows well against the green and red.

4 VIBURNUM. Many viburnums are grown for their fragrant spring flowers (*see* pp. 3, 25); others for their autumn foliage and berries. V. *davidii* (4) is a dwarf evergreen with leathery leaves and handsome blue berries. The berries, however, are borne only on female plants and then only if at least one male is present to fertilize them, so it is essential to be sure that the circumstances are right for producing fruit.

Most viburnums have red or occasionally black or yellow fruits. The garden forms of the wild plant V. *opulus* (Guelder Rose) are very decorative. The form *xanthocarpum* has large bunches of amber berries which hang through the winter, as the birds never seem to touch them. V. *opulus* 'Notcutt's variety' has bunches of very large clear red berries. V. *betulifolium*, when mature, produces drooping clusters of red currant-like berries on an 8–9 ft. bush.

5 LEYCESTERIA formosa. The attraction of this hardy Himalayan plant lies in the claret-coloured bracts which enclose the flowers and, later, the reddish-purple fruit. These are beloved of birds and as a result seeds are scattered and tend to grow up all over the place. The shrub, which has a bamboo-like growth and rich green leaves, is about 6 ft. tall.

AMPELOPSIS heterophylla. A vine-like fruiting climber with porcelain blue-black speckled fruits, which are in effect little grapes. It comes from the Far East and needs a hot sunny wall, though ampelopses, such as A. *veitchi*, the small-leaved Virginia Creeper, are suitable to grow on north walls.

SKIMMIA. An evergreen, moderate-sized shrub which makes a good show of bright orange-red berries set against pale green foliage, which last well. The most commonly planted has been S. *japonica* which, being single sexed, will flower only on female bushes when there is also a male bush. The hybrid S. x. *foremanii* is self-fertilizing and will grow on any soil, and S. *reevesiana* is shorter and does well on acid soils. Skimmias will grow in sun or half shade.

BERBERIS (Barberry). This is a vast group of prickly shrubs with a rich show of autumn berries. The best fruiting species are those which flower late (June or July). These also have rich autumn leaf colour. A good choice might be: B. x. *carminea* 'Barbarossa' or 'Buccaneer' with long clusters of large berries, the former scarlet and the latter coral-crimson; B. *aggregata* 'Sibbertoft Coral' with darker berries; and B. *prattii laxipendula*, a new variety with long sprays of bright pink berries. B. *wilsonae* 'Tom Thumb' is a dwarf variety suitable for rock gardens. *See* also p. 23.

1 SYMPHORICARPUS 'MOTHER OF PEARL'   2 CLERODENDRON FARGESII   3 CORNUS ALBA SIBERICA

4 VIBURNUM DAVIDII   5 LEYCESTERIA FORMOSA

EVERLASTING FLOWERS AND SEEDPODS

Flowers for drying should be cut just before they are fully open, and then tied in bunches and hung upside down in a dry airy place. Seedpods are cut when they are dry and papery, and then also hung up until required.

1 L U N A R I A **annua (Honesty).** This plant is more often grown for its flat, papery, moon-shaped seed-heads than its June to July flowers; though these, which vary from white to rich purple, are quite attractive. Lunaria does well in semi-shade and can be grown as a biennial (*see* p. 33). Once it has been grown in the garden it will usually seed itself and come up every year afterwards.

SPECIES: *Lunaria annua* 'Munstead Purple', 3 ft.; *variegata*, 3 ft., crimson flowers, variegated foliage; *L. rediviva*, 2–3 ft., white and violet, a perennial variety, with smaller seedpods.

2 A M M O B I U M **alatum grandiflorum** (*ammos* =sand, *bio* =to live). An Australian plant, best treated as a half-hardy annual. It will grow in any ordinary soil and grows about 1½ ft. tall.

3 X E R A N T H E M U M **annuum** (*xeros* =dry, *anthos* = flower). These hardy annuals grow about 2 ft. tall and prefer light soil. The flowers keep their colours of pink, lavender, and white particularly well when dried.

4 H E L I C H R Y S U M **bracteatum** (*helios* =sun, *chrysos* = golden). Most helichrysums are shrubs (*see* p. 65), but this everlasting species from Australia is a half-hardy annual, growing 2–3 ft. tall and with a wide range of colours from white and yellow to dark blood-red. The dried flowers keep their colours excellently.

5 L I M O N I U M **sinuatum (Statice).** This Sea Lavender is a perennial, but is best grown in the garden as a half-hardy annual, or a hardy annual in mild districts. Many pastel shades have been developed.

The perennial herbaceous *L. latifolium* also dries very well. It grows 2–3 ft. tall and has slender, loosely-branched stems bearing small blue or lavender flowers (*see* p. 148).

P H Y S A L I S **franchetii (Chinese Lantern).** This and the rather less hardy *P. alkekengi*, the Bladder Cherry, are perennials from China and Japan, which have rather insignificant white flowers and very showy, orange and scarlet, bell- or lantern-shaped calyces surrounding the fruits, which dry well. *P. franchetii* will grow in any soil in any unwanted corner, and unless restrained may spread further than it is wanted.

O T H E R E V E R L A S T I N G P L A N T S. Several plants, both annuals and perennials, described elsewhere in this book are suitable for drying and winter decoration. (1) ANNUALS. Helipterum (*helios* =sun, *pteron* =wing) is a half-hardy annual of the daisy family, the flowers being not unlike helichrysum. Molucella (Bells of Ireland), which is hardier, have enlarged pale green calyces which turn an attractive ivory colour when dried. *See* also p. 126.

(2) PERENNIALS. Acanthus has long spikes with purple calyces (*see* p. 157). Achillea, solidago, and anaphalis (*see* p. 151) all provide good yellow colouring for the winter vase, and anaphalis has decorative silver or grey-green foliage. Artemisia is silvery white with an aromatic scent (*see* p. 150). Catananche (*see* p. 123), which is not unlike xeranthemum, provides pinks and blues, Echinops, the Globe Thistle (*see* p. 115) and eryngium, the Sea Holly (*see* p. 155) provide blues and grey-greens. Hydrangea heads (*see* p. 145), if cut late in the season and kept in water until they become papery, turn a good maroon colour. A lightness and softness in a dried flower arrangement is attained by using *Gypsophila paniculata* (*see* p. 148).

Some wild-flower seed-heads also are very effective: for example, the split-open capsules of Roast-beef Plant, *Iris foetidissima* — though the orange-red seeds tend to fall out unless carefully handled. The dead flower-heads of Teasel, *Dipsacus fullonum*, turn an attractive brown and are a good shape.

1 LUNARIA ANNUA   2 AMMOBIUM ALATUM GRANDIFLORUM   3 XERANTHEMUM ANNUUM
4 HELICHRYSUM BRACTEATUM   5 LIMONIUM SINUATUM

MID AND LATE SUMMER LILIES

The majority of garden lilies flower in early to mid July, depending on the season, though some flower as late as September. Although the species are interesting to grow, and the reasonably easy ones mentioned below might well be included in any gardens, there is no doubt that the modern hybrids, because of their ease of cultivation and great beauty, are most likely to give satisfaction. Before reading a description of lilies one should know the difference between a 'strain' and a 'clone'. A clone represents one original lily, the offspring of which have arisen from normal division or from bulblets produced from the scales of the bulb, and therefore will be exactly alike. A strain, on the other hand, represents the offspring of a number of lilies of similar breeding but raised from seed; the bulbs will produce flowers very much alike but not identical. As the latter is the quicker and easier method of raising stocks, such lilies are always cheaper.

1 EMERALD STRAIN is one of the group of hybrids resulting from the crossing of the yellow semi-reflexed *L. henryi* and various trumpet lilies, followed by selection and intercrossing. The flowers are a translucent, pure, cold white with a green flush at opening. They are about 5 ins. across, and about a dozen are borne in a pyramid on 4- to 6-ft. stems in July. Other good strains are 'African Queen', apricot or orange with a bronzy exterior, and 'Golden Splendour', a lovely soft yellow with maroon outside, which may have up to fifteen flowers in the head. These are about 4 ft. high. The Olympic hybrids, with the white, yellow-throated, brown-streaked *L. leucanthum centifolium* in their breeding, have open, bowl-shaped trumpet flowers in white, cream, lemon-yellow, and soft pink, and flower in July-August, and are very vigorous.

Of species with trumpet flowers, the best-known is *L. regale*, with its scented white flowers with sulphur-yellow throat and pinkish exterior, and its offspring 'Royal Gold'. Others to be considered are *L. sargentiae*, also white and scented and about 5 ft. tall, and the Creelman hybrids, white with a brown or green exterior, which will go up to 6 ft., and are hybrids of the two just mentioned.

2 BRIGHT STAR is another hybrid with *L. henryi* blood and is a clone. It has the wide, flaring, flat, open flowers of a distinct group. The flowers are silvery white with a vivid orange centre which tends to spread up the petals. They may be up to 5½ ins. across and up to fourteen heads on a 3-ft. stem. Another good clone of this type is 'Stardust', also with white petals and a small green star in the orange centre. This lily may grow up to 5 ft. tall. 'Golden Sunburst' is a strain of this type, varying from lemon to gold. Closely allied is the 'Heart's Desire' strain, with shallow bowl-shaped flowers in white, cream, or pale orange.

3 L. SPECIOSUM (**Red Champion**) is a selected ruby-red strain of the Japanese *L. speciosum*, which has 5-in. flowers on 3-ft. stems. There are white and pink varieties, as well as the similar ruby-carmine 'Numazu Beauty'. These lilies do not flower until September and therefore must be grown in a sheltered sunny place; in cold areas they are better grown in pots.

L. Speciosum was concerned in the original cross with the well-known *L. auratum* which produced *L. x parkmannii*. Of recent years many such hybrids have been produced, particularly in New Zealand and Australia, as well as in America. They, like *L. auratum*, may have flowers 9- to 12-ins. across on 6- to 7-ft. stems; but they are still expensive, and most gardeners are wiser to grow a good strain of the white, yellow-rayed, purple-spotted *L. auratum* itself, or one of its varieties. These latter lilies flower in late July and August.

4 CROESUS is a 4-ft. lily, golden yellow with black spots, one of the Mid-Century Hybrids (*see* p. 69), which have *L. tigrinum* blood. There are usually six flowers on a stem. This is rather earlier-flowering than the others on this page, and may be in flower by late June or early July.

Two easy lilies of similar shape in yellow to orange shades are the hybrids of the west-coast lilies of America, 'Shuksan', light orange with dark maroon spots, and the Bellingham Hybrids, mostly yellow-orange to orange-red. They may have as many as twenty flowers on 5-ft. stems.

L. henryi, which is used so much in developing new varieties, is an easy lily but has poor weak stems and therefore always needs staking. All the lilies with its blood will grow on limy soils, as also those bred from *L. regale* and *L. leucanthum centifolium;* but *L. speciosum* and *auratum* and their hybrids will not tolerate lime. Books on lily culture should be consulted for cultural details. For earlier-flowering lilies, *see* p. 69.

1 GREEN MOUNTAIN HYBRID, 'EMERALD STRAIN'
2 SUNBURST TYPE, 'BRIGHT STAR'
3 SPECIOSUM 'RED CHAMPION'
4 MID-CENTURY HYBRID 'CROESUS'

MINIATURE GARDENS

In recent years the growing of alpine plants in old stone troughs and sinks has become increasingly popular. It is surprising how well many of the small and more difficult plants thrive under these conditions. Whilst old stone is the best and most attractive material, suitable containers can be made of cement (with or without peat added to the mixture), or out of half barrels. Glazed sinks are not so suitable or attractive.

The placing of the garden is important, and this must depend on what plants are grown — whether they need full sun or prefer cool shady conditions. A draughty site should be avoided. It is better to raise the garden on pillars made from weathered brick or stone so that the final height is approximately 2 ft. from the ground. This is a comfortable height for looking at the plants and also reduces the danger from slugs and other pests.

Drainage is all important. Most troughs have a hole at the side or at one end, and when setting the trough in position, a slight tilt should be given towards the hole so that water can drain out satisfactorily. It is wise to test this before filling the trough. If there is no hole, then one must be made with a hammer and chisel. A large piece of broken crock (flower pot) or stone should be placed over the hole to prevent the soil running out, and then a layer some 3 ins. thick of broken stone or clinker should be placed over the whole of the bottom of the trough. This is to ensure perfect drainage. A layer of rough turf fibre or leaves on the top of the drainage layer prevents the soil being washed through. Finally comes the layer of soil which should fill up the trough to just below the brim. In order to have room for these layers and enough depth of soil for the plants, the trough should be at least 6, preferably 9, ins. deep.

The soil should be a gritty mixture, such as the John Innes seed mixture without fertilizer. This suits the vast majority of alpine plants; but for ericaceous species, such as rhododendrons, and plants such as *Primula marginata* (p. 21), and *Gentiana sino-ornata* (p. 34), more peat should be used and the soil should be lime free. Finally, the effect is improved if a few pieces of stone are inserted, for these give the impression of a miniature outcrop of rock. Tufa or weathered Westmorland stone are suitable, but not pieces of brick, concrete, or even flint. The rocks should be half buried in the soil.

When choosing what plants to grow, the size the plant will eventually reach, its season of flowering, and its preference for sun or shade must all be taken into consideration. Quickly-spreading rampant plants are to be avoided, but cushion plants which spread slowly and those which will fall over the side of the trough are more suitable. Some of the miniature spring bulbs can be included. Plants with attractive foliage as well as flower are valuable, and it is well worth finding room for one or two dwarf conifers to give interest in the winter. A list of possible choices is given at the end, with a page reference to the place in the book where each is illustrated or described.

Before planting, the soil must be allowed a few days to settle and become firm. After planting, it is a good plan to cover the surface with a half-inch layer of dull-grey stone chippings. These not only give the garden a natural effect but act as a mulch in summer to prevent drying out, and in the winter they keep the collar of the plants drier and so prevent rotting off — which can be a serious danger. A trough measuring about 2 ft. by 2½ ft. will accommodate about twelve or sixteen slow-growing plants, depending on the amount of rock used.

The 'garden' must, of course, be kept weeded, and in the summer must not be allowed to get too dry. In very dry weather the drainage hole can be stopped up to preserve moisture; otherwise a

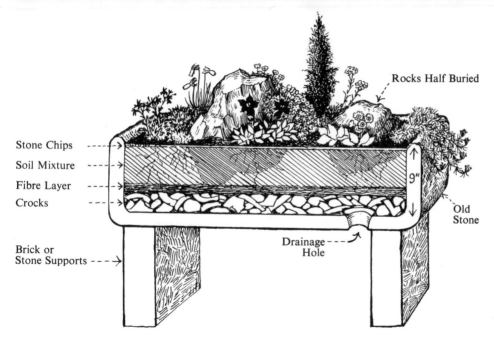

Labels on the illustration:
- Rocks Half Buried
- Stone Chips
- Soil Mixture
- Fibre Layer
- Crocks
- 9"
- Old Stone
- Brick or Stone Supports
- Drainage Hole

SECTION OF STONE TROUGH

good watering in the evening is best. In winter wet weather, a cloche or sheet of glass put over the trough will protect the plants from damp, which they dislike more than cold.

SUITABLE MINIATURE-GARDEN PLANTS

Spring

Androsace sempervivioides, 20
Aethionema 'Warley Rose', 43
Alyssum serpyllifolium, 40
Armeria caespitosa, Bevan's var., 80
Crocus chrysanthus; C. minimus, 11
Erinus alpinus, 43
Gentiana verna, 34
Iris histrioides; I. danfordiae, 11
Morisia monantha, 21
Narcissus asturiensis, 10
Primula marginata, 21
Ranunculus alpestris, 44
Saxifrages, Kabschia and Engleria groups, 21
Soldanella villosa, 21

Summer

Allium flavum nanum, 70
Antennaria dioica minima, 88
Asperula caespitosa lilaciflora, 42
Campanula allionii, 80
Dianthus alpinus, 78
Globularia bellidifolia, 80
Helichrysum milfordae, 91
Myosotis rupicola, 32
Papaver alpinum, 82
Phlox douglasii 'Violet Queen', 40
Penstemon rupicola, 90

Saxifraga aizoon minutifolia
Sempervivums, 91
Veronica prostrata nana, 40

Autumn

Acaena microphylla, 88
Anagallis tenella, 140
Cyclamen europaeum, 176
Gentiana farreri; G. saxosa, 177
Leucojum autumnale, 182
Linaria alpina, 134
Oxalis lobata, 44
Sedum cauticola, 176

Dwarf Shrubs

Cytisus hirsutus demissus, 67
Hebe x 'Carl Teschner', 66
Helianthemum lunulatum, 65
Helichrysum selago, 42
Hypericum empetrifolium, 64
Teucrium subspinosum, 90

Conifers (not illustrated)

Chamaecyparis obtusa nana
Juniperus communis compressa
Pinus sylvestris beauvronensis

CLASSIFYING AND NAMING OF GARDEN PLANTS

This book is concerned only with the seed-bearing cultivated plants, and of these only with those which have the seed or seeds enclosed in an outer covering of some sort, such as the shell of a nut or the pod of a pea. These are called Angiosperms in contrast to the Gymnosperms, or naked seeded plants, such as the conifers. The Angiosperms are divided into two classes; the Monocotyledons, the seedlings of which have only one seed leaf, such as Iris, Tulip, and Narcissus; and the Dicotyledons, which have two seed leaves. This latter is far the larger class. The classes are divided into families, such as Compositae and Labiatae, in which there is what may be called a broad family resemblance. The Compositae, for example, all have numerous small, more or less inconspicuous flowers called florets arranged closely on a disc, with or without a showy outer ring of ray florets, as in the daisy; the Labiatae have flowers which all have a distinct lower lip (*see* pages 105 and 153). The families are divided into genera. The generic name, such as Alyssum, Berberis, Phlox, means that all the plants with that name have certain features in common, usually associated with the flower, fruit, and seed, which are not found in other genera. Individuals in the genus which have the same and constant distinctive characters are known as species: for example, Alyssum *maritimum*, *A. saxatile*, *A. spinosum*. All these have the special generic characters of Alyssum but differ in other respects, as may be seen by reference to the Plates. The specific name may be an indication of where a plant grows: *maritimum* means near the sea; *alpinum*, in mountains; *palustris*, in marshes. The name may indicate the discoverer or introducer, such as Berberis *darwinii* after the naturalist Charles Darwin; or the country of its origin: Rosa *chinensis* or Linaria *maroccana* (Morocco). It may show the size or colour of the flower: Magnolia *grandiflora*, large-flowered, or Helleborus *atrorubens*, black-red in colour. Cyclamen *vernum* flowers in the spring; Helenium *autumnale* flowers in the autumn, and so on.

Two species of a genus may cross-fertilize naturally in the wild or in the garden, usually by means of insects; but the majority of hybrids, as they are called, have been produced artificially by the hand of man. A primary hybrid (first cross) is indicated by x between the name of the genus and the name given to the hybrid. For example, Hypericum *calycinum* crossed with *H. patulum* (*H. calycinum x H. patulum*) gives the hybrid, *H. x moserianum:* similarly Viburnum *x bodnantense* (*V. fragrans x V. grandiflorum*). The plants raised from the seeds of such crosses will not necessarily be exactly alike; if the horticulturist selects a particularly good one for cultivation and propagation, it is then given a name and is then known as a 'cultivar' (cultivated variety), such as *V. x bodnantense* 'Dawn'. All plants of a cultivar distributed must have been propagated from the original by cuttings, division, or grafting, and then form a 'clone'. Seedlings from it, if it produces seed, cannot be called 'Dawn', for they may not come true. In some families, such as Cyclamen, where cross-fertilization does not take place, no hybrids exist; in others, such as orchids, they are extremely plentiful.

Apart from hybrids, seedlings of plants vary among themselves to different degrees. If any one shows advantages in habit of growth, colour of flower, or foliage or fruit, which it is desired to bring into general cultivation, it also must have a cultivar name, such as Acer *platanoides* 'Crimson King', and no other Acer *platanoides* is allowed this name. At one time Latin names were often used for such variants: for example, Acer *platanoides drummondii* (*drummondii* referring to the botanist Drummond), but since 1954 this has not been allowed. Also one should now no longer speak of Armeria *caespitosa* Bevan's variety, for example, but *A. caespitosa* 'Roger Bevan'. A second Latin name is allowed only to the botanist who wants to distinguish a variation occurring in a natural state, such as Crocus *longiflorus melitensis*, the form of this crocus found only in Malta and differing from the Crocus *longiflorus* from Italy.

In the course of time in some genera, such as Iris, Lilium, and Delphinium, so many different plants have been raised by hybridization and seedling selection that the original parentage is unknown, and then only the genus and the cultivar name is recorded — as, for example, Iris 'Golden Hind', Delphinium 'C. F. Langdon', Lilium 'Shuksan'.

PLANNING A GARDEN

In these short notes we have in mind small gardens cultivated, with or without occasional help, by the owner who wishes to grow a selection of the plants illustrated or similar ones. The planning of large gardens is best left to the professional landscape gardener.

The garden to be planted may be a new one on uncultivated soil, or it may have been in existence for some years. If a new site, the first thing to discover is the nature of the soil, whether acid, neutral, or limy; information on this is important, because, for example, rhododendrons and heathers will not grow on a limy soil, whereas many plants, such as flowering cherries delight in it (*see* list p. 199). Neutral or slightly acid soils will grow most plants. The County Horticultural Adviser will always give advice about soils. Further, a selection of plants is also governed by whether the soil is sandy, or a loam or clay soil. If it is a light loam it will grow almost everything. Assuming one cannot afford to import fresh soil, the basis of a successful garden is to choose the plants which will grow with ordinary care in the soil available. It is helpful to observe what is growing in other gardens in the immediate neighbourhood, and particularly in the nearest nursery. If there is a local horticultural society, it is well worth joining it, for much may be learned from other gardeners. Never try to fill the garden until you know the most suitable kinds of plants for it.

In an old garden the existing plants give a clue to those which are suitable, and it is wiser not to dig up things until you are quite sure they are not plants or shrubs which you want, or ones which will afford temporary shelter for new ones until these have grown up. Ideas for improvement will come gradually, as one watches the garden from day to day, in all weathers.

As well as knowing about the soil, it is important to understand the climate of the garden which, apart from the general climate of the district, is influenced by the amount of sun it receives and the direction of the winds to which it is most subject. If possible, shelter from the north, northeast, and east should be provided by a fence, hedge, or screening of some kind. The sunny and shady parts of the garden need different kinds of plants (*see* lists p. 200), and what may be planted in the shady part depends on what throws the shade. Shade from buildings or from trees some way outside the garden offer minor problems compared with shade from trees within the garden which impoverish and dry out the soil. Ash, birch, chestnut, large conifers. elm, or poplar are not suitable in a small garden and are better replaced with modest flowering trees, which will give the amount of shade needed and will allow plants to be grown close to them. Fences and hedges, unless very tall, throw little shade in the summer when it is most wanted, so some shade trees are needed.

It is useful to plan the garden on paper with a rough sketch. On this you should note the warmest place when cold winds are blowing, for this will be the place for any tender plants you may wish to grow. In deciding where to put a lawn do not choose a place more than half in shade; otherwise the lawn will be damp and unsatisfactory for most of the year. If there are hedges, put the paths near these to make clipping easy. Also the soil near a hedge is not good for a flower bed. Paths 2-ft. wide are sufficient in a small garden. Grass paths, though very pretty, are troublesome in upkeep, and unless very wide they soon show signs of wear. When making a path, whether of gravel, bricks, or stone slabs, there must be a layer underneath of broken brick or any kind of rubble to give proper drainage.

The gardener should make up his mind what kind of plants he wants to grow, for everything cannot be grown in one small garden, and a better effect can usually be produced by selecting certain types of plants only and growing enough of these to make a good show. Again, the amount of time available for cultivating the garden must be considered. No good garden of any kind can be made without trouble and labour, and anyone who does not enjoy the labour had better not garden. But some kinds of plants give more work than others. Annuals are time-consuming and so is a rockery to some extent; whereas a shrubbery is less work, and floribunda roses (p. 99) of all plants, probably produce the greatest show for the least labour.

If florists' flowers, such as chrysanthemums (p. 181), delphiniums (p. 85), or roses (p. 101) are to be grown, it is advisable to make long rectangular or oval beds not more than 6-ft. wide, so that they can be reached from either side without trampling on the soil. The same is true of an herbaceous border, though this can with advantage have a less formal outline. Although a hedge makes an attractive background for herbaceous plants, for the reasons given the hedge needs to be a little way back, with a path running between it and the border. A wall or a fence makes a good background, but these are in demand for climbing plants, and the protected south wall is in great demand for growing the more tender plants. Small flowering trees and shrubs can make a good backing to a south-facing border.

Annuals and biennials are suitable for showy beds in front of the house, for patches in front of shrub borders, or for empty spaces in the herbaceous border. Spring-flowering biennials (p. 33) can be followed by half-hardy annuals (p. 141), and annuals can be planted where bulbs have died down. If rock plants are to be grown, the beds must be raised above ground level. The soil excavated for the paths may be used for this. The actual building of a rockery is a specialist matter, and a book on this subject should be consulted. Even a small garden must have a place for a compost heap, preferably in two or three compartments. It must be hidden from sight, perhaps by a low hedge. A cold frame is also invaluable for rooting cuttings, for bringing tender plants through thè winter, and for many other purposes.

Properly designed and studied, there is no part of even the smallest garden which cannot contain something interesting in flower or foliage at most times of the year. This book is especially designed to show what plants are in flower at the different seasons.

A few special points:
1. *Soil.* Imperfect soils can be improved so that year by year they become more amenable. A very light and sandy soil, and therefore dry, can be improved by digging in compost continually and also moss peat, spent hops, or hop manure. Except for the last, these are all improved by adding a mixed fertilizer, preferably organically based. Heavy clay can be improved also by compost, and by sand or grit and unrotted leaves. If the ground is dug in the autumn and left rough for the frost to act on the lumps in the winter, the soil will break up into a much more manageable tilth in the spring.

2. *Protecting tender plants.* An attractive and successful garden can be made by growing only plants which are hardy in the district; but sooner or later gardeners want to experiment with the less hardy plants. Many of these may be brought through a normal winter if given a little protection. In the first place they must be planted in a position protected from the north and east winds and where the early sun does not shine on them while the frost is still present. A west-facing wall is best. The body of a shrub may be protected with cut branches of an evergreen such

as yew, or with straw or hay shaken among the branches and replaced if the wind blows it away. The ground round the roots should be compacted and the soil kept moist, except when frost makes this impossible. A mulch is not helpful in the winter as this prevents the warmth of the soil passing to the air above. Herbaceous plants can be protected by a light covering of bracken or straw in the severe weather. Small plants are best protected by some form of cloche, over which a sack may be placed when severe frost is expected.

3. *What to avoid.* In a small garden, avoid shrubs which run at the roots, and certain herbaceous plants which spread too fast (*see* list p. 201). Do not grow hedge plants which are too greedy or spread their roots too far, such as privet or Cupressus *macrocarpa*. Lonicera *nitida* makes a very good low hedge.

Do not expect everything you plant to succeed; even expert gardeners lose a certain number of plants from one cause and another, so do not be discouraged by a few failures.

PLANTS FOR SPECIAL SOILS OR SITUATIONS

These lists are mainly confined to the plants described in this book and are by no means exclusive. They give, however, some indication of what can or cannot be grown in particular conditions. There are, as well, many plants which are not particular about the type of soil or situation available.

LIME-LOVING PLANTS

Rock-garden Plants

Aethionema 43
Alyssum 41, 67
Anacyclus 91
Aubrietia 41
Dryas octopetala
Saxifrages, Kabschias 21

Bulbs, Corms, etc.

Anemone blanda 9
Anemone pulsatilla 35
Fritillaria 31
Iris (except American species) 5, etc.
Lilium candidum 68

Herbaceous Plants

Pinks and Carnations 79 etc.
Eremurus 72
Euphorbia 13, 134
Viola odorata 4

Shrubs

Cistus 65
Daphnes (except D. odora) 3, etc.
Halimiocistus 64
Lavendula 105
Lilac 59
Malus 185
Prunus viii, 25, 60
Rosmarinus 105
Tamarix 158

LIME TOLERATORS WITH PLENTY OF HUMUS

Rock-garden Plants

Corydalis cashmeriana (not chalk) 45
Dodecatheon 45
Erica carnea 2
Gentiana acaulis 34
Gentiana farreri 177

Climbing Plants

Tropaeolum speciosum 162

Herbaceous Plants

Lithospermum fruticosum 38
Lupins (not chalk) 77

Shrubs

Camellia 27
Cytisus (some) 59, 67
Eucryphia x intermedia
Hamamelis (not chalk) 3
Magnolia 25
Ulex 23

LIME-HATING PLANTS

Rock-garden Plants
Erica ciliaris, cinerea etc. 176
Lithospermum diffusum 40
Gentiana sino-ornata 176

Climbing Plants
Trachelospermum 164

Herbaceous Plants
Meconopsis 38

Shrubs
Acacia dealbata 102
Azaleas 57
Corylopsis pauciflora 27
Desfontainea 102
Eucryphia glutinosa 171
Kalmia 57
Menziesia 56
Rhododendron 57
Vaccinium 57

PLANTS FOR HOT SUNNY PLACES

Rock-garden Plants
Aethionema 43
Alyssum spinosum 67
Asperula arcadiensis 43
Erinacea 66
Helichrysum 43, 91
Iberis 66, 134
Penstemon pinifolius 91
Saponaria 41
Sedums 91, 177
Sempervivums 91

Herbaceous Plants
Centaurea 87, 115
Helichrysum 191
Oenothera 109, 127
Penstemon 169
Salvia 105, 108, 127, 153
Statice 148, 191
Verbascum 113
Catananche 123

Bulbs, Corms, etc.
Most summer bulbs 69, 71, 73, 117, 173, 175
Some spring bulbs 11, 31
Iris stylosa 5

Annuals
Calandrinia 142
Mesembryanthemum 143
Salvia splendens 127
Zinnia 137

Shrubs
Anthyllis 64
Caryopteris 171
Cistus 65
Genista 61
Helianthemum 65
Hibiscus 171
Lavendula 105
Spartium 158
Thymus 89, 104

PLANTS FOR FULL OR PARTIAL SHADE

Rock-garden Plants
Arenaria balearica 42
Chiastophyllum oppositifolium 49
Cyclamen 7, 177
Dodecatheon 45
Haberlea 45
Mentha requienii 89
Ramonda 45

Bulbs, Corms, etc.
Anemone ranunculoides 7
Erythronium 7
Galanthus (except G. elwesii) 7

PLANTS FOR FULL OR PARTIAL SHADE—*continued*

Shrubs

Berberis darwinii 23
Daphne laureola 13
Deutzia 59
Hamamelis 3
Hypericum 65, 161
Rhododendron 57

Herbaceous Plants

Actaea spicata 118
Ajuga 36
Alchemilla 35
Astrantia 119
Anemone hepatica 5
Bergenia 17
Convallaria 51

Disporum 50
Epimedium 13, 49
Euphorbia wulfeni 13
Hacquetia (Dondia) 13
Helleborus 5, 13
Hosta 73
Meconopsis 38
Polygonatum 51
Pulmonaria 17
Rodgersia 75
Sanguinaria 49
Smilacina 51
Saxifraga umbrosa 49
Tiarella 49
Uvularia 50
Vinca 17

PLANTS FOR NORTH WALLS

Ampelopsis veitchi 188
Clematis montana (not full shade) 63
Clematis spooneri (not full shade) 62
Clematis tangutica (not full shade) 164
Cotoneaster horizontalis 184
Forsythia suspensa 22
Garrya elliptica (in mild districts) 1

Hydrangea petiolaris 144
Jasminum nudiflorum 3
Kerria japonica 24
Lonicera (Honeysuckle) 164
Pyracantha 187
Tropaeolum speciosum 162
Roses, climbing, various 97

SPREADING PLANTS, NOT FOR SMALL GARDENS

Herbaceous Plants

Campanula rapunculoides 110
Centaurea (some varieties) 114
Chrysanthemum maximum (old varieties) 122
Physalis franchettii 190

Shrubs

Rhus typhina (Stag's Horn Sumach) 158
Rose species which sucker 92
Old Garden Roses which sucker 94
Spiraea menziesii 60

HOW TO OBTAIN PLANTS

It is a pity to put a great deal of work into growing inferior plants when better plants could be grown quite as easily. A little trouble at the beginning, therefore, in choosing well and then finding out where to obtain your choice will make all the difference to the success of the garden. Not many places are not within reach of a reliable nursery. There is much to be said for using a local nursery if there is a good one, for the soil and the climate are likely to be the same as those in your own garden, and you can see for yourself which plants flourish. But do not buy from an inferior nursery even though it may be close at hand, as you may get poor stock or plants which are not what they purport to be. In any case, as you get more ambitious, you will want things you cannot obtain locally, and so it is worth collecting the catalogues of two or three well-known general nurseries and studying them. Plants from such nurseries are sent so well packed that they travel easily, and it is worth the cost of the carriage to be sure you have the right plant. A weekly gardening paper is invaluable as a guide in this respect. But do not be tempted by cheap lots and wonderful-sounding bargains offered in some advertisements, unless these come from nurseries of high repute.

When buying seeds for your garden, it is essential to be sure that you are buying a first-class strain from one of the reliable seedsmen. It is important that the seed should be fresh and not old stock. To sow stale polyanthus seed, for example, is asking for failure. Seed bought from a reliable seedsman is certain to be fresh.

For all the big groups of garden plants there are specialist growers, and these naturally have a much larger selection, as well as the newest varieties. If you want the best selection of roses, chrysanthemums, dahlias, lilies, irises, heaths, dianthus, delphiniums, violas, rock plants, or flowering shrubs, you can get the catalogue of a specialist nursery. A visit to the annual Chelsea Flower Show will give you all the information you want. You can become a member of the Royal Horticultural Society, the Alpine Garden Society, the National Rose Society, the Delphinium Society, etc., and visit their specialist shows.

It is well worth trying to build up a small gardener's library, especially of books which give more information about important special groups such as roses and rock plants. There are available excellent inexpensive paperback series written by first-class authorities which give reliable information on what to grow.

Gardening should be a social activity which should include visiting other people's gardens and exchanging experiences. Many herbaceous border plants, rock plants, pinks, etc., need at intervals to be lifted and divided in the late autumn or spring, and then is the time to exchange plants to the advantage of everyone. If you join a local horticultural society it will put you in touch with other keen gardeners.

INDEX